U0362138

※涉外法律人才培养系列教材※

国际投资仲裁案例选读

裁决原文＊中英对照

Selected Readings of International Investment
Arbitration Cases

焦洪宝　编著

南开大学出版社

天　津

图书在版编目(CIP)数据

　　国际投资仲裁案例选读：汉、英 / 焦洪宝编著. —
天津：南开大学出版社，2021.1
　　涉外法律人才培养系列教材
　　ISBN 978-7-310-06015-3

　　Ⅰ.①国… Ⅱ.①焦… Ⅲ.①国际投资法学－国际仲
裁－案例－教材－汉、英 Ⅳ.①D996.4

中国版本图书馆 CIP 数据核字(2021)第 000691 号

国际投资仲裁案例选读
GUOJI TOUZI ZHONGCAI ANLI XUANDU

南开大学出版社出版发行
出版人：陈　敬
地址：天津市南开区卫津路 94 号　　邮政编码：300071
营销部电话：(022)23508339　营销部传真：(022)23508542
http://www.nkup.com.cn

三河市同力彩印有限公司印刷　全国各地新华书店经销
2021 年 1 月第 1 版　　2021 年 1 月第 1 次印刷
260×185 毫米　16 开本　14.25 印张　284 千字
定价：45.00 元

如遇图书印装质量问题,请与本社营销部联系调换,电话:(022)23508339

目　　录（Content）

编者的话

本书选取了国际投资仲裁领域 16 个重要案例，摘编了这些外国投资者与东道国政府间争端案件的仲裁裁决书，按照案例研读的体例进行中英文对照，汇编成本教材，供法学本科生和研究生开设国际投资法、国际投资案例仲裁等课程使用，也可供从事涉外法律业务的法律工作者研习使用。

该教材选读的案例，大部分是从投资争端解决国际中心（ICSID）的数百件案例中选取，还有一部分是由国际常设仲裁院、北美自由贸易区仲裁委会员、斯德哥尔摩商会仲裁院、联合国国际贸易法委员会仲裁庭审理的相关国际投资仲裁案例。案例争议的焦点问题不仅涉及最惠国待遇、最低标准待遇、公平公正待遇、国民待遇、征收补偿标准等国际投资领域的实体待遇问题，也涉及仲裁管辖、保护伞条款、岔路口条款、裁决撤销、仲裁反请求、裁决执行等国际投资仲裁的程序性法律问题，还尤其注意特别引入了与中国有关的一些案件。

由于这些案例较为典型，被国际投资法学习和研究者、投资领域实务专家所普遍重视和关注，其中大部分也曾被国际经济法或国际投资法的教材、著作甚至新闻媒体提及、援引或专门评析过。案例按照裁决作出的时间排序，有部分早期案例在国际投资法的经典教材中有过分析，读者可进一步结合本教材给出的材料做深入研读；有的案例因争议较大而受到国际投资仲裁法律实务界持续关注，乃至目前仍不断有新的进展，在本教材汇编过程中也注意收集同一案件在不同审理机构所获得的不同进展，从而有助于实务领域人士从整体上厘清案例的来龙去脉。通过此次对裁决原文的中英文对照选读，读者可更为直观、全面、准确地掌握案例相关的国际投资仲裁法律制度及其在实践中的发展，还可帮助提高法律英语水平，奠定从事涉外法律工作的基础。

作为涉外法律人才培养系列教材中的一册，希望本教材能够成为卓越涉外法律人才培养适用的特色专业训练教材，并在使用过程中获得广大师生、读者的批评与指正，以便编者予以修正和完善。

编　者
2020 年 12 月

案例一　挪威诉美国案

Norway v. United States of America（1922）（Permanent Court of Arbitration）

选读理由（Selected Reason）

1922 年挪威诉美国的"挪威船主求偿仲裁案"是国际判例上关于间接征收的第一个案例，内容涉及的是美国接收挪威船主们的船只的问题。第一次世界大战前，美国设立了一个公司，接收境内的各种船舶以及船舶的材料、机器和设备。由于美国这一措施也适用于美国私人公司基于契约为挪威船主们建造的船只，涉及接收了外国人的财产，由此引发起挪威王国要求美国政府赔偿，并通过海牙常设仲裁法院设立了临时仲裁庭进行仲裁。本案对理解间接征收的法律概念具有重要的指导意义。

仲裁申请情况（The Request for Arbitration）

Whereas the United States and the Kingdom of Norway are Parties to the Convention for the Pacific Settlement of International Disputes signed at the Hague, on October 18, 1907, which replaced by virtue of Article 91 there of as between the contracting powers the original Hague Convention of July 29, 1899;

Whereas the United States and Norway signed on April 4, 1908, a general Arbitration Convention in which it was agreed.

Desiring to settle amicably certain claims of Norwegian subjects against the United States arising, according to contentions of the Government of Norway, out of certain requisitions by the United States Shipping Board Emergency Fleet Corporation;

Considering that these claims have been presented to the United States Shipping Board Emergency Fleet Corporation and that the said Corporation and the claimants have failed to reach an agreement for the settlement thereof;

Considering, therefore, that the claims should be submitted to arbitration conformable to the Convention of the 18th of October, 1907, for the pacific settlement of international disputes and the Arbitration Convention concluded by the two Governments April 4, 1908, and renewed by agreements dated June 16, 1913 and March 30, 1918 respectively;

鉴于美国和挪威王国是 1907 年 10 月 18 日在海牙签署的《和平解决国际争端公约》的缔约国，该公约根据其第 91 条取代了 1899 年 7 月 29 日原海牙公约；

鉴于美国和挪威于 1908 年 4 月 4 日达成一致意见签署了一项一般仲裁协定。

希望按照挪威王国的友好解决针对美国的索赔，这些索赔是由挪威国民对美国航运委员会应急船队公司提出的请求而引发的。

考虑到这些索赔已提交给美国航运委员会应急船队公司，并且上述公司和索赔人未能就解决这些索赔达成协议；

因此，考虑到这些索赔应按照 1907 年 10 月 18 日《和平国际争端解决公约》和 1908 年 4 月 4 日两国政府缔结并分别于 1913 年 6 月 16 日和 1918 年 3 月 30 日通过协议续签的仲裁协定提交仲裁；

It is common ground between the Parties to this arbitration that the fifteen claims against the United States are presented by the Government of the Kingdom of Norway, which Government, and not the individual claimants, "is the sole claimant before this Tribunal". The claims arise out of certain actions of the United States of America in relation to ships which were building in the United States for Norwegian subjects at a time, during the recent Great War, when the demand for ships was enormous, owing to the needs of the armies and to the losses of mercantile ships.

本仲裁的当事人之间有一个共同点，即对美国的 15 项索赔是由挪威王国政府提出的，挪威政府而非个别索赔人"是本法庭的唯一索赔人"。这些索赔是由美国的与船舶有关的诉讼引起的。这些船是在美国为挪威国民在最近的一次大战期间所建造的，由于军队的需要和商船的损失，在当时对船舶的需求量巨大。

For some time before the United States declared war, the shortage of shipping was serious both in European countries and in the United States. In these circumstances, Norwegian subjects, amongst others, directed their attention to the possibilities of shipbuilding in the United States. From July 1915 onwards, various contracts were placed by Norwegian subjects with shipyards in the United States. Meanwhile, from the Summer of 1916 onwards, the United States Government took a series of steps for the protection of its interests and these steps made possible the later "mobilisation for war purposes of the commercial and industrial resources of the United States".

在美国宣布参加第一次世界大战之前的一段时间里，欧洲国家和美国的航运严重短缺。在这种情况下，挪威王国的国民和其他国家的人把注意力集中在美国造船的可能性上。从1915年7月开始，挪威国民与美国造船厂签订了各种各样的合同。与此同时，从1916年夏天开始，美国政府采取了一系列保护其利益的措施，这些措施使得后来的"为战争目的调动美国的商业和工业资源"成为可能。

The United States declared war against Germany on April 6th, 1917. Already by the United States Shipping Act of September 1916 the United States Shipping Board had been established "for the purpose of encouraging, developing and creating a naval auxiliary and naval reserve and a merchant marine to meet the requirements of the commerce of the United States with its territories and possessions and with foreign countries".

美国于1917年4月6日对德国宣战。而在此之前根据1916年9月的《美国航运法》，美国航运委员会成立，"以鼓励、发展和建立海军辅助船、海军预备役以及商业船队，满足美国领土和属地与外国之间的商要需求为目标"。

On the day of the declaration of war by the United States (April 6th 1917) the Shipping Board exercised this authority and formed the United States Shipping Board Emergency Fleet Corporation to carry out, in general, the purposes set forth in section 11 of the Act. All the stock of this corporation was owned by the United States. Though its certificate of Incorporation of April 16th 1917, provided "that the existence of this corporation shall be perpetual," it had been laid down in section 11 of the Act that "at the expiration of five years from the conclusion of the present European War the operation of vessels on the part of any such corporation in which the United States is then a stockholder shall cease and the said corporation stand dissolved... The vessels and other property of any such corporation shall revert to the board".

在美国宣战的当天（1917年4月6日），航运委员会行使了这一权力，成立了美国航运委员会应急船队公司，以实现美国航运法第11条所述的目标。这家公司的所有股份都归美国政府所有。虽然它在1917年4月16日的公司注册证中规定"公司永久存续"，但在航运法第11条中已经规定了"在当前欧洲战争结束后五年内，在美国仍作为该公司股东的情况下该公司的任何船舶均将停止营运，该公司将解散……该等公司的船舶及其他财产应归还航运委员会"。

For some time before the declaration of war the question of requisitioning ships by the United States had been considered and the fact that early in 1917 a large proportion of the shipyards in the United States was engaged with contracts for foreign shipowners led to various proposals and negotiations into which it is unnecessary to enter here. On the 4th of March 1917 (after the severance of diplomatic relations between the United States and Germany on

February 3rd 1917), a Naval Emergency Fund Act was passed. This Act authorized and empowered the President, "in addition to all other existing provisions of law" within the limits of the appropriation available, "to place an order with any person for such ships or war material as the necessities of the Government, to be determined by the President, may require and which are of the nature, kind, and quantity usually produced or capable of being produced by such person." Such orders were given precedence over all other orders and compliance was made obligatory. In the case of noncompliance, the President was authorized to "take immediate possession of any factory or of any part thereof." The President was furthermore empowered, under the same penalty, "to modify or cancel any existing contract for the building, production, or purchase of ships or war material", to place an order for the whole or any part of the output of a factory in which ships or war material were being built or produced, and to "requisition and take over for use or operation by the Government any factory or any part thereof." In all cases where these powers were exercised, provision wasmade for "just compensation" to be determined by the President, with the customary provision for an appeal to the courts. Then on June 15th 1917, two months after the declaration of War, further important powers were given to the President by the Emergency Shipping Fund Provision of the Urgent Deficiencies Act.

在宣战前的一段时间里，美国一直在考虑征用船只的问题，这一事实 1917 年初美国的大部分船厂与外国船主签订合同时所进行的各种各样的要约建议和谈判都成为不必要的。1917 年 3 月 4 日（在美国与德国断绝外交关系的 1917 年 2 月 3 日之后），《海军紧急资助法》通过。该法案授权总统"除所有其他现有法律规定外"在现有拨款范围内可以"根据总统所确定的政府的需求，向任何人发出订单，要求其提供通常生产或能够生产的相应性能、类型和数量的船只或其他战争物资""此类订单优先于所有其他订单，必须遵守"。在不服从的情况下，总统被授权"立即拥有接管任何工厂或其任何部分"。在这一处罚措施中，总统还被授权"修改或取消任何现有的建造、生产或购买船舶或战争物资的合同"，订购建造或生产船舶或战争物资的工厂所生产的全部或部分产品，以及"由政府征用和接管任何工厂或其任何部分以供使用或运营"的规定。在行使这些权力的所有情况下，都规定了总统可决定给予"公平补偿"，还一般性地规定了可向法院起诉的条款。1917 年 6 月 15 日，即宣战两个月后，《紧急匮乏法》的紧急航运资助条款赋予总统更多的重要权力。

The details of the claims, both as originally presented in the Case of the Kingdom of Norway and as finally presented in the course of the oral argument, are as follows:

挪威王国最初在案件中提出的和在口头辩论过程中最终提出的索赔详情如下：

Number of claim.	Name of Claimant.	Amounts originally claimed. $	Amounts including interest. $	Amounts finally claimed. (Without addinginterest claimed.) $
1	The Manitowoc Shipping Corporation	731,500.00	1,028,220.24	766,500.00
2	The Manitowoc Shipping Corporation	731,500.00	1,028,220.24	766,500.00
3	The Baltimore Steamship Company	1,507,860.28	2,120,679.93	1,542,187.50
4	The Vard II Steamship Company	1,944,877.26	2,731,749.47	1,957,200.00
5	The Sörlandske Lloyd Company	1,617,000.00	2,273,753.21	1,837,000.00
6	The Östlandet Steamship Company	2,390,960.00	3,363,311.07	2,478,960.00
7	Jacob Prebensen Jr	148,987.50	209,850.03	396,937.50
8	The Tromp Steamship Company	257,737.50	361,745.30	396,937.50
9	The Maritim Corporation	278,400.00	392,492.40	417,600.00
10	The Haug Steamship Company	413,460.94	580,093.48	417,600.00
11	The Mercator Corporation	434,123.44	609,083.36	438,262.50
12	The Sörlandske Lloyd Corporation	196,875.00	277,871.43	451,875.00
13	H. Kjerschow	447,250.00	627,500.16	415,875.00
14	Harry Borthen	146,875.00	207,300.90	451,875.00
15	E. & N. Chr. Evensen, Incorporated	421,875.00	591,788.29	451,875.00
	Totals	11,669,281.92	16,403,659.51	13,223,185.00

The claim made by the United States in reference to Page Brothers amounted to $22,800. The validity of this claim was totally denied by the Kingdom of Norway.

美国就佩奇兄弟公司提出的索赔金额为 22800 美元。挪威王国完全不认可这一主张。

仲裁结果（Award）

For these reasons the Tribunal of Arbitration decides and awards that：

I. The United States of America shall pay to the Kingdom of Norway the following sums：

In claim No. 1 by the Skibsaktieselskapet "Manitowoc" the sum of $845,000.

In claim No. 2 by the Skibsaktieselskapet "Manitowoc" the sum of $845,000.

In claim No. 3 by the Dampskibsaktieselskapet "Baltimore" the sum of $1,625,000.

In claim No. 4 by the Dampskibsaktieselskapet "Vard II" the sum of ＄2,065,000.

Out of this amount of ＄2,065,000 the United States are entitled to retain a sum of ＄22,800 in order that this sum be paid to Page Brothers；

In claim No. 5 by the Aktieselskapet Stirlandske Lloyd the sum of ＄2,045,000.

In claim No. 6 by the Dampskibsaktieselskapet Östlandet the sum of ＄2,890,000.

In claim No. 7 by Jacob Prebensen jun. the sum of ＄160,000.

In claim No. 8 by the Dampskibsaktieselskapet "Tromp" the sum of ＄160,000.

In claim No. 9 by the Aktieselskapet "Maritim" the sum of ＄175,000.

In claim No. 10 by the Aktieselskapet "Haug" the sum of ＄175,000.

In claim No. 11 by the Aktieselskapet "Mercator" the sum of ＄190,000.

In claim No. 12 by the Aktieselskapet Sörlandske Lloyd the sum of ＄205,000.

In claim No. 13 by H. Kjerschow the sum of ＄205,000.

In claim No. 14 by Harry Borthen the sum of ＄205,000.

In claim No. 15 by E. & N. Evensen the sum of ＄205,000.

II. The claim made by the United States of America on behalf of Page Brothers is disallowed as against the Kingdom of Norway，but a sum of ＄22,800 may be retained by the United States as stated under claim No. 4 above.

Done at The Hague，in the Permanent Court of Arbitration，October 13th，1922.

The President：James Vallotton

The Secretary-General：Michiels Van Verduynen

基于这些原因仲裁庭决定并裁决如下：

一、美国应向挪威王国支付下列款项：

1. 第 1 号索赔案件赔偿 Skibsaktieselskapet "Manitowoc" 金额为 84.5 万美元。

2. 第 2 号索赔案件赔偿 Skibsaktieselskapet "Manitowoc" 金额为 84.5 万美元。

3. 第 3 号索赔案件赔偿 Dampskibsaktieselskapet "Baltimore" 金额为 162.5 万美元。

4. 第 4 号索赔案件赔偿 Dampskibsaktieselskapet "Vard II" 金额为 206.5 万美元。

在这 206.5 万美元中，美国有权保留一笔 2.28 万美元的款项，以便支付给佩奇兄弟。

5. 第 5 号索赔案件赔偿 Aktieselskapet Stirlandske Lloyd 金额为 204.5 万美元。

6. 第 6 号索赔案件赔偿 Dampskibsaktieselskapet Ostlandet 金额为 289 万美元。

7. 第 7 号索赔案件赔偿 Jacob Prebensen jun 总额 16 万美元。

8. 第 8 号索赔案件赔偿 Dampskibsaktieselskapet "Tromp" 金额为 16 万美元。

9. 第 9 号索赔案件赔偿 Maritim 股份公司的金额为 17.5 万美元。

10. 第 10 号索赔案件赔偿 Haug 股份公司的金额为 17.5 万美元。

11. 第 11 号索赔案件赔偿 Mercator 股份公司的金额为 19 万美元。

12. 第 12 号索赔案件赔偿 Sörlandske Lloyd 股份公司的金额为 20.5 万美元。

13. 第 13 号索赔案件赔偿由 H. Kjerschow 的金额为 20.5 万美元。

14. 第 14 号索赔案件赔偿在 Harry Borthen 的金额为 20.5 万美元。

15. 第 15 号索赔案件赔偿 E. & N. Evensen 金额为 20.5 万美元。

二、美国为佩奇兄弟公司向挪威主张的索赔被驳回，但是上述第 4 项赔偿内容中的 2.28 万美元款项可由美国保留。

1922 年 10 月 13 日，常设仲裁法院，裁决于海牙

总统：詹姆斯·瓦洛顿

秘书长：米歇尔斯·范·维尔杜伦

裁决原因（Reasons for the Award）

Was the Claimants' Property taken?

The Fleet Corporation sent a general order of requisition by telegram to almost all the shipyards of the United States on August 3rd and 4th, 1917, but it did not send any detailed order of requisition, giving the particular ships or contracts to which the requisition was intended to apply. Nor did the Corporation state precisely to what extent each of the yards was requisitioned. The Tribunal cannot regard this notice as sufficient as regards foreign owners of shipbuilding contracts, except for the purpose of preventing any transfer to a foreign flag or to foreign ownership or any other change to the status quo which could have been detrimental from the point of view of national defence.

This telegraphic order of August 3rd, sent to the shipyards only, ordered the completion of all vessels "with all practicable despatch", and referred to a letter which was to follow. The order contained in the letter of August 3rd expressly requisitioned not only the ships and the material, but also the contracts, the plans, detailed specifications and payments made, and it even commandeered the yards (depriving them of their right to accept any further contracts). In spite of this the United States have contended that there was no requisition, except of "physical property" and have strongly maintained that the word "contract" in the letter of 3rd August only referred to commitments for material. It is common ground that the United States ordered the shipyards not to accept after August 3rd 1917, any further progress payments under the contracts from the private owners, but that subsequent progress payments were made by some of the former owners to the shipbuilders.

索赔人的财产被征用了吗？

美国航运委员会应急船队公司于 1917 年 8 月 3 日和 4 日通过电报向美国几乎所有的船厂发送了一份普通的征用命令，但没有发送任何详细的征用命令，给出所拟征用的具体船舶或合同。该公司也没有准确说明每一个船厂被征用的程度。仲裁庭不能将本通知视为对订立船舶建造合同的外国船主的充分通知，这个通知的目的只是从国防的角度阻止向外国船旗国或外国船主交付船只，或防止出现可能有害于现状的其他变动。

这张 8 月 3 日只发给船厂的电报命令，要求结束所有船舶的实际发货，并提及随后的信件。8 月 3 日信件中的命令不仅明确地征用了船只和材料，还征用了合同、计划、详细的规格和付款，甚至征用了船厂（剥夺了他们接受任何其他合同的权利）。尽管如此，美国仍声称，除了"有形财产"外，没有任何征用，并强烈主张 8 月 3 日信函中的"合同"一词仅指材料的投入。各方的共识是美国命令造船厂在 1917 年 8 月 3 日之后不接受任何私人船主根据合同支付的进度款，但随后仍有一些前船主支付进度款给造船者。

The Corporation seemed to have forgotten that it had assumed certain contractual obligations, and in particular to have ignored the fact that the retention of the money of the claimants without restoring the ships was obviously unlawful. Such action was not only contrary to international law, but also to the municipal law of the United States. The amounts of the progress payments should have been refunded at the time of the requisitioning of the ships. There can be no excuse for waiting until 1919 to make an assessment of these amounts.

The Corporation could not have entertained any doubt after October 6th, 1917, that an immediate settlement of the claims was imperative. The Corporation may have intended, up to October 6th, 1917, to settle accounts with regard to these claims, namely so long as it was expected that the property of the claimants would be restored at the end of the war. More especially the Corporation should not have had any doubt with regard to Claims 13 to 15 as to the legality of its action according to municipal law as well as under international law, after it had informed the ship builders not to go on with these contracts. The Tribunal is therefore of opinion:

1. That, whatever the intentions may have been, the United States took, both in fact and in law, the contracts under which the ships in question were being or were to be constructed.

2. That in fact the claimants were fully and for ever deprived of their property and that this amounts to a requisitioning by the exercise of the power of eminent domain within the meaning of American municipal law.

应急舰队公司似乎忘记了它承担了某些合同义务，特别是忽略了这样一个事实，即在不归还船舶的情况下保留索赔人的钱显然是非法的。这种行为不仅违背了国际法，而且违背了美国的《市政法》。进度款应在船舶征用时即予以退还，而没有理由直到1919年才对这些数额进行估算。

在1917年10月6日之后，公司不应再有任何怀疑，即立即解决索赔是必要的。截至1917年10月6日，公司就应该做好准备确定这些索赔的数额，并计划在战争结束时对索赔人的财产予以赔付。更重要的是，在公司通知造船商不要继续履行这些合同之后，公司不应对第13号至第15号索赔中对其根据市政法和国际法采取的行动的合法性产生任何怀疑。因此，法庭认为：

1. 不管意图是什么，美国实际上和在法律上都接收了正在建造或将要建造相关船舶所依据的合同。

2. 事实上，索赔人被完全地、永久地剥夺了财产。这相当于美国《市政法》意义上的征用权的行使。

The Date on which Claimant's property was effectively requisitioned.

It appears from the minutes of October 4th, 1917, that at that date the Members of the United States Shipping Board, held strongly divergent views with regard to the requisitioning of foreign vessels. While the majority proposed "that the Board conform its action with reference to foreign tonnage to the action already taken by the Board with reference to the British and French ships", Vice-Chairman Stevens presented the following resolution: that vessels building for Norwegian account, commandeered by the Emergency Fleet Corporation, be transferred to American Corporations to be formed by their owners, on condition that they voluntarily charter the vessels to the Board, bare boat or time charter, at Board's option, for the period of the war and six months thereafter, at the general requisition rate established by the Board, and reimburse the Corporation for all expenditure incurred in the completion of thevessels. The motion not being seconded, the Vice-Chairman moved "that the question is of such international importance that it be referred to the President. "

This motion also not being seconded, the Chairman of the Shipping Board, after having stated to the Board that the decision arrived at was to "retain the title to the tonnage for the present", wrote to Dr. Fridtjof Nansen, at Washington D. C. , on October 6th 1917, as follows:

"After careful inquiry into the present and prospective war needs of the United States and of the Allies.... the Board has concluded that it is its duty to retain for urgent military purposes, all vessels building in this country for foreign account, title to which was commandeered by the United States on August 3rd. The decision includes necessarily the vessels building for Norwegian account.... I need not add that it is our intention to compensate the owners of commandeered vessels, be they American, Allied or Neutral, to the full measure required by the generous principles of American Public Law".

索赔人的财产被有效征用的日期

从 1917 年 10 月 4 日的会议记录来看，当时美国航运委员会的委员对征用外国船只持有强烈的不同意见。尽管多数人提议"委员会将其对外国船舶采取的行动与委员会已经针对英国和法国船舶采取的行动相一致"，但副主席史蒂文斯提出了以下解决方案：由应急船队公司征用的为挪威账户下的船舶，应由其船主交付给美国公司，他们可以自愿按照委员会的意见选择以光船租赁或定期租船的形式将船只租给委员会，期限为战争期间和战争结束后的六个月内，具体提供船只的比例按照委员会确定的征用比例执行，船主要向公司偿还所有船舶建造完成之前的所有开支。这项动议没有得到附议，副主席表示："这个问题具有国际重要性，必须提交总统处理。"

提交总统处理的动议也没有得到附议。1917 年 10 月 6 日，航运委员会主席在向委员会说明所作出的决定是"保留目前吨位船舶的所有权"后，写信给华盛顿特区的 Fridtjof Nansen 博士，内容如下：

"在对美国和盟国目前和未来的战争需求进行仔细调查之后……委员会得出结论，正在美国国内为外国账户建造的所有船舶，均有义务保留下来以满足紧急军事目的，其所有权于 8 月 3 日被美国征用。该决定必然包括为挪威账户建造的船舶。……我不需要补充，我们会补偿被征用船只的所有人，无论他们是美国的、盟国的还是中立的，以达到美国公法慷慨原则所要求的全部程度。"

The law governing the Arbitration.

The Fifth Amendment to the Constitution of the United States provides: "No person... shall be... deprived of life, liberty, or property without due process of law; nor shall private property be taken for public use, without just compensation."

It is common ground that in this respect the public law of the Parties is in complete accord with the international public law of all civilised countries.

The inviolability of the private property of a foreign citizen is a question of public policy, and it is for the courts in the United States, as well as in other countries, to settle conflicts thatmay arise between the respect for private property, and the "power of eminent domain", as is called in the United States the power of a sovereign state to expropriate, take or authorize the taking of any property within its jurisdiction which may be required "public good" or for the "general welfare".

仲裁适用的法律

《美国宪法》（第五修正案）规定："未经正当法律程序，不得剥夺任何人的生命、自由或财产；未经正当赔偿，不得将私人财产用于公共用途。"

在这方面达成的共识是，双方的公法完全符合所有文明国家的国际公法。

外国公民私有财产的不可侵犯性是一个公共政策问题，美国和其他国家的法院应解决尊重私有财产和"征用权"之间可能产生的冲突，美国将征用权称为主权国的权力，由国家基于"公共利益"或"公共福利"的需要而对其管辖范围内的任何财产进行征收、取得或授权取得。

It has been proved that the claimants lost the use and possession of their property through an exercise by the United States of their power of eminent domain. When, for instance, on October 6, 1917, the Shipping Board informed Dr. Nansen that the United States had taken the "title", the Board implicitly admitted that the ownership of all the liens, rights and equities set forth in the fifteen shipbuilding contracts had been transferred to the United States by operation of law. As the United States have taken up the position and have acted in such a way that such transfer of the property implied cancellation or "destruction" of the Jura in personam or in rem, it must be adjudged and awarded, in conformity with the American doctrine and jurisprudence itself, that this action of the United States is equivalent to the taking of private property as defined in the fifth Amendment of their Constitution.

Whether the action of the United States was lawful or not, just compensation is due to the claimants under the municipal law of the United States, as well as under the international law, based upon the respect for private property.

事实证明，通过美国行使其征用权，索赔人失去了对其财产的使用和占有。例如，1917 年 10 月 6 日，当航运委员会通知南森博士美国已取得"所有权"时，航运委员会含蓄地承认，15 份造船合同中规定的所有的留置权、合同权利和权益的权利已依法转让给美国。由于美国已经采取了立场，并采取了这样的行动，即财产的转让意味着取消或"破坏"了对人权或对物权，根据美国本身的学说和法理，必须判决和裁决美国的这一行动等同于根据宪法第五修正案的规定征用取得私有财产。

无论美国的行为是否合法，根据美国的《市政法》和国际法，基于对私有财产的尊重，应对索赔人给予公正的赔偿。

The amount of compensation

The Tribunal cannot agree, nevertheless, with the contention of the United States that no compensation should be given to the claimants over and above the sums offered by the United States, namely ＄2,679,220. The United States say that there can be no liability, and that therefore there should be no compensation, when the contract has been destroyed or rendered-void, or delayed, in consequence of "force majeure" or "restraint of princes and rulers" and a fortiori when the contract has been a "purchase of chances", after the requisition.

This last contention was accepted by Norwegian Courts. These Norwegian judgment sare not to be disregarded, as they support the Tribunal's opinion adverse to the view that the compensation should be based upon the mere reimbursement of expenses. Such judgments are conclusive evidence that some of the assignees were imprudent.

赔偿数额

不过，仲裁庭不能同意美国的论点，即不应向索赔人支付超过美国可提供的金额（即 2679220 美元）的赔偿。美国表示，在合同因"不可抗力"或"君主禁令"而被破坏或被宣布无效或延迟时，以在合同被征用后被"购买机会"这一更为有力的事由下，不应承担任何责任，因此不应进行赔偿。

挪威法院接受了最后一个有关"购买机会"的论点。挪威的这些判决不容忽视，因为它们支持仲裁庭的意见，反对认为赔偿应仅以报销费用为基础的观点。这些判决是确凿的证据，表明了有些合同受让人是不谨慎的。

Just compensation should have been paid to the Claimants or arranged with them on the basis of the net value of the property taken:

1. On the 6th October, 1917, for use, during the war (whenever such use was possible without destroying the property, according to the contract, state of completion of ship, etc.), and

2. At the latest on the 1st July 1919, as damages for the unlawful retaining of the title and use of the ships after all emergency ceased;

Or

On the 6th October, 1917, as full compensation for the destruction of the Norwegian property.

After careful comparative examination of the results of the two systems above described, the Tribunal is of opinion that the compensation hereinafter awarded is the fair market value of the claimants' property.

公正的赔偿应当已经根据以下被征用财产的净值向索赔人完成支付或与索赔人达成协议：

1. 在 1917 年 10 月 6 日，在战争期间被使用的财产（在此期间只要可能被使用，且不会破产财产，并根据合同、船舶完工状态等情况确定）。

2. 最迟在 1919 年 7 月 1 日，所有紧急情况停止后仍被非法保留船舶所有权和使用船舶的损害赔偿；或者在 1917 年 10 月 6 日，对挪威财产破坏的全部赔偿。

经仔细比较上述两种制度的结果后，仲裁庭认为，下文判给的赔偿金是申请人财产的公平市场价值。

The Tribunal is competent to allow interest as part of the compensation ex aequo et bono, if the circumstances are considered to justify it. So far as interest after the date of this award is concerned, the Parties decided in the Agreement of 30th June 1921, that "any amount granted by the award rendered shall bear interest at the rate of six per centum per annum from the date of the rendition of the decision until the date of payment".

如果情况被认为是合理的，法庭有权允许利息作为公平合理补偿的一部分。就本裁决日期后的利息而言，双方在1921年6月30日的协议中决定，"裁决所授予的任何金额应以年息百分之六计息，从裁决提交之日起至付款之日止"。

In coming to the conclusion that interest should be awarded, the Tribunal has taken into consideration the facts that the United States have had the use and profits of the claimants' property since the requisition of five years ago, and especially that the sums awarded as compensation to the claimants by the American Requisition Claim Committee have not been paid; finally that the United States have had the benefit of the progress payments made by Norwegians with reference to these ships. The Tribunal is of opinion that the claimants are entitled to special compensation in respect of interest and that some of the claimants are, in view of the circumstances of their cases, entitled to higher rates of interest than others. The claimants have asked for compound interest with half-yearly adjustments, but compound interest has not been granted in previous arbitration cases, and the Tribunal is of opinion that the claimants have not advanced sufficient reasons why an award of compound interest, in this case, should be made.

在得出应给予利息的结论时，仲裁庭考虑了自5年前被征用以来，美国已经有了对索赔人财产的使用和收益的事实，特别是美国征用索赔委员会授予索赔人的赔偿金。尚未支付；最后，美国受益于挪威人就这些船舶支付的进度款。仲裁庭认为，索赔人有权就利息获得特别补偿，而就其案件的情况而言，有些索赔人有权获得较其他人更高的利率。索赔人要求每半年调整一次计取复利，但在以前的仲裁案件中没有给予复利，仲裁庭认为索赔人没有提出充分的理由以表明应当做出支持复利的裁决。

The Tribunal is of opinion that it is just to allow a lump sum to each claimant in respect of interest for a period of five years from 6th October, 1917. Such lump sums have been included in the total amounts of compensation awarded in respect of each claim. As the Tribunal is of the opinion that full compensation should have been paid, including loss of progress payments etc., at the latest on the day of the effective taking, and as the Tribunal has assessed the net value of the property and has decided to award damages as on that date, interest should, contrary to the claim of Norway, not run before that date as previous interest is included in the estimate of the net value.

仲裁庭认为，向每名申请人一次性支付一笔从1917年10月6日起计算的5年期的利息是公正的。这笔一次性付款已经包含在给每项索赔的赔偿总额中。仲裁庭认为，全部赔偿款，包括进度款的损失，应在征用生效的当日完成支付。仲裁庭已经评估了财产的净值，并决定以该日期为依据判付损害赔偿金，则相应的利息不可以像挪威索赔时主张的那样，在该日期以前开始计算，因为此前的利息已经包含在净值的估算中。

About The Claim of Page Brothers

The Tribunal has carefully examined the facts and documents submitted in this claim and has come to the decision that the non-receipt of the balance of their commission by Page Brothers on the further progress payments made by the Fleet Corporation after it requisitioned the contract, was due solely to the action of the United States. It is not within the jurisdiction of the Tribunal to decide the question whether Page Brothers have any claim against the United States or any of its citizens. But the Tribunal is of opinion that, as the evidence now stands, Page Brothers have no claim against the Kingdom of Norway or against any Norwegian subject.

关于佩奇兄弟的主张

法庭已仔细审查了本案中提交的事实和文件，并作出裁决，认为佩奇兄弟公司未收到其关于应急船队公司在征用合同后所应支付的后续进度款相应的佣金，完全是由于美国的行为造成的。仲裁庭无权裁决佩奇兄弟是否对美国或其公民提出任何索赔。但仲裁庭认为，就目前的证据来看，佩奇兄弟公司没有针对挪威王国或任何挪威国民的索赔权。

案件影响（Impact of the Case）

本案是挪威政府与美国政府关于挪威国内一些船主在美国造船公司委托造船合同利益被征用而要求美国政府予以赔偿的案件。美国为应对第一次世界大战，向其国内的造船厂发布征用命令，将正在建造的船舶交归政府所有和使用。相应地，订购这些船只的挪威船主已经支付的造船资金和在征用命令下达后因不知情而继续支付的造船进度款，当然应得到退还。然而美国政府方面迟迟未予赔付。经过一些国内的法庭审理程序，挪威政府与美国政府就解决该项争议达成仲裁协议，由常设国际仲裁院出面组织仲裁庭进行了仲裁，从而形成了本裁决。

美国因对德国宣战的需要而发布的征收命令涉及正在建造中的 437 艘船。本裁决涉及的迟迟没有解决赔偿问题的挪威国民的 15 艘船，在 1922 年 8 月 11 日提出的索赔总额为 13223185 美元，除此之外，挪威王国还要求以每年 7% 的利率计息并每半年计一次复利，其索赔总额截至 1922 年 9 月 1 日超过 1800 万美元。仲裁庭考虑了在战时因船舶稀缺、人力与材料价格上涨等因素，同时也考虑了因被征用等原因人为被降低租金或船舶购买价格等因素，并适当考虑了利息，最终做出了大约 1500 万美元的赔偿额决定。本案对于政府征收命令下对商业造船合同履行的影响构成了政府对造船厂一方在合同项下地位的接管，并进而认定构成了对委托造船船主在造船合同项下权益的征收的论述，阐明了征收所具有的剥夺私有财产权的实质含义，也否认了美国一方以该合同因不可抗力而不应承担责任的抗辩。

思考问题（Questions）

1. 征收征用权是国家主权的构成部分吗？在何种情况下法院可否决征收征用？
2. 为何认为本案是间接征收而非直接征收？

案例二　真空盐业诉加纳案

Vacuum Salt Products Limited v. Government of The Republic of Ghana（1994）（ICSID Case No. ARB/92/2）

选读理由（Selected Reason）

　　本案是关于 ICSID 适格申请人的争议案件。一家在 1966 年 11 月 4 日由希腊国民及其兄弟在加纳注册成立的公司，在与政府达成的一份租赁合同履行过程中发生争议。在该公司以外国投资者身份向 ICSID 中心提请仲裁后，仲裁庭裁决对该案不予受理。本案涉及投资仲裁管辖的争议事项，仲裁庭在本案裁决中体现的观点对理解公约管辖权相关条款具有重要指导意义。

仲裁申请情况（The Request for Arbitration）

On 28th May 1992 the International Centre for Settlement of Investment Disputes （ "ICSID" or "the Centre"） received the Request for Arbitration （ "the Request"） in this case submitted by "Thacher Proffitt & Wood As CASES 73 Attorneys for Claimant Vacuum Salt Products Limited" （ "Vacuum Salt" or "Claimant"） . The Request essentially alleged that Vacuum Salt had suffered both a breach and progressive expropriation of its contractual rights to develop a salt production and mining facility in the Ada-Songor Lagoon in the Republic of Ghana （ "Ghana" or "Respondent"） . In particular, the Request alleged "continual violation" by Ghana of a lease agreement between Vacuum Salt and Ghana dated 22th January 1988 "and a predecessor agreement," "ultimate repudiation of the ［1988］ Lease Agreement" by Ghana by decision of 24th April 1992 and "its expropriation of the business and property of Vacuum Salt." The Request asserted that the parties had consented to ICSID arbitration in paragraph 36 (a) of the said lease agreement:

1992 年 5 月 28 日，解决投资争端国际中心（简称"ICSID"或"中心"）收到撒切尔·普罗菲特—伍德律师事务所代表第 73 号案件的原告真空盐业有限公司（简称"真空盐业"或"申请人"）提交的仲裁申请书（简称"申请书"）。申请书的基本内容是诉称真空盐业在加纳共和国（简称"加纳"或"被申请人"）的阿达松厄拉贡地区发展盐业生产和采矿设施时其在合同项下的权益遭受了违约侵害和逐步征收。具体而言，申请书诉称加纳持续违反 1988 年 1 月 22 日真空盐业与加纳之间的租赁合同和一份此前的协议，加纳在 1992 年 4 月 24 日决定对 1988 年的租赁合同予以撤销并对真空盐业的企业和资产予以征收。申请书主张双方在上述租赁合同的第 36 条（a）款同意由 ICSID 仲裁：

Any dispute or difference between the parties arising out of or in connection with this Agreement or any agreed variation thereof or in respect of the interpretation or enforcement of the provisions of this document or any agreed variation or as to the rights, duties or liabilities of either party shall unless the parties agree to submit to any procedures available in Ghana for the settlement of such dispute be submitted at the instance of any party to the jurisdiction of the International Centre for the Settlement of Investment Disputes for settlement by reconciliation [sic] or arbitration pursuant to the Convention of [sic] the Settlement of Investment Disputes between States and Nationals of other States.

双方之间的任何争议或分歧，无论是因本协议而产生的或与本协议有关的，还是由此而造成的任何双方认可存在的异议，有关本协议条款的解释或执行，有关任何一方权利、义务或责任方面双方均认可存在的异议，除双方同意在加纳提交给可适用的程序予以解决以外，任何一方均有权向国际投资争端解决中心提请解决，适用《解决国家与他国国民之间投资争端公约》进行和解或仲裁。

The Request premised jurisdiction ratione personae on the fact that Ghana is a State Party to the Convention on the Settlement of Investment Disputes between States and Nationals of Other States ("Convention" or "ICSID Convention") and that although Vacuum Salt is "a corporation organized under the Companies Code, 1963 (Act 179), of Ghana," "in the 1988 Lease Agreement, the parties agreed that because Vacuum Salt is controlled by a Greek national, it should be treated as a foreign corporation for the purposes of the Convention…" The second clause of Article 25 (2) (b) of the Convention provides: "National of another Contracting State" means:… any juridical person which had the nationality of the Contracting State party to the dispute on that date ["the date on which the parties consented to submit such dispute to… arbitration"] and which, because of foreign control, the parties have agreed should be treated as a national of another Contracting State for the purposes of this Convention."

申请书主张仲裁管辖权的事实依据是,加纳是《解决国家与他国国民之间投资争端公约》（简称"公约"或"ICSID 公约"）的成员国,且虽然真空盐业是依据加纳 1963 年《公司法》（第 179 号法令）设立的公司,但在 1988 年租赁合同中,双方同意基于真空盐业受一个希腊人控制,真空盐业应被视为公约项下的外国公司。公约第 25 条第（2）款（b）项第 2 句规定"另一缔约国国民系指:……在争端双方同意将争端交付仲裁之日,具有作为争端一方缔约国国籍的任何法人,而该法人因受外国控制,双方同意为了本公约的目的,应看作是另一缔约国国民"。

As relief the Request sought "A declaration that the illegal acts of [Ghana]… are null and void abinitio;"

An order for restitutio in integrum, or, alternatively, "damages measured according to the value of the 1988 Lease Agreement for the remainder of its term and all other property seized or damaged by" Ghana;

Damages… for the… breaches of contract, illegal acts and expropriation of Vacuum Salt's property;

"Lost profits, including loss of investment opportunities in the Songor Lagoon;"

"Interest; and Costs and expenses including attorneys' fees."

申请书寻求的救济包括:"裁决认定加纳的违法行为是无约束力的、完全无效的。""裁决恢复原状或由加纳按照 1988 年租赁合同的总值计算赔偿剩余年期的损失予以赔偿,并赔偿其他被征收或损坏的财产损失""赔偿因违反合同、非法行为和对真空盐业财产征收造成的损失。""利润损失,其中包括在松厄拉贡地区投资机会的损失。""利息,以及包括律师费在内的费用、开支。"

仲裁结果（Award）

The tribunal awards as follows:

1. The Request for Arbitration herein registered 11 June 1992 is dismissed for lack of jurisdiction.

2. Each party shall bear the expenses incurred by it in connection with the proceedings.

3. Each party shall pay one half the fees and expenses of the members of the Tribunal and the charges for the use of the facilities of the Centre.

Done at the Peace Palace, The Hague

The Netherlands

1 February 1994

本仲裁庭裁决如下：

1. 由于无管辖权，拒绝受理 1992 年 6 月 11 日登记的仲裁申请。

2. 各方均应承担由此而产生的一切费用。

3. 仲裁庭成员费用和"中心"设施的使用费，双方各付一半。

裁决于荷兰，海牙，和平宫

1994 年 2 月 1 日

裁决原因（Reasons for the Award）

Since it is agreed that Vacuum Salt is and has at all material times been a corporation organized under the 1963 Companies Code of Ghana and hence could not be regarded as "a national of another [ICSID] Contracting State" within the definition of the first clause of Article 25 (2) (b) of the Convention, the Tribunal can have jurisdiction ratione personae in regard to Vacuum Salt only if in respect of it the requirements of the second clause of Article 25 (2) (b) of the Convention are satisfied.

既然双方同意真空盐业是而且在实质上都一直是一个依加纳 1963 年《公司法》而注册成立的公司。因此，按《公约》第 25 条第（2）款（b）项中第一句的定义，这就不可能被视为"中心的另一缔约国国民。"只有在符合《公约》第 25 条第（2）款（b）项中第 2 句的要求的情况下，仲裁庭才对真空盐业基于其诉讼主体资格而具有管辖权。

The Tribunal therefore turns to consider that question, for the parties' agreement to treat Claimant as a foreign national "because of foreign control" does not ipso jure confer jurisdiction. The reference in Article 25 (2) (b) to "foreign control" necessarily sets an objective Convention limit beyond which ICSID jurisdiction cannot exist and parties therefore lack power to invoke same no matter how devoutly they may have desired to do so. See Report of the Executive Directors on the Convention on the Settlement of Investment Disputes between States and Nationals of Other States, ICSID Doc. 2, 18 March 1965, para. 25, at 9 ("While consent of the parties is an essential prerequisite for the jurisdiction of the Centre, consent alone will not suffice to bring a dispute within its jurisdiction. In keeping with the purpose of the Convention, the jurisdiction of the Centre is further limited by reference to the nature of the dispute and the parties thereto. ") .

　　因为外国控制并非自然而然地给予管辖权，仲裁庭还需要考虑双方在协议中同意将原告视作他国国民的问题。第 25 条第（2）款（b）项中对"外国控制"的描述给《公约》设立了一个客观界限，超越此限，"中心"就无管辖权，而且当事人双方也就无权援引这一法规，即便他们双方可能很虔诚地希望能这么做。请见解决国家和他国国民间投资争端公约执行董事会报告，中心文件第 2 号，1965 年 3 月 18 日，第 25 段第 9 节（尽管当事人同意是中心取得管辖权的必要前提，但仅仅同意不足以使中心获得管辖权。为保障公约目的的实现，中心管辖权还要受到争议及争议当事方性质的限制。）

　　The facts initially relevant to the issue of foreign control as regards Vacuum Salt are not in dispute. It is conceded that as of 22 January 1988 Mr. Gerassimos Alexis Panagiotopulos, a Greek national resident in Ghana since 1942, held 20 percent of the shares of vacuum Salt. It is agreed that on that date three banks owned by Ghana, i. e. , National Investment Bank, Development Finance and Holdings Limited and National Savings and Credit Bank, held ten percent each, and that the remaining 50 percent was held by private Ghanaian nationals (including one company) as follows: Albert Adamako 10 percent, Appenteng Mensah & Co. 31 percent, Kwesi Ehna (also known as Robert John Hayfron-Benjamin) 2. 5 percent, Kabutey Olaga 1. 5%, Ernest Orgle 5. 0%.

　　真空盐业最初由外国控制的事实，双方并无争议。双方均承认，1988 年 1 月 22 日，耶拉西莫斯·亚历克西斯·帕纳吉奥托普罗斯，一个自 1942 年就居住在加纳的希腊人，持有真空盐业 20% 的股份。双方也都认可，在当时加纳的三家银行，国家投资银行、金融发展控股银行和国家储蓄信用银行，分别持有 10% 的股票，剩下的 50% 的股票是由以下加纳国民私人所有（包括一家公司）：阿尔伯特·阿达马科 10%，阿彭滕·门萨公司 31%，奎西·埃纳（又名罗伯特·约翰·海夫隆—本杰明）2.5%，卡布蒂·奥拉加 1.5 percent，欧内斯特·奥格尔 5.0 percent。

　　The Tribunal notes, and itself confirms, that "foreign control" within the meaning of the second clause of Article 25 (2) (b) does not require, or imply, any particular percentage of share ownership. Each case arising under that clause must be viewed in its own particular context, on the basis of all of the facts and circumstances. There is no "formula. " It stands to reason, of course, that 100 percent foreign ownership almost certainly would result in foreign control, by whatever standard, and that a total absence of foreign shareholding would virtually preclude the existence of such control. How much is "enough," however, cannot be determined abstractly. Thus, in the course of the drafting of the Convention, it was said variously that "interests sufficiently important to be able to block major changes in the company" could amount to a "controlling interest" (*Convention History*, Vol. 11, 447); that "control could in fact be acquired by persons holding only 25 percent of" a company's capital (id., 447 – 448); and even that "51% of the shares might not be controlling" while for some purposes "15% was sufficient" (id., 538). As Amerasinghe has said, "the concept of 'control' is broad and flexible... [The question is... whether the nationality chosen represents an exercise of a reasonable amount of control to warrant its choice on the basis of a reasonable criterion."

仲裁庭提出并证实,《公约》第 25 条第 (2) 款 (b) 项第 2 句并未要求,也未表明 "外国控制" 应具体占有多少百分比的股份。涉及该条规定所引起的每一案例都应当依照其具体事实、内容和情况分别审查,无 "公式" 可套。当然,毫无疑问地,百分之百的国外拥有自然可以视为外国控制。反之,国外不拥有任何股份,外国控制也就不存在。但是究竟要拥有多少股份才 "够格" 为外国控制却无法抽象地来决定。因此,在起草公约的过程中,众说纷纭:"利益之大,足以阻止公司中的重大变革" 应构成 "控制利益"(《公约立法史》,第 11 卷,第 447 页);"要拥有一个公司 25% 股份即可在事实上获得控制权"(同上,第 447—448 页);甚至有 "51% 的股份可能不构成控制" 但某些情况下 "15% 已足够"(同上,第 538 页)。正像阿迈拉辛格所说:"控制概念既广泛又灵活……问题是,所选择的国籍是否代表能行使控制权的合理数量,以便根据合理的标准作出。"

It is significant that nowhere does there appear to be any material evidence that Mr. Panagiotopulos either acted or was materially influential in a truly managerial rather than technical or supervisory vein. At all times he was subject to the direction of the Managing Director, Mr. Appenteng, who himself apparently controlled the largest single block of shares (31 percent held by Appenteng Mensah & Co.), and who in turn responded to the board of directors, of which Mr. and Mrs. Panagiotopulos were but two members. Nowhere in these proceedings is it suggested that Mr. Panagiotopulos, as holder of 20 percent of Vacuum Salt's shares, either through an alliance with other shareholders, through securing a significant power of decision or managerial influence, or otherwise, was in a position to steer, through either positive or negative action, the fortunes of Vacuum Salt. The fact that it was truly his "brain-child" and, if such be the case, that his technical advice generally was heeded and even proved to be indispensable, does not fuse with his 20 percent shareholding to render him capable of strongly influencing critical decisions on important corporate matter. This is reflected in the board minutes under review, where he invariably delivered the "technical report," and, while temporarily styled General Manager or Deputy Managing Director, also reported on the company's financial status. In the end, the entire proceedings, even viewed in the light most favorable to Claimant, are instinct with the sense that Mr. Panagiotopulos, for all his admitted talents, was not in any sense "in charge".

没有任何具体的实在的证据可以表明，除了技术监督之外，帕纳吉奥托普罗斯先生在具体的实际的管理中有何影响力，这是十分重要的。自始至终，他都听命于执行董事阿彭滕先生，他拥有的股份显然是最大的一股（阿彭滕·门萨公司持股31%），他要向董事会汇报工作，该董事会中帕纳吉奥托普罗斯先生及其夫人只是其中的两名董事成员。在本案的诉讼程序中，从未有任何事实表明，拥有真空盐业20%的股份的帕纳吉奥托普罗斯先生试图通过与其他股东们的联盟确保他的重要决策权或在管理上施加影响，或其他方面来确定自己的位置，用赞成或否定的方法来左右真空盐业的命运。即使真空盐业是他的"智力产儿"确实名副其实，而且他的技术指导常引起重视，甚至被证明是不可缺少的，再加上其拥有20%股份；尽管如此，也没能使得他在公司的重大问题决策中起决定性的作用。这点可从仲裁庭审查的董事会记录中看出，尽管他总是向董事会提交"技术报告"，而且还偶尔被称为总经理或副执行董事，制作公司财务状况的财务报告。最终，即使以最有利于原告的角度来看，整个诉讼程序充分证明帕纳吉奥托普罗斯先生尽管才华公认，但并没有任何"大权在握"的迹象。

The Tribunal is constrained to conclude that the presumption from the fact of consent that the requirements of the second clause of Article 25 (2) (b) were satisfied in this case on 22 January 1988 is rebutted. Admittedly, "it would be difficult to challenge later such a stipulation [under Article 25 (2) (b)] agreed to by the Contracting State concerned, regardless of the objective situation," The Tribunal finds the Request here, however, to be such a case. Simply stated, accepting jurisdiction in the particular circumstances of this case, in our view, "would permit parties to use the Convention for purposes for which it was clearly not intended." We do not find here indications of foreign control of Vacuum Salt such as to justify regarding it as a national of an ICSID Contracting State other than Ghana. In our estimation, the drafters of the Convention, and specifically of the second clause of Article 25 (2) (b), cannot have contemplated that a case such as this one would bring into play an international dispute settlement regime designed to promote greater private international investment by providing a forum for the resolution of any ensuing disputes between a State and a national of another State.

For the reasons set forth above, the Tribunal finds that it lacks jurisdiction and, accordingly, the Request for Arbitration herein must be dismissed.

仲裁庭不得不做出结论，这个案子，仅仅从1988年1月22日签约同意就认定《公约》第25条第（2）款（b）项第2句的要求得到满足的假设是不成立的。我们承认，无论客观情况如何，想对有关缔约国所同意的这样一个条款［第25条第（2）款（b）项］而后提出异议是十分困难的。但仲裁庭发现本案的仲裁申请恰是如此。简单地说，依我们看来，对此案的具体情况实施管辖权"将会允许当事方不按其原宗旨来运用、执行公约"。在此，我们并未发现任何迹象足以表明真空盐业被外国控股，因而无法律依据认为它是解决投资争端国际中心加纳之外的其他缔约国的国民。我们认为，公约起草者，尤其是第25条第（2）款（b）项的起草者，无法预料到像这样一个案子的解决会用到国际争端解决制度。因为它是用为一个国家和其他国家国民的争端提供解决平台的办法来促进更多的国际私人投资。

由于以上所述理由，本仲裁庭裁决对此案无管辖权。因此，拒绝受理仲裁申请。

案件影响（Impact of the Case）

在本案立案后，加纳司法部长1992年10月26日致函"中心"，反对"中心"对此案的管辖，根据是原告"本来就是一家加纳公司"，"并未被外国控制而且双方从来就没有协议说应享受另一签约国的国民待遇。"仲裁庭分析了双方当事人同意将争议提交仲裁的时间点，即签署租赁合同的1988年1月22日时点上，申请人真空盐业公司的股份分布情况及实际控制人情况，并对公约第25条第（2）款（b）项中视为其他缔约国法人的情况进行了详尽的分析，认为双方同意并不代表可以突破客观情况。本案中申请人真空盐业主张公司受希腊国籍股东控制，然而相关证据表明该持公司20%的股东并未对公司的经营管理有重大影响，而另一加纳国民控制公司31%股权并担任着公司执行董事，故认定申请人未被外国人控制，从而无法对本案行使管辖权。

本案是一个较为极端的个案。因为之前中心处理的很多案件中，并无必要区分"同意视为外国国民"和"外国投资者控制"这两种情况，通常双方在协议中认可投资者可视为外国国民，一般均是以该投资者确由外国投资者控制为基础。但在本案中，尽管涉案投资合同中加纳同意将双方争议提交中心解决，但客观事实是，该公司并非由外国投资者控制。这一案例的裁决结果澄清了公约视为其他缔约国国民的有关条款应如何具体适用。

思考问题（Questions）

1. ICSID行使管辖权所针对的仲裁主体的适格性应如何认定？
2. 如何认定公司的实际控制人？

案例三　马菲基尼诉西班牙案

Emilio Agustín Maffezini v. The Kingdom of Spain（2000）（ICSID Case No. ARB/97/7）

选读理由（Selected Reason）

　　本案争议主要涉及 ICSID 是否拥有管辖权。本案涉案金额虽然不大（3000 万比塞塔大约相当于 187 万元人民币），但仍成为国际投资法历史上金光闪闪的存在，主要是因为案件涉及国际投资法领域很多体系性的问题，比如最惠国待遇条款适用于争端解决问题、国有企业的行为可否归责于国家等问题。

仲裁申请情况（The Request for Arbitration）

　　On July 18, 1997, the International Centre for Settlement of Investment Disputes（ICSID or the Centre）received from Mr. Emilio Agustín Maffezini a Request for Arbitration against the Kingdom of Spain. The request concerned a dispute arising from treatment allegedly received by Mr. Maffezini from Spanish entities, in connection with his investment in an enterprise for the production and distribution of chemical products in the Spanish region of Galicia.

　　1997 年 7 月 18 日，国际投资争端解决中心（简称为 ICSID 或中心）收到埃米利奥·奥古斯丁·马菲基尼先生的请求，要求对西班牙王国进行仲裁。这项仲裁请求涉及的争端是因马菲基尼先生声称其从一家西班牙企业实体获得的待遇所引起的，这和他投资于在西班牙加利西亚地区生产和销售化学品的企业有关。

　　The Claimant, Mr. Emilio Agustín Maffezini, is a national of the Argentine Republic

(Argentina), with his domicile in Buenos Aires, Argentina. In 1989, Mr. Emilio Agustín Maffezini decided to embark on the production of various chemical products in Galicia, Spain, by establishing and investing in a corporation named Emilio A. Maffezini S. A. (EAMSA). EAMSA was incorporated under the laws of Spain on November 15, 1989. Mr. Maffezini subscribed to 70% of the capital for 35 million Spanish Pesetas, paying 66. 36% thereof at the time of incorporation, with the balance to be paid at a later time. The Sociedad para el Desarrollo Industrial de Galicia, a Spanish entity whose legal status will be discussed below, subscribed to 30% of the capital or 15 million Spanish Pesetas. A third nominal shareholder was included to comply with the legal requirements relating to the incorporation, but that share was immediately repurchased by Mr. Maffezini. A contract was also made for the repurchase of SODIGA's shares by Mr. Maffezini. This contract provided for an interest rate of 12%. That rate was lower than the current market rate of 16. 6% and reflected a preferential arrangement. SODIGA also granted a loan of 40 million Spanish Pesetas to the newly incorporated company, at a preferential interest rate, to be applicable at least for the first year. Various subsidies were requested from and approved by the Spanish Ministry of Finance and the Xunta de Galicia.

申请人埃米利奥·奥古斯丁·马菲基尼先生是阿根廷共和国（阿根廷）国民，其住所位于阿根廷布宜诺斯艾利斯。1989 年，马菲基尼先生决定在西班牙加利西亚建立并投资一家名为 Emilio A. Maffezini S. A. （EAMSA）的公司，开始生产各种化工产品。EAMSA 于 1989 年 11 月 15 日根据西班牙法律成立。马菲基尼先生以 3500 万西班牙比塞塔认购了 70% 的股份，在公司成立时支付了 66. 36% 的资本金，剩余部分将在以后支付。西班牙加利西亚工业发展公司（SODIGA，一个西班牙企业实体，其法律地位将在下文中讨论）以 1500 万西班牙比塞塔认购了 30% 股份。另外公司还有一个第三方名义股东，以符合与公司成立有关的法律要求，但该股东的股份很快被马菲基尼先生回购。马菲基尼先生还签订了一份回购 SODIGA 股份的合同，此合同规定了 12% 的利率，这一利率低于当时 16. 6% 的市场利率，反映出一种优惠安排。SODIGA 还向新成立的公司提供了 4000 万西班牙比塞塔的贷款，并至少在第一年适用优惠利率。西班牙财政部和加利西亚政府给该公司批准了多种补贴。

Information on prospective markets was requested from various Spanish government agencies. At the same time, EAMSA proceeded to hire a private consulting firm in order to identify the appropriate plot of land to buy and to undertake a study on the costs of construction and whatever other requirements the new company might have to begin production. On the basis of this study the land was purchased and contracts concluded with various firms and suppliers. SODIGA, for its part, had also undertaken an economic evaluation of the project in order to decide whether to participate in it.

On June 24, 1991, an environmental impact assessment (EIA) study was filed with the Xunta de Galicia, the government of the Autonomous Region of Galicia. Additional information was requested and provided, and the EIA was finally cleared on January 15, 1992. Before such clearance was obtained, work commenced on readying the land for construction. Construction of the plant itself was also begun.

西班牙各政府机构要求提供有关未来市场的信息。与此同时,EAMSA 开始聘请一家私人咨询公司,以确定要购买的合适地块,并对新公司开始生产所需的建设成本和其他要求进行研究。在此研究的基础上,新公司购买了土地并与不同的公司和供应商签订合同。SODIGA 也对该项目进行了经济评估,以决定是否参与该项目。

1991 年 6 月 24 日,公司向加利西亚自治区政府提交了一份环境影响评估(EIA)报告。在进一步补充提供资料后,环境影响评估报告最终于 1992 年 1 月 15 日获得通过。在获得通过之前,为实施建设而进行的土地准备工作已经开展,工厂本身的建设也开始了。

While these preparations for the implementation of the project were in progress, EAMSA began to experience financial difficulties. A capital increase was agreed to, new loans were requested and applications for additional subsidies were made. Some of these efforts did not succeed, however. A transfer of 30 million Spanish Pesetas was made from a personal account of Mr. Maffezini to EAMSA, under circumstances that will be considered below.

In early March 1992, Mr. Maffezini ordered the construction to stop and the dismissal of EAMSA employees. In June 1994 an attorney working for Mr. Maffezini approached SODIGA with an offer inviting it to cancel all outstanding debts owed it by EAMSA and Mr. Maffezini in exchange for EAMSA's assets. SODIGA indicated that it would accept this offer provided Mr. Maffezini was willing to add 2 million Spanish Pesetas. This proposal was rejected by Mr. Maffezini. The Argentine embassy in Madrid was then asked by Mr. Maffezini to intervene. After an exchange of more correspondence, SODIGA indicated, on June 13, 1996, that it was willing to accept the original proposal made by Mr. Maffezini's attorney. Mr. Maffezini did not follow up on SODIGA's latest proposal. Not long there after he instituted the ICSID proceedings described above.

虽然项目实施的这些准备工作正在进行中,但 EAMSA 开始遇到财务困难。公司采取了让股东同意增加资本,申请新贷款和额外补贴的措施,但其中一些努力没有成功。在以下情况下,3000 万西班牙比塞塔被从马菲基尼先生的个人账户转账到EAMSA 账户。

1992 年 3 月初,马菲基尼先生下令停止施工并解雇 EAMSA 员工。1994 年 6 月,一名为马菲基尼先生工作的律师向 SODIGA 提议要求其取消 EAMSA 和马菲基尼先生对其所欠的所有未清偿的债务，以换取 EAMSA 的资产。SODIGA 表示，如果马菲基尼愿意增加 200 万西班牙比塞塔，它将接受这个提议。但这一要价被马菲基尼先生拒绝了。阿根廷驻马德里大使馆随后被马菲基尼先生要求进行干预。在多次相互致函后，SODI-GA 于 1996 年 6 月 13 日表示，愿意接受马菲基尼先生的律师最初提出的报价。马菲基尼没有跟进 SODIGA 的最新提议。不久后他提起上述 ICSID 程序。

Based on the foregoing facts, Mr. Maffezini has submitted four main contentions to this Tribunal. First, that because of SODIGA's status as a public entity, all of its acts and omissions are attributable to the Kingdom of Spain. Second, that the project failed because of the wrong advice given by SODIGA with regard to the costs of the project, which turned out to be significantly higher than originally estimated. Third, that SODIGA was also responsible for the additional costs resulting from the EIA since EAMSA was pressured to make the investment before the EIA process was finalized and before its implications were known. Fourth, that Mr. Maffezini had not agreed to a loan to EAMSA for 30 million Spanish Pesetas and that the transfer of this amount from his personal account to EAMSA was irregular.

基于上述事实，马菲基尼先生已向本法庭提出四项主要观点。第一，由于 SODIGA 具有一个公共实体的法律地位，其所有行为和疏忽都可归因于西班牙王国。第二，项目失败是由于 SODIGA 就项目成本给出的错误建议，项目所需成本远超过最初的估算。第三，SODIGA 还应负责因环境影响评估而产生的额外费用，因为在环境影响评估程序最终确定之前以及在环境影响评价的结果已知之前，EAMSA 迫于压力而进行了投资。第四，马菲基尼先生没有同意向 EAMSA 提供 3000 万西班牙比塞塔的贷款，而且将这笔款项从他的个人账户转移到 EAMSA 账户是不正常的。

On October 30, 1997, the Secretary-General of the Centre registered the request, pursuant to Article 36 (3) of the ICSID Convention. On this same date, the Secretary-General, in accordance with Institution Rule 7, notified the parties of the registration of the request and invited them toproceed to constitute an Arbitral Tribunal as soon as possible.

After consulting with the parties, the Tribunal scheduled a first session for August 21, 1998. On August 20, 1998, counsel for the Respondent hand-delivered a document containing Spain's objections to the jurisdiction of the Centre.

the Tribunal, addressing the other objections to jurisdiction raised by Spain, concluded that the Claimant had made out aprima facie case that he had standing to file this case, that the Sociedad para el Desarrollo Industrial de Galicia Sociedad Anonima (SODIGA S. A. or SODIGA) was a State entity acting on behalf of the Kingdom of Spain and that the dispute came into being after both the Argentine-Spain and the Chile-Spain BITs had entered into force. On these basis, the Tribunal concluded that the Centre had jurisdiction and that the Tribunal was competent to consider the dispute between the parties in accordance with the provisions of the Argentine-Spain BIT.

1997 年 10 月 30 日，中心秘书长根据 ICSID 公约第 36 条（3）款的规定，登记了此项要求。同日，秘书长根据机构细则 7，将申请登记的情况通知当事人，并要他们尽快组成仲裁庭。

在与当事各方协商后，仲裁庭定于 1998 年 8 月 21 日举行第一届会议。1998 年 8 月 20 日，被告的律师亲手递交了一份文件，其中载有西班牙对中心管辖权的异议。

仲裁庭处理了西班牙提出的对管辖权的其他反对意见，得出结论说，索赔人提出了一项初步证据，证明他有资格提起这一案件，加利西亚工业发展公司（SODIGA S. A. 或 SODIGA）是代表西班牙王国行事的一个国家实体，争端是在阿根廷—西班牙双边投资协定和智利—西班牙双边投资协定生效后产生的。基于此，仲裁庭得出结论，中心具有管辖权，仲裁庭有资格根据阿根廷—西班牙双边投资协定的规定审理当事各方之间的争端。

仲裁结果（Award）

For the reasons stated above the Tribunal unanimously decides that：

（1）The Kingdom of Spain shall pay the Claimant the amount of ESP 57,641,265. 28（fifty-seven million six hundred forty one thousand two hundred and sixty-five Spanish pesetas and 28 cents）.

（2）Each of the parties shall bear the entirety of its own expenses and legalfees for its own counsel.

（3）All other claims are dismissed.

鉴于上述理由，仲裁庭一致决定：

（1）西班牙王国应向索赔人支付 57664261. 28 比塞塔。

（2）每一方均自行承担所发生的全部费用和律师费用。

（3）驳回其他请求。

仲裁原因（reasons for the decisions）

Exhaustion of Domestic Remedies

The Kingdom of Spain first challenges the jurisdiction of the Centre and the competence of the Tribunal on the ground that the Claimant failed to comply with the requirements of Article X of the Bilateral Investment Treaty between Argentina and Spain. Article X of this Treaty reads as follows:

"Article X Settlement of Disputes Between a Contracting Party and an Investor of the other Contracting Party

1. Disputes which arise within the terms of this Agreement concerning an investment between an investor of one Contracting Party and the other Contracting Party shall, if possible, be settled amicably by the parties to the dispute.

2. If the dispute cannot thus be settled within six months following the date on which the dispute has been raised by either party, it shall be submitted to the competent tribunal of the Contracting Party in whose territory the investment was made.

3. The dispute may be submitted to international arbitration in any of the following circumstances:

a) At the request of one of the parties to the dispute, if no decision has been rendered on the merits of the claim after the expiration of a period of eighteen months from the date on which the proceedings referred to in paragraph 2 of this Article have been initiated, or if such decision has been rendered, but the dispute between the parties continues;

b) If both parties to the dispute agree thereto,

Respondent makes two interrelated arguments based on Article X. The first is that Article X (3) (a) requires the exhaustion of certain domestic remedies in Spain and that Claimant failed to comply with this requirement. The second contention is that Claimant did not submit the case to Spanish courts before referring it to international arbitration as required by Article X (2) of the BIT. "

西班牙王国首先对该中心的管辖权和仲裁庭的管辖权提出质疑,理由是索赔人未能遵守阿根廷和西班牙之间的双边投资协定第 10 条的要求。该条约第 10 条规定如下:

"第十条 一缔约国与另一缔约国投资者之间争端的解决:

1. 本协定条款内发生的一缔约方投资者与另一缔约方之间的投资争端,如有可能,应由争端各方友好解决。

2. 如果在任何一方提出争端之日起 6 个月内,争端不能得到解决,则应将争端提交在其领土内进行投资的缔约方的有管辖权的法庭。

3. 有下列情形之一的,可以提交国际仲裁:

a) 应争端一方要求,如果在本条第(2)款所指的诉讼开始之日起满 18 个月后,仍未就是否应当赔偿作出决定,或虽已作出该决定,但双方之间的争议依然存在;

b) 如果争议双方同意,则

被申请人根据第十条提出了两个相互关联的论点。第一个论点是，第 10 条第（3）款（a）项要求在西班牙用尽某些国内补救措施，而索赔人未能遵守这一要求。第二个论点是，索赔人在根据双边投资协定第 10 条第（2）款的规定将案件提交国际仲裁之前，没有将案件提交西班牙法院。"

Most Favored Nation Clause

The argument based on the most favored nation clause raises a number of legal issues with which international tribunals are confronted from time to time. As is true of many treaties of this kind, Article Ⅳ of the BIT between Argentina and Spain, after guaranteeing a fair and equitable treatment for investors, provides the following in paragraph 2:

"In all matters subject to this Agreement, this treatment shall not be less favorable than that extended by each Party to the investments made in its territory by investors of a third country."

As noted above, the Argentine-Spain BIT provides domestic courts with the opportunity to deal with a dispute for a period of eighteen months before it may be submitted to arbitration. However, Article 10 (2) of the Chile-Spain Bilateral Investment Treaty, imposes no such condition. It provides merely that the investor can opt for arbitration after the six month period allowed for negotiations has expired. Claimant contends, consequently, that Chilean investors in Spain are treated more favorably than Argentine investors in Spain. He argues, accordingly, that the most favored nation clause in the Argentine-Spain BIT gives him the option to submit the dispute to arbitration without prior referral to domestic courts.

申请人基于最惠国待遇条款的论点提出了国际仲裁庭不时面临的一些法律问题。正如许多此类条约的情况一样，阿根廷和西班牙在保证对投资者的公平和公平待遇后，在第（2）款中规定了以下内容：

"在本协议规定的所有事项中，这种待遇不应低于每一缔约方对第三国投资者在其领土内进行的投资所给予的待遇。"

如上所述，阿根廷—西班牙双边投资协定给国内法院用 18 个月的期限处理争议提供了机会，然后争议才能被提交国际仲裁。然而，《智利—西班牙双边投资协定》第 10 条（2）款并未规定此类条件。它只规定，在允许的六个月谈判期限到期后，投资者可以选择仲裁。因此，申请人辩称，智利在西班牙的投资者比阿根廷在西班牙的投资者受到更好的待遇。因此，他认为，阿根廷—西班牙双边投资协定中最惠国条款允许他选择将争议提交仲裁，而无须事先提交国内法院。

From the above considerations it can be concluded that if a third party treaty contains provisions for the settlement of disputes that are more favorable to the protection of the investor's rights and interests than those in the basic treaty, such provisions may be extended to the beneficiary of the most favored nation clause as they are fully compatible with theejusdem generis principle. Of course, the third-party treaty has to relate to the same subject matter as the basic treaty, be it the protection of foreign investments or the promotion of trade, since the dispute settlement provisions will operate in the context of these matters; otherwise there would be a contravention of that principle. This operation of the most favored nation clause does, however, have some important limits arising from public policy considerations that will be discussed further below.

根据上述考虑，可以得出结论，如果第三方条约中包含的解决争端的条款比在基础条约中的条款更有利于保护投资者的权益，则此类条款可以扩展到最惠国条款的受益人，因为按照同类规则它们是完全相同的。当然，第三方条约必须与基础条约涉及相同的主题，无论是保护外国投资还是促进贸易，因为争端解决条款将在这些事项的背景下运作；否则将违反这一原则。然而，最惠国条款的这种运作确实有一些重要的限制，这些限制来自公共政策考虑，将在下文进一步讨论。

In light of the above considerations, the Tribunal is satisfied that the Claimant has convincingly demonstrated that the most favored nation clause included in the Argentine-Spain BIT embraces the dispute settlement provisions of this treaty. Therefore, relying on the more favorable arrangements contained in the Chile-Spain BIT and the legal policy adopted by Spain with regard to the treatment of its own investors abroad, the Tribunal concludes that Claimant had the right to submit the instant dispute to arbitration without first accessing the Spanish courts.

鉴于上述考虑，仲裁庭认为，申请人已令人信服地证明阿根廷—西班牙双边投资协定中包含的最惠国待遇条款的适用范围及于该条约的争端解决条款。因此，根据智利—西班牙条约中包含的更为有利的安排以及西班牙对本国投资者在国外的待遇所采取的法律政策，仲裁庭得出结论，原告有权将当前的纠纷提交仲裁，而无须先向西班牙法院提起诉讼。

SODIGA's status in the Kingdom of Spain

The Claimant arguesthat the actions and omissions affecting his investment are attributable toan entity owned and operated by the Kingdom of Spain. SODIGA, the Claimant argues, is not only owned by several State entities, but it is alsounder the control of the State and operated as an arm of the State for the purposes of the economic development of the region of Galicia. Accordingly, as a State entity, its wrongful acts or omission may be attributed to the State. The Respondent maintains, however, that SODIGA is a privatecommercial corporation established under the commercial laws of Spainand that, consequently, its activities are those of a private entity. Ownership of part of the shares of SODIGA by State entities, the Respondentargues, does not alter the private commercial character of the corporationnor does it transform SODIGA into a State agency. Its acts or omissions cannot, therefore, be attributed to the State.

申请人辩称，影响其投资的行为和疏忽可归因于西班牙王国拥有和经营的实体。SODIGA 不仅归几个国家实体所有，而且还受国家控制，是为加利西亚地区的经济发展而作为国家的一个部门运作。因此，作为一个国家实体，其不法行为或不作为可归因于国家。但是，被告认为，索迪加是一家根据西班牙商业法成立的私人商业公司，因此，其活动属于私人实体。被申请人辩称，国有实体对 SODIGA 部分股份的所有权既不会改变公司的私人商业性质，也不会将 SODIGA 转变为国有机构。因此，它的作为或不作为不能归因于国家。

The question whether or not SODIGA is a State entity must beexamined first from a formal or structural point of view. Here a finding that the entity is owned by the State, directly or indirectly, gives rise to arebuttable presumption that it is a State entity. The same result will obtainif an entity is controlled by the State, directly or indirectly. A similar presum ption arises if an entity's purpose or objectives is the carrying out of functions which are governmental in nature or which are otherwise normally reserved to the Statc, or which by their nature are not usually carried out by private businesses or individuals.

必须首先从形式或结构的角度来研究 SODIGA 是否是一个国家实体的问题。如果发现该实体直接或间接为国家所有，则会产生一个可反驳的推定，即该实体为国家实体。如果一个实体被国家直接或间接控制，也会得到同样的结果。如果一个实体的目的或目标是履行政府性质的职能，或通常保留给国家的职能，或其性质通常不是由私营企业或个人履行，则也会产生类似的推定。

Because of the many forms that State enterprises may take and thus shape the manners of State action, the structural test by itself may notal ways be a conclusive determination whether an entity is an organ of the State or whether its acts may be attributed to the State. An additional testhas been developed, a functional test, which looks to the functions of or role to be performed by the entity. Although, as noted above, neither the ICSID Convention nor the Argentine-Spain BIT define a Contracting State, the drafting history of the Convention does cover an analogous situation: whether mixed economy companies or government-owned corporations may be considered under the definition of a "national of a Contracting State". While recognizing, of course, that definitions of different terms are not usually inter changeable and that, in this case, a "Contracting State" is different from a "national of a Contracting State", there are sufficient similarities which would allow us to utilize jurisprudence developed for one definition in the context of the other. Thus, adetermination as to the character of state-owned enterprises in the context of whether it is a "national of a Contracting State", may also be relevant indetermining whether a state enterprise may be subsumed within the definition of the term "Contracting Party". In this connection, it is relevant tonote, as explained by a leading authority on the Convention, that it would seem that "a mixed economy company or government-owned corporation should not be disqualified as a 'national of another Contracting State' unless it is acting as an agent for the government or is discharging an essentially governmental function".

由于国有企业可以采取多种形式，从而形成国家行为方式，因此，对一个实体本身进行结构检验并不总是能够对其是否是国家机关，或者其行为是否可以归因于国家形成决定性的结论。另外还有一个检验标准即职能检验，它关注实体的职能或其扮演的角色。尽管如上所述，ICSID 公约和阿根廷—西班牙都没有界定何谓一个缔约国，但该公约的起草历史确实涵盖了一个类似的情况：无论是混合经济公司还是国有公司，都可以被考虑为"缔约国国民"。当然，虽然认识到不同术语的定义通常是不可互换的，在本案情况下，"缔约国"不同于"缔约国国民"，但有足够的相似性使我们能够在另一个定义的上下文中发挥自由裁量权界定一个定义。因此，在确定国有企业是否为"缔约国国民"的情况下，确定国有企业的性质也可能与确定国有企业是否可纳入"缔约国"一词的定义有关。在这方面，有必要注意到，正如公约的一个主管当局所解释的那样，"一个混合经济公司或政府所有的公司不应被取消'另一缔约国国民'的资格，除非它是政府的代理人或正在履行基本的政府职能"。

This functional test has been applied, in respect of the definition of a national of a Contracting State, in the recent decision of an ICSID Tribunal on objections to jurisdiction in the case of Ceskoslovenska Obchodni Banka, A. S. v. the Slovak Republic. Here it was held that the fact of State owner ship of the shares of the corporate entity was not enough to decide the crucial issue of whether the Claimant had standing under the Convention as a national of a Contracting State as long as the activities them selves were "essentially commercial rather than governmental in nature". By the same token, a private corporation operating for profit while discharging essentially governmental functions delegated to it by the State could, under the functional test, be considered as an organ of the State and thus engage the State's international responsibility for wrong fulacts.

这一对缔约国国民进行功能检验的方法，在ICSID 法庭最近就对塞科斯洛文斯卡·奥布乔德尼·班卡诉斯洛伐克共和国管辖权裁决中得到应用。该案认为，国家拥有法人实体股份的事实不足以决定申请人是否具有公约中的缔约国国民的地位，因为他们的活动在本质上基本上是商业性质的而非政府性质的。同样地，一个以盈利为目的的私营公司，如果同时履行国家赋予它的基本政府职能，在职能检验标准下，也可以被视为国家的一个机构，从而使国家对错误行为承担国际责任。

SODIGA was created by a decree issued by the Ministry of Industry which authorized the

National Institute for Industry (Instituto Nacionalde Industria), a national State agency, to establish SODIGA. The characterization of the Ministry and the Institute as State entities is not disputed in this case. Furthermore, in spite of the fact that the government chose to create SODIGA in the form of a private commercial corporation, it did so by providing that the Instituto Nacionalde Industria would own no less than 51% of the capital. In fact, as of December 31, 1990, the percentage of governmentally owned capital of SODIGA had increased to over 88%, including the stock holdings of the Xunta de Galicia, also a state entity in charge of the executive power in the Autonomous Community of Galicia, several savings and loans associations, other regional development agencies and the Banco Exterior de España.

SODIGA 是由工业部颁布的一项法令创建的，该法令授权一家国家政府机构即国家工业研究所建立 SODIGA。在本案中，将该工业部和研究所定性为国家实体并无争议。此外，尽管政府选择以私人商业公司的形式创建 SODIGA，但政府还是通过国家工业研究所持有其不少于 51% 的股权。事实上，截至 1990 年 12 月 31 日，SODIGA 的政府所有资本比例已增至 88% 以上，其中包括控制加利西亚自治区行政权力的政府实体、加利西亚政府、几个储蓄和贷款机构、其他地区发展机构和西班牙对外银行所持有的股份。

The preamble to the decreedeclares that one of the purposes for SODIGA's creation is the promotion of regional industrial development of the Autonomous Region of Galicia. Furthermore, it can be seen that it was the intent of the Government of Spain to utilize SODIGA as an instrument of State action. Among its functions was the undertaking of studies for the introduction of new industries into Galicia, seeking and soliciting such new industries, investing in new enterprises, processing loan applications with official sources of financing, providing guarantees for such loans, and providing technical assistance. Moreover, either through the Instituto Nacional de Industria or directly, SODIGA was charged with providing subsidies and offering other inducements for the development of industries. Many of these objectives and functions are by their very nature typically governmental tasks, not usually carried out by private entities, and, therefore, cannot normally be considered to have a commercial nature.

该法令的序言宣布，SODIGA 的创建目的之一是促进加利西亚自治区的区域工业发展。此外，可以看出，西班牙政府意图利用 SODIGA 作为国家行动的工具。其职能之一是开展向加利西亚引进新产业的研究、寻找和招揽此类新产业、投资新企业、利用官方融资提供贷款、为此类贷款提供担保以及提供技术援助。此外，无论是通过国家工业研究所还是直接，SODIGA 都被指控为工业发展提供补贴和其他优惠政策。很多目标和职能在其本质上都是典型的政府任务，通常并不由私人实体执行，因此通常不能被认为具有商业性质。

In view of the fact that SODIGA meets both the structural test of State creation and capital ownership and the functional test of performing activities of a public nature, the Tribunal concludes that the Claimant has made out aprima facie case that SODIGA is a State entity acting on be half of the Kingdom of Spain.

鉴于 SODIGA 既符合由国家创造和拥有的结构检验标准，又符合执行公共性质活动的职能检验标准，仲裁庭得出结论，申请人已初步证实 SODIGA 是代表西班牙王国行事的国家实体。

Whether SODIGA is responsible

The second main contention by the Claimant, as noted above, is that the project failed because SODIGA provided faulty advice regarding the cost of the project, which turned out to be significantly higher than originally estimated. According to the Claimant, the first draft investment project was based on a report by SODIGA, dated May 1989, which was made in order to determine the viability of the project. Claimant submits that the final cost of the investment would have been 300% higher had the project been completed.

In this connection, the Tribunal must emphasize that Bilateral Investment Treaties are not insurance policies against bad business judgments. While it is probably true that there were short comings in the policies and practices that SODIGA and its sister entities pursued in the here.

relevant period in Spain, they cannot be deemed to relieve investors of the business risks inherent in any investment. To that extent, it is clear that Spain cannot be held responsible for the losses Mr. Maffezini may have sustained any more than would any private entity under similar circum stances.

如上文所述，索赔人的第二个主要论点是，项目失败是因为 SODIGA 就项目成本提供了错误的建议，结果发现，该建议明显高于最初的估计。根据申请人的说法，第一个投资项目方案是基于 SODIGA 于 1989 年 5 月提交的一份报告，该报告旨在确定项目的可行性。申请人认为，如果项目完成，投资的最终成本将会高出 300%。

在这方面，法庭必须强调，双边投资协定不是防止不良商业判断的保险。虽然 SODIGA 及其姐妹实体在西班牙这一相关时期所实施的政策和做法可能存在缺陷，但不能认为这些缺陷和做法可以减轻投资者在任何投资中固有的商业风险。在这方面，西班牙显然不能对马菲基尼先生这样的任何私营实体在类似情况下可能遭受的损失负责。

The Claimant also contends that SODIGA is responsible for the additional costs resulting from the EIA because EAMSA was pressured to go ahead with the investment before that process was finalized and its implications were known. This pressure, according to Claimant, was exercised for political reasons by the authorities of the Xunta de Galicia and the local municipality. Claimant's decision to stop the construction work was directly related to this additional increase in the costs of the project.

The Tribunal holds that the Kingdom of Spain and SODIGA have done no more in this respect than insist on the strict observance of the EEC and Spanish law applicable to the industry in question. It follows that Spain cannot be held responsible for the decisions taken by the Claimant with regard to the EIA.

申请人还主张，SODIGA 对环境影响评估引起的额外费用负有责任，因为 EAMSA 在这一进程最后确定并知道其影响之前受到了继续投资的压力。申请人说，这种压力是由当局和加利西亚政府出于政治原因施加的。申请人之所以决定停止建筑工程建设，与这项额外增加的费用直接有关。

仲裁庭认为西班牙王国和 SODIGA 在这方面所做的只是坚持严格遵守适用于有关行业的欧洲经济共同体和西班牙法律。因此，西班牙不能对申请人就环境影响评估作出的决定负责。

The Claimant also contends that 30 million Spanish Pesetas were transferred from his personal account as a loan to EAMSA, despite the fact that he had not consented to the loan. The Claimant also complains of anumber of irregularities attributable to the private banks that managed his accounts, and that these acts also engage the responsibility of the Banco de España, Spain's Central Bank.

申请人还诉称，其个人账户中的 3000 万西班牙比塞塔被作为贷款转移至 EAMSA 账户，但他并未同意为 EAMSA 提供贷款。申请人还提及管理其账户的私人银行存在许多违规行为，这些行为也由西班牙中央银行负责。

The order to transfer was given by Mr. Soto Baños on February 4, 1992. The underlying financial commitment, however, never came to be formalized in a contract binding on Mr. Maffezini, nor was the loan approved by the board of EAMSA, either before or after the transfer of the funds. The Tribunal also finds that Mr. Soto Baños was not acting in this operation as the personal representative of Mr. Maffezini but as an official of SODIGA. Because SODIGA was an entity charged with theim plementation of governmental policies relating to industrial promotion, it performed a number of functions not normally open to ordinary commercial companies. Handling the accounts of EAMSA as a participating company, managing its payments and finances and generally intervening on its behalf before the Spanish authorities without being paid for these services, are all elements that responded to SODIGAs public nature-and responsibility. Moreover, the manner in which the private banks conducted themselves in this case with regard to the loan, can be explainedin large measure only because of their recognition that SODIGA's ordersand instructions were entitled to be honored because of the public functions it performed in Galicia.

索托·巴约先生于 1992 年 2 月 4 日下达了移交令。然而，这项暗地里进行的融资安排，从来没有正式地出现在对马菲基尼有约束力的合同中，EAMSA 董事会也没有在资金转移之前或之后批准该贷款。仲裁庭还发现，索托·巴约先生并非作为马菲基尼先生的个人代表，而是作为 SODIGA 的一名官员参与这项行动。由于 SODIGA 是一个负责执行与工业促进有关的政府政策的实体，因此它获得了一些通常不向普通商业公司开放的职能。作为一家参股公司，处理 EAMSA 的账目，管理其付款和财务，并代表西班牙当局的利益对这些行为进行干预，而不支付这些服务的费用，这些都是 SODIGA 所具有的公共实体的性质和职能的反映。此外，私人银行之所以参与到此次款项划转行为中，在很大程度上可以解释，因为他们认识到，由于 SODIGA 在加利西亚履行的公共职能，SODIGA 的命令和指示应当得到执行。

Because the acts of SODIGA relating to the loan cannot be considered commercial in nature and involve its public functions, responsibility for them should be attributed to the Kingdom of Spain. In particular, the seacts amounted to a breach by Spain of its obligation to protect the investment as provided for in Article 3 (1) of the Argentine-Spain Bilateral Investment Treaty. Moreover, the lack of transparency with which this loan transaction was conducted is incompatible with Spain's commitment to ensure the investora fair and equitable treatment in accordance with Article 4 (1) of the same treaty.

由于索迪加与贷款有关的行为在性质上不能被视为商业行为，也不能涉及其公共职能，因此对这些行为的责任应归于西班牙王国。尤其是，这些行为构成西班牙违反了其与阿根廷双边投资协定第 3 条第（1）款规定的保护投资的义务。此外，此次资金划转缺乏透明度，这与西班牙在同一协定第 4 条第（1）款承诺的确保投资者获得公平待遇的规定不符。

Since the funds were with drawn from a time-deposit account of Mr. Maffezini, it is appropriatein this case to order the payment of interest compounded on an annualbasis from February 4, 1992 until the date of the Award. The Tribunal considers reasonable to fix as interest rate the LIBOR rate for the Spanishpeseta for each annual period since February 4, 1992 and for the proportion that corresponds to the period between February 4, 2000 and the dateof the A-ward. The interests therefore amount to ESP 27,641,265.28.

Accordingly, the Tribunal finds that the total amount of compensation, including interest, that the Kingdom of Spain is to pay the Claimantis ESP 57,641,265.28. The Kingdom of Spain shall make such payment within a period of 60 days as of the dateof this Award. Should the payment of this amount not be made within the period specified above, the amount shall accrue interests at a rate of 6% perannum, compounded monthly, as of the date of the Award to the date of payment.

由于资金是从马菲基尼先生的定期存款账户中提取的，因此在这种情况下，最好从 1992 年 2 月 4 日至裁决作出的日期，每年计取复利。仲裁庭认为，有理由自 1992 年 2 月 4 日起按照每年的伦敦银行同业拆借利率计算应支付的西班牙比塞塔的利息，并自 2000 年 2 月 4 日至裁决作出日计取相应比例的利息。因此，利息总额为 27641265.28 西班牙比塞塔。

因此，仲裁庭认为，西班牙王国将向申请人支付的赔偿总额（包括利息）为 57641265.28 西班牙比塞塔。西班牙王国应在本裁决作出之日起 60 天内支付该款项。如果未在上述规定的期限内支付该笔款项，则该笔款项自裁决之日起至支付之日应按 6% 的年利率计息，按月计取复利。

案件影响（Impact of the Case）

此案裁决开启了国际投资法中的最惠国待遇条款解释的魔盒。西班牙和阿根廷签订的 BIT 为国内法院争取了 18 个月的审理期限，若国内法院在此期限内未作出裁决，或作出裁决，但争议仍在，就可以诉诸国际仲裁。但本案中阿根廷投资者在未向西班牙国内法院起诉的情况下，根据最惠国待遇条款直接援引了西班牙和智利的 BIT，主张提起投资争端时不必符合 18 个月国内诉讼的条件。仲裁庭分析了西班牙和阿根廷签订的 BIT 中最惠国待遇条款使用了"all matters"的措辞，认为该最惠国待遇条款的适用范围涵盖争端解决方面的待遇，支持了申请人直接提起国际仲裁的主张，确立了仲裁庭对本案的管辖权。

本案的另一难题是国有企业的行为是否应由被仲裁的西班牙政府负责。案中国有企业具有招商引资职能，申请人主张其行为应当归责于国家。仲裁庭援引了国际法委员会的《国家责任条款草案》，认为裁定国有企业是否承担国家责任时，要通过两条法律标准，第一个标准是结构标准，第二个标准是职能标准。仲裁庭随后类比了国有企业可作为外国投资者提起仲裁的案例，从反方向推理，认为即便一个私营公司是盈利性的，但只要从事了国家授权的政府职能，就可以依据职能标准认定为国家机构，其错误行为可归责于国家。

思考问题（Questions）

1. 西班牙和阿根廷 BIT 生效时间是 1992 年 9 月 28 日，此案争议事实主要发生在

1989 年至 1992 年上半年，而马菲基尼 1997 年 7 月才提出仲裁请求，本案仲裁庭是如何认定本案的争议适用西班牙和阿根廷 BIT 的？

2. 如何分辨地方政府招商引资企业履行与投资者之间投资协议的行为是否具有国家行为的性质？

案例四　萨利尼诉摩洛哥案

Salini Costruttori S. P. A. and Italstrade
S. P. A. v. Kingdom of Morocco（2001）
（ICSID Case No. ARB/00/4）

选读理由（Selected Reason）

萨利尼诉摩洛哥案中两家意大利建筑公司参与竞标获得了摩洛哥首都拉巴特高速公路的建设工程，随后因为种种原因延期交付工程，摩洛哥一方因此拒绝履行相应的付款义务。在多次交涉无果的前提下，两家意大利公司作为联合申请人向 ICSID 提出仲裁申请，要求摩洛哥政府履行合同并赔偿相应的损失。这是一起因为承包涉外工程而产生争议遂诉至 ICSID 进行仲裁的案件，对于后来的 ICSID 仲裁庭分析自身对案件管辖权的有无重大影响。案中的"Salini 标准"被后来的 ICSID 仲裁庭应用至今，对学术界和实务界都有重大意义。

仲裁申请情况（The Request for Arbitration）

A dispute has been referred to the Arbitral Tribunal between the following Italian companies: Salini Costruttori S. P. A. Italstrade S. P. A. and the Kingdom of Morocco. The Societe Nationale des Autoroutes du Maroc（hereinafter "ADM"）, incorporated in 1989 as a limited liability company, builds, maintains and operates highways and various road-works, in accordance with the Concession Agreement concluded with the Minister of Infrastructure and Professional & Executive Training, acting on behalf of the State. In August 1994, within the context of this Agreement, ADM issued an international invitation to tender for the construction of a highway joining Rabat to Fes.

The above mentioned Italian companies submitted a joint tender for the construction of section No. 2 Khemisset-Meknes Ouest (West Meknes) , which is approximately 50 kilometres long. The construction of this section was awarded to the Italian companies for a price of MAD 280,702,166. 84 and JPY 3,122,286,949. 50. The negotiations that followed the award of section No. 2 resulted in the signature of Contract 53/95 on October 17, 1995.

意大利公司萨利尼建筑股份公司、意大利贸易股份公司和摩洛哥之间的争端已提交仲裁庭。摩洛哥国家高速公路公司（以下简称"摩洛哥高速公司"）成立于 1989 年，是一家有限责任公司，根据基础设施与专业管理培训部长达成的特许协议，代表国家建造、维护和运营高速公路和各种道路工程。1994 年 8 月，在这项特许协议的范围内，摩洛哥高速公司发出一项国际邀请，招标建设一条连接拉巴特和费斯的公路。

上述意大利公司联合投标承建这一工程的第 2 标段西赫米塞特至梅克内斯（西梅克内斯），长约 50 公里。这一段工程以 280702166. 84 摩洛哥道拉姆和 3122286949. 50 日元的价格授予合同给这两家意大利公司。之后两方进行了谈判，并于 1995 年 10 月 17 日签署了第 53/95 号合同。

The two Claimants created the Groupement d'Entreprises Salini-Italstrade (hereinafter "the Group") for the performance of the contract giving rise to the present dispute. The Group is not a legal entity. As a result, the Italian companies take part in the present arbitration as joint Claimants.

两个申请人成立了萨利尼—意贸公司集团（以下简称"集团"），以履行引发当前争议的合同。该集团不是一个法律实体。因此，两家意大利公司作为共同申请人参加了本次仲裁。

A provisional Taking Over of the work took place on July 31, 1998. The works were completed on October 14, 1998. The works therefore took 36 months to complete, 4 months longer than stipulated in the contract (32 months) . The final Taking Over took place on October 26, 1999.

工程的临时接收工作于 1998 年 7 月 31 日进行。工程于 1998 年 10 月 14 日完成。因此，完成工程用了 36 个月，比合同规定时间（32 个月）长 4 个月。最后的接收在 1999 年 10 月 26 日进行。

A draft of the final account was sent to the Italian companies by ADM. They signed it on March 26, 1999 (with reservations) . On April 29, 1999, the Italian companies sent ADM's Head Engineer a memorandum setting out the reasons for the reservations put forward: technical reservations, exceptionally bad weather, project upheaval, modifications concerning the dimensions of the work, extension of contractual time limits, financial burdens, unforeseeable fluctuations of the value of the Yen.

On September 14, 1999, following the rejection of all of their claims by ADM's Head Engineer, the Italian companies sent a memorandum relating to the final account to the Minister of Infrastructure, in accordance with Article 51 of the Cahier des Clauses Administratives Generales [Book of General Administrative Clauses]. No reply was received from either the Minister of Infrastructure or ADM.

摩洛哥高速公司向意大利公司致送了一份结算草案，意大利公司于 1999 年 3 月 26 日有保留地签署了该结算草案。1999 年 4 月 29 日，意大利公司向摩洛哥高速公司的总工程师发送了备忘录，阐述了提出保留意见的原因：技术疑难、异常恶劣的天气、工程变更大、工程范围调整、合同期限延长、资金负担、不可预见的日元价值的波动。

1999 年 9 月 14 日，在摩洛哥高速公司的总工程师驳回了他们的所有主张后，意大利公司按照《一般行政条款手册》第 51 条的规定，向基础设施部长提交了一份有关结算的备忘录。基础设施部长和摩洛哥高速公司均未给出任何答复。

On May 1, 2000, the Italian companies filed a Request for Arbitration against the Kingdom of Morocco with ICSID. The Secretary-General registered the Request on June 13, 2000. The Italian companies claimed ITL 132,639,617,409, as compensation for damages suffered.

The Kingdom of Morocco raised an objection to jurisdiction in a letter sent to ICSID on July 17, 2000. A hearing dealing exclusively with the questions of the admissibility of the Request and the Arbitral Tribunal's jurisdiction was held in Paris on May 3, 2001.

2000 年 5 月 1 日，两家意大利公司向 ICSID 提交了对摩洛哥的仲裁请求。秘书长于 2000 年 6 月 13 日登记了这项请求。这两家意大利公司索赔 132639617409 意大利里拉作为损失赔偿。

摩洛哥在 2000 年 7 月 17 日给 ICSID 的信中对管辖权提出异议。2001 年 5 月 3 日在巴黎举行了一次专门解决请求的可受理性问题和仲裁庭管辖权问题的听证会。

In their Request for Arbitration, the Italian companies base the jurisdiction of ICSID on Article 8 of the Treaty between the Government of the Kingdom of Morocco and the Government of the Republic of Italy for the reciprocal promotion and protection of investments, signed on July 18, 1990, which came into force on January 1, 1992 in favour of Italian investors, by way of letters exchanged between the Ministers of Foreign Affairs for both Governments, dated November 26, 1991. The Kingdom of Morocco no longer contests the coming into force of this Bilateral Investment Treaty for the protection of investments.

The Kingdom of Morocco has raised various objections to the referral of this matter to the Arbitral Tribunal. It maintains, on the basis of Article 8 of the aforementioned Treaty, that the

Request is not admissible because it is premature（Ⅰ）, that the Tribunal has no jurisdiction ratione personae andratione materiae（Ⅱ）and that the Italian companies have waived all jurisdiction other than that of the administrative courts of Rabat（Ⅲ）.

在他们的仲裁请求中，意大利公司基于1990年7月18日签署、1991年11月26日通过两国政府的外交部长换文后于1992年1月1日生效的《摩洛哥政府和意大利共和国政府相互促进和保护投资协定》第8条有关保护意大利投资者的内容，主张ICSID有管辖权。摩洛哥王国对这项保护投资的双边投资协定的生效不持异议。

摩洛哥对将此事提交仲裁庭审理提出了各种反对意见。它主张，根据上述条约第8条，这项请求不应该被受理，因为：①该请求为时过早；②仲裁庭没有属人管辖权和属事管辖权；③意大利公司放弃了除拉巴特行政法院以外的所有管辖权。

仲裁结果（Award）

The Tribunal declares that it has jurisdiction over the Italian companies' claims, as they are formulated, but specifies that it does not have jurisdiction over mere breaches of thecontract concluded between the Italian companies and ADM that do not simultaneously constitute a violation of the Bilateral Treaty.

July 16, 2001

仲裁庭宣布对上述意大利公司的索赔拥有管辖权，像他们所共同构想并做出具体规定的那样，仲裁庭对仅违反了意大利公司与摩洛哥高速公司之间签订的合同，而不同时构成违反双边协定的行为没有管辖权。

2001年7月16日

裁决原因（Reasons for the Award）

The inadmissibility of the request due to its premature nature

In its memorials on jurisdiction and its oral presentations, the Kingdom of Morocco states that the Claimants'request was premature under Article 8. 2 of the Bilateral Treaty. Essentially, it maintains that this provision required: that the grounds for complaint contained in the Request for Arbitration be presented in the form of a request for amicable settlement addressed to the Kingdom of Morocco at least six months before the Request for Arbitration was filed; that these grounds for complaint constitute violations of the Bilateral Treaty, the arbitration proceedings provided for under Article 8.2 being inseparable from the other provisions of the said Treaty.

仲裁请求因提交过早而不应被受理问题

摩洛哥王国在其关于管辖权的法律意见和口头陈述中声明,根据双边条约第8条第(2)款的规定,请求人提出要求为时过早。大体上,它他认为这一规定要求:仲裁请求书中所载的申请事由应以友好解决请求书的形式在提交仲裁请求前至少六个月提交给摩洛哥王国;这些申请事由违反了双边条约,第8条2款规定的仲裁程序与上述条约的其他条款不可分割。

This second argument concerns the question of theratione materiae jurisdiction of the Tribunal. As a result, it will be assessed during the examination of this issue. With regard to the assertion that the Request is premature, the only pertinent point to ascertain is whether the Italian companies actually made the request for amicable settlement referred to in paragraphs 1 and 2 of Article 8.

Concerning the first argument, the Respondent alleges that the Italian companies' claims were sent to ADM's Chief Executive Officer (Head Engineer) and the Minister of Infrastructure, in his capacity as ADM's President and not that of Minister. Thus, these claims could not have been transmitted to the Kingdom of Morocco. The Italian companies contend that such a request was made and produce the documents in support of this assertion: memorandum setting out claims relating to the final account, presented to the Minister of Infrastructure and President of ADM, on September 14, 1999; letter sent to the Ambassador of Morocco in Rome, dated April 10, 1998; letter sent to the Prime Minister of Morocco, dated May 15, 1998.

第二个争辩观点涉及仲裁庭的属事管辖权问题。因此,将在审查本争议问题时对其进行评估。关于请求过早的主张,唯一需要确定的是,意大利公司是否真的提出了第8条第1款和第2款所述的友好解决请求。

关于第一个争辩观点,被申请人主张,意大利公司的索赔要求被送交给了摩洛哥高速公司首席执行官(总工程师)和基础设施部长,但其职责只是摩洛哥高速公司的总裁而并不是部长。因此,这些要求不可能转交给摩洛哥王国。意大利公司主张说,他们提出了这样的要求,并出示了支持这一主张的文件:1999年9月14日提交给基础设施部部长和摩洛哥高速公司总裁有关阐明与结算的主张的备忘录;1998年4月10日发送给摩洛哥驻罗马大使的信;1998年5月15日发给摩洛哥总理的信。

Article 8 of the Bilateral Treaty provides that:

"1) All disputes or differences, including disputes related to the amount of compensation due in the event of expropriation, nationalisation, or similar measures, between a Contracting

Party and an investor of the other Contracting Party concerning an investment of the said investor on the territory of the first Contracting Party should, if possible, be resolved amicably.

2）If the disputes cannot be resolved in an amicable manner within six months of the date of the request, presented in writing, the investor in question may submit the dispute either:

a）To the competent court of the Contracting Party concerned;

b）To anad hoc tribunal, in accordance with the Arbitration Rules of the UN Commission on International Trade Law;

c）To the International Centre for Settlement of Investment Disputes (ICSID), for the application of the arbitration procedures provided by the Washington Convention of March 18, 1965 on the settlement of investment disputes between States and nationals of other States.

3）The two Contracting Parties shall refrain from handling, through diplomatic channels, all questions pertaining to an arbitration or to pending legal proceedings, as long as these proceedings have not come to an end and that one of the said Parties has not complied with the judgment of the arbitral tribunal or the designated ordinary court, within the term for enforcement fixed by the judgment or to be otherwise established, on the basis of the rules of international or national law applicable in the case. "

双边条约第 8 条规定:

"1）缔约国一方与缔约国另一方投资者之间关于该投资者在前述第一缔约方领土上的投资的所有争议或分歧,包括与征收、国有化或类似措施的应付赔偿金额有关的争议。如有可能,应友好解决。

"2）如果在提出书面请求之日起六个月内未能以友好方式解决争议,则相关投资者可提交争议:

"a）向有关缔约方的主管法院提出;

"b）根据联合国国际贸易法委员会的仲裁规则,提交特别法庭;

"c）提交国际投资争端解决中心（ICSID）适用 1965 年 3 月 18 日关于解决国家与他国国民之间投资争端的《华盛顿公约》规定的仲裁程序。

"3）缔约双方应避免通过外交途径处理与仲裁或未决法律程序有关的一切问题,只要这些程序尚未结束,且其中一方还未能在判决所确定的或根据案件所适用国际或国内法规则以其他方式所确定的执行期限内,履行仲裁委员会或指定的一般法院的判决。"

Under the title "Representation of the Owner", Article 23 of theCahier des Clauses Administratives Generales provides that: "In all the general texts mentioned in Article 2, the functions are attributed as follows:

——Minister-President

——Head Engineer-Chief Executive Officer"

在业主代表标题下,《一般行政条款手册》第23条规定"第二条所提及的所有条款,职责分配给:部长暨董事长,总工程师暨总裁。

The Kingdom of Morocco rightly emphasises the fact that the CCAP, a contractual document whose purpose is to govern the relations between ADM and the Italian companies, cannot amount to the attribution of the function of President of ADM to the Minister. But, it cannot infer that the CCAP has removed the Contractor's claims from the Minister's control to place them under the distinct control of the President of ADM. The confusion surrounding the positions held by the Minister, which results from the organisation of structures of implementation put in place by the Moroccan Authorities regarding highways, cannot be invoked to uphold the premise that what the Minister was aware of in one of his capacities, as can be implied from the reference to Article 51 of theCahier des Clauses Administrative Particulieres, was unknown to him in another capacity.

摩洛哥王国正确地强调了这样一个事实,即《一般行政条款手册》是一份旨在管理摩洛哥高速公司和意大利公司之间关系的合同文件,不能据此将摩洛哥高速公司总裁的职能转交由部长承担。但是,不能推断《一般行政条款手册》已经将承包商的索赔从部长的控制中移除,将其置于摩洛哥高速公司总裁的明确控制之下。围绕,由摩洛哥当局对高速公路实施管理的结构组织而带来的部长所担任的职位的混乱,不能被援引来支持这样一个主张,即部长以某一身份所了解的情况,正如《特别行政条款》第51条所暗示的那样,在另一身份上他并不知道。

Therefore, the Tribunal concludes that the various above-mentioned documents constitute a written request aimed toward the amicable settlement of the dispute and satisfy the requirement set out in the Bilateral Treaty in relation to the addressee of the request.

The Request for Arbitration was submitted on May 4, 2000, 8 months after the transmission of the memorandum setting out the claims relating to the final account, presented to the Minister of Infrastructure and President of ADM on September 14, 1999. This last document is the most recent of those considered by this Tribunal as constituting an attempt to reach an amicable settlement prior to arbitration.

因此,仲裁庭的结论是,上述各种文件构成了一项以友好方式解决争议的书面请求,并满足在双边协定中就致送请求书所规定的要求。

仲裁请求书于2000年5月4日提交,即在1999年9月14日提交基础设施部部长和摩洛哥高速公司总裁的备忘录(其中列出了与结算有关的索赔)发送8个月后。最后一份文件是本仲裁庭认为在仲裁前试图达成友好解决的最新的文件。

Objections to the jurisdiction of the arbitral tribunal

The Kingdom of Morocco considers that the Italian companies are bound by Article 18 CCAP that refers to a procedure provided for by Articles 50 and 51 of the CCAG, which gives the courts of Rabat jurisdiction over disputes arising from the performance of the contract for services.

Generally, ICSID jurisdiction arises from the consent of the Parties to the dispute; that is to say, a Contracting State and the national of another Contracting State. Concerning the formal conditions required in order to have valid consent, Article 25.1 of the Washington Convention (hereinafter "the Convention") states only one condition: that the consent be given in writing. Regarding the moment at which consent must be expressed, one may deduce from the Convention that it must have been given prior to the filing of a request for conciliation or arbitration, since this request must, in order to be registered, state the date and the nature of the documents relating to the consent of the Parties.

对仲裁庭的管辖异议问题

摩洛哥王国认为，意大利公司受《特别行政条款》第18条的约束，该条指的是《一般行政条款手册》第50条和51条规定的程序，该程序赋予拉巴特法院对履行服务合同产生的争议的管辖权。

一般来说，ICSID的管辖权是由争端各方的同意产生的，也就是说，一个缔约国和另一个缔约国的国民。关于获得有效同意所需的正式条件，《华盛顿公约》（以下简称"公约"）第25条1款只规定了一个条件：书面同意。关于必须表示同意的时刻，从公约中可以推断出，必须在提交调解或仲裁请求之前提出，因为为了登记该请求，必须说明与各方同意有关的文件的日期和性质。

The Tribunal notes that the fact that a State may act through the medium of a company having its own legal personality is no longer unusual if one considers the extraordinary expansion of public authority activity. In order to perform its obligations, and at the same time take into account the sometimes diverging interests that the private economy protects, the State uses a varied spectrum of modes of organisation, among which are in particular semi-public companies, similar to ADM, a company mostly held by the State which, considering the size of its participation (over 80%), directs and manages it. All these factors resolutely imprint a public nature on the said company.

Thus, since ADM is an entity, from a structural as well as a functional point of view, which is distinguishable from the State solely on account of its legal personality, the Tribunal, in spite of the observations of July 2, 2001 made by the Kingdom of Morocco, concludes that the Italian companies have shown that ADM is a State company, acting in the name of the

Kingdom of Morocco.

仲裁庭注意到，如果考虑到公共权力活动的异常扩大，一个国家可以通过一个拥有自己法人资格的公司作为媒介行事的事实就不再是不寻常的了。为了履行其职责，同时考虑到私营经济所保护的有时分散的利益，国家采用了各种各样的组织模式，其中特别是半公开公司，类似于摩洛哥高速公司，一家从持股规模（80%以上）来看主要由国家控制、领导和管理的公司。所有这些因素都给这家公司赋予了公众公司的性质。

鉴于摩洛哥高速公司是一个实体，且从结构和功能的角度来看，它与国家的区别仅在于其法律人格，因此，尽管摩洛哥王国于 2001 年 7 月 2 日发表了意见，但仲裁庭仍得出结论，意大利公司已证明摩洛哥高速公司是一个国家公司，代表摩洛哥王国行事。

Article 1 of the Bilateral Treaty provides that:

"Pursuant to the present Agreement,

"I. the term 'investment' designates all categories of assets invested, after the coming into force of the present agreement, by a natural or legal person, including the Government of a Contracting Party, on the territory of the other Contracting Party, in accordance with the laws and regulations of the aforementioned party. In particular, but in no way exclusively, the term 'investment' includes:

"a) chattels and real estate, as well as any other property rights such as mortgages, privileges, pledges, usufructs, related to the investment;

"b) shares, securities and bonds or other rights or interests and securities of the State or public entities;

"c) capitalised debts, including reinvested income, as well as rights to any contractual benefit having an economic value;

"d) copyright, trademark, patents, technical methods and other intellectual and industrial property rights, know-how, commercial secrets, commercial brands and goodwill;

"e) any right of an economic nature conferred by law, or by contract, and any licence or concession granted in compliance with the laws and regulations in force, including the right of prospecting, extraction and exploitation of natural resources;

"f) capital and additional contributions of capital used for the maintenance and/or the accretion of the investment;

"g) the elements mentioned in (c), (d) and (e) above must be the object of contracts approved by the competent authority."

The construction contract creates a right to a "contractual benefit having an economic value" for the Contractor, mentioned in Article 1 (c). The Contractor also benefits from a "right of an economic nature conferred...[...]...by contract" dealt with by Article l (e). Moreover, the Respondent does not deny that the rights of the Italian companies are of the same nature as those referred to in (c) and (e) of Article 1.

双边条约第一条规定：

"根据本协议，

一、'投资'一语是指本协定生效后，一个自然人或法人，包括缔约国一方政府，根据上述缔约国的法律和法规，在另一缔约国领土上的所有类型的投资资产。'投资'一词具体包括但不限于以下：

a）与投资有关的动产和不动产，以及任何其他财产权利，如抵押、特权、质押、用益权；

b）国家或者社会团体的股份、证券、债券或者其他权益、证券；

c）资本化债务，包括再投资收入，以及享有任何具有经济价值的合同利益的权利；

d）版权、商标、专利、技术方法和其他知识产权、专有技术、商业秘密、商业品牌和商誉；

e）法律或合同授予的任何经济性质的权利，以及根据现行法律法规授予的任何许可或特许权，包括勘探、开采和开发自然资源的权利；

f）用于维持和/或增加投资的资本和额外出资；

g）上述（c）、（d）、（e）项所述要素必须是主管机关批准的合同的标的。"

施工合同为第1条（c）款所述的承包商创造了获得"具有经济价值的合同利益"的权利。承包商还受益于第1条（e）款所述的"……合同授予的经济性质的权利"。此外，被申请人不否认意大利公司的权利与第1条（c）款和（e）款所述的权利具有相同性质。

The Tribunal notes that there have been almost no cases where the notion of investment within the meaning of Article 25 of the Convention was raised. However, it would be inaccurate to consider that the requirement that a dispute be "in direct relation to an investment" is diluted by the consent of the Contracting Parties. To the contrary, ICSID case law and legal authors agree that the investment requirement must be respected as an objective condition of the jurisdiction of the Centre.

仲裁庭注意到，几乎没有任何案件提出《公约》第25条所指的投资概念。然而，如果认为争端"与投资直接相关"的要求经缔约方同意可予以淡化，则是不准确的。相反，ICSID判例法和法学的作者同意，投资要求必须作为中心管辖权的客观条件予以遵守。

The contributions made by the Italian companies are set out and assessed in their written submissions. It is not disputed that they used their know-how, that they provided the necessary equipment and qualified personnel for the accomplishment of the works, that they set up the production tool on the building site, that they obtained loans enabling them to finance the purchases necessary to carry out the works and to pay the salaries of the workforce, and finally that they agreed to the issuing of bank guarantees, in the form of a provisional guarantee fixed at 1.5% of the total sum of the tender, then, at the end of the tender process, in the form of a definite guarantee fixed at 3% of the value of the contract in dispute. The Italian companies, therefore, made contributions in money, in kind, and in industry.

意大利公司的"投入"在其提交的书面文件中提出并得到了相应的评估。以下是无可争议的事实：完成工程，他们使用他们的专有技术，提供必要的设备和合格的人员，在建筑工地上安装生产设备，获得贷款使他们能够为实施工程所需的采购提供资金，并支付工人的工资。最后，他们同意签发金额为总投标价格 1.5% 的临时担保形式的银行担保，并在投标程序结束后，提供担保金额为争议合同价 3% 的明确的保证。因此，意大利公司在货币、实物和物资领域都进行了投入。

Although the total duration for the performance of the contract, in accordance with the CCAP, was fixed at 32 months, this was extended to 36 months. The transaction, therefore, complies with the minimal length of time upheld by the doctrine, which is from 2 to 5 years.

根据《特别行政管理条款》，履行合同的总期限固定为 32 个月，该期限被延长至 36 个月。因此，该交易符合该原则所支持的最短时间，即 2—5 年。

With regard to the risks incurred by the Italian companies, these flow from the nature of the contract at issue. The Claimants, in their reply memorial on jurisdiction, gave an exhaustive list of the risks taken in the performance of the said contract. Notably, among others, the risk associated with the prerogatives of the Owner permitting him to prematurely put an end to the contract, to impose variations within certain limits without changing the manner of fixing prices; the risk consisting of the potential increase in the cost of labour in case of modification of Moroccan law; any accident or damage caused to property during the performance of the works; those risks relating to problems of co-ordination possibly arising from the simultaneous performance of other projects; any unforeseeable incident that could not be considered as force majeure and which, therefore, would not give rise to a right to compensation; and finally those risks related to the absence of any compensation in case of increase or decrease in volume of the work load not exceeding 20% of the total contract price.

关于意大利公司所承担的风险，这些风险来自所讨论的合同性质。申请人在其关于管辖权回复的法律意见中，详细列出了履行上述合同所承担的风险。这中间值得注意的是，与业主的特权相关的风险，允许业主提前终止合同，允许业主在一定范围内实施变更而不改变定价方式。这些风险还包括在摩洛哥法律修订的情况下劳动力成本可能增加的风险，在工程实施过程中对财产造成的任何事故或损害，与同时实施的其他项目的协调问题引起的有关风险，任何因不被视为不可抗力而不会产生补偿权的不可预见事件，以及最后，如果工作量的增加或减少不超过合同总价的20%则不给予任何补偿的风险。

Lastly, the contribution of the contract to the economic development of the Moroccan State cannot seriously be questioned. In most countries, the construction of infrastructure falls under the tasks to be carried out by the State or by other public authorities. It cannot be seriously contested that the highway in question shall serve the public interest. Finally, the Italian companies were also able to provide the host State of the investment with know-how in relation to the work to be accomplished.

Consequently, the Tribunal considers that the contract concluded between ADM and the Italian companies constitutes an investment pursuant to Articles 1 and 8 of the Bilateral Treaty concluded between the Kingdom of Morocco and Italy on July 18, 1990 as well as Article 25 of the Washington Convention.

最后，合同对摩洛哥国家经济发展的贡献不容置疑。在大多数国家，基础设施的建设都是由国家或其他公共机构承担的任务。毫无疑问，该高速公路是在为公众利益服务。最后，意大利公司还能够为所投资的东道国提供与待完成工程有关的专有技术。

因此，仲裁庭认为，根据1990年7月18日摩洛哥王国与意大利签订的双边协定第1条和第8条以及《华盛顿公约》第25条，摩洛哥高速公司与意大利公司签订的合同构成投资。

案件影响（Impact of the Case）

《华盛顿公约》未对"投资"的定义做出明确的规定，而依世界银行董事会《关于〈华盛顿公约〉的报告》的解释，"投资"的定义可由争端当事方自主决定，公约没有必要对此进行详细的解释或界定。国际投资条约中对"投资"的定义方式一般被认为有3种，一是以资产为基础的投资定义，二是以企业为基础的投资定义，三是以交易为基础的投资定义。这其中资产为基础的定义最为常见，但"一切资产"或者"任何资产"的表述使得投资的外延无限扩大，结果就是诉诸投资争端解决机制的案件越来越多。ICSID实践中仲裁庭逐渐形成了对投资定义的限制解释，以此来缩小仲裁庭的管辖范围。在Salini v. Morocco一案最早确立了投资应该具备四要素的观点。

本案最终由双方达成了和解而终止了仲裁程序。在本案的管辖权裁定中，仲裁庭采取了限制解释的方法确立了判断一项"投资"是否存在的四项标准，成为后来仲裁庭判断 ICSID 是否享有管辖权经常采用的标准：一、实质性的投入；二、持续一定的时间；三、双方对交易承担风险；四、促进东道国的经济发展。"符合主体要件的实质性投入"是对投资者主体的认定和实际投入的衡量；"持续一定时间"则是使"投资"区别于一般的国际贸易；"不可避免的风险"则是 ICSID 致力于保护投资者利益的目的之一；"对东道国经济发展有贡献"则是暗含了《华盛顿公约》对外国投资的希冀。本案对于后来 ICSID 仲裁庭分析自身对案件管辖权有着很大的影响，"Salini 标准"被后来的 ICSID 仲裁庭不断应用而且继续进行推陈出新。后来 ICSID 在 Joy Mining v. Egypt 案发展了"Salini 原则"，在原先的"四要素"基础上提出了五要素说。该案仲裁庭认为，要构成公约第 25 条规定下的投资，相关资产或行为必须符合以下条件：一定持续期间、有预期利润或收入、承担一定风检、数额较大、能够促进东道国经济发展。Phoenix v. Czech 案在前一个案件的基础上，提出了投资必须具备六要素：金钱或财产贡献、一定的持续期间、一定的风险、为促进东道国经济活动发展而经营、投入的资产符合东道国法律的规定、投入真实的资产。这些案例在适用投资限制性定义的大致方法上与"Salini 原则"基本保持了一致。

思考问题（Questions）

1. 投资合同约定的争端解决方式为何不能对抗提交 ICSID 的仲裁请求权？

2. 摩洛哥主张该工程建设合同依其国内法是服务合同而非投资合同，应如何辨别该合同的性质以及以何为依据认定一项投资是否促进东道国经济发展？

案例五　梅赛尼斯公司诉美国案

Methanex Corporation v. United States of America（2005）（In the Matter of an International Arbitration under Chapter 11 of the North American Free Trade Agreement and The UN CITRAL Arbitration Rules）

选读理由（Selected Reason）

　　本案是一起有关《北美自由贸易协定》的争议案件。1999 年，加拿大梅赛尼斯公司认为美国加州出台的关于环境保护的禁令使其在美的投资遭受了损失。因其存在环境危害性，加利福尼亚州宣布至迟自 2002 年 12 月 31 日起禁止销售和使用被称为 MT-BE（甲基叔丁基醚）的汽油添加剂。仲裁庭在本案中体现的观点对在何种情况下应接受法庭之友的意见书以及国际投资争端中仲裁庭对待外国投资者的偏向具有重要意义。

仲裁申请情况（The Request for Arbitration）

　　The Claimant, Methanex Corporation（"Methanex"）, initiated this arbitration against the Respondent, the United States of America（the "USA"）, on 3rd December 1999 under Chapter 11 of the North American Free Trade Agreement（"NAFTA"）, as a Canadian investor. As formulated in its Original Statement of Claim of 3rd December 1999, Methanex claimed compensation from the USA in the amount of approximately US $ 970 million（together with interest and costs）, resulting from losses caused by the State of California's ban on the sale and use of the gasoline additive known as "MTBE"（methyl tertiary-butyl ether）which was then intended to become legally effective on 31st December 2002. MTBE is a synthetic, volatile, colourless and organic ether, with a turpentine-like taste and odour. Methanex was (and remains) the world's largest producer of methanol, a feedstock for MTBE. It has never produced or sold MTBE.

1999 年 12 月 3 日，根据《北美自由贸易协定》第 11 章的规定，申请人梅赛尼斯公司（简称梅赛尼斯）以加拿大投资者的身份向被申请人美利坚合众国（简称美国）提起仲裁。于 1999 年 12 月 3 日提出的仲裁申请书正本中，梅赛尼斯公司向美国索赔约 9.7 亿美元（连同利息和费用），理由是加利福尼亚州禁止销售和使用被称为 MTBE（甲基叔丁基醚）的汽油添加剂而造成的损失，这一禁令将于 2002 年 12 月 31 日具有法律效力。MTBE 是一种合成的、挥发性的、无色的和有机的醚，具有松节油的味道和气味。梅赛尼斯公司曾是（并且现在仍然是）世界上最大的甲醇生产商，甲醇是 MTBE 的原料。它从未生产或销售过 MTBE。

The claimant, Methanex Corporation ("Methanex"), is a company originally incorporatedunder the laws of Alberta and then continued under the Canada Business Corporations Act. Methanex is a producer and marketer of methanol with production facilities located in North America, New Zealand and Chile.

Methanex Methanol Company ("Methanex US") is a Texas general partnership of two companies, Methanex Inc. and Methanex Gulf Coast Inc., both incorporated under the laws of the State of Delaware. Methanex owns, indirectly, 100% of the shares of both partners. Methanex Fortier, Inc. ("Methanex Fortier") is a company incorporated under the laws of the State of Delaware. Methanex owns, indirectly, 100% of the shares of Methanex Fortier.

The respondent, United States of America as represented by the Department of State, is the governmental body, under the provisions of the North American Free Trade Agreement ("NAFTA"), with responsibility for responding to arbitration claims arising from actions taken by the federal and state governments of the United States of American (the "United States").

申请人梅赛尼斯公司（梅赛尼斯），是一家最初根据阿尔伯塔省法律成立的公司，然后根据加拿大商业公司法继续营业。梅赛尼斯是一家甲醇生产商和销售商，生产设施位于北美、新西兰和智利。

梅赛尼斯甲醇公司（美国梅赛尼斯）是梅赛尼斯公司和梅赛尼斯墨西哥湾公司两家均根据特拉华州法律注册成立的公司在得克萨斯州的普通合伙企业。梅赛尼斯间接拥有两个合伙人100%股份。梅赛尼斯福蒂尔公司（梅赛尼斯福捷）是一家根据特拉华州法律成立的公司，梅赛尼斯间接拥有梅赛尼斯福捷100%的股份。

根据《北美自由贸易协定》（"NAFTA"）的规定，被申请人，即国务院代表的美利坚合众国，是政府机构，负责对美利坚合众国政府（美国）联邦和州政府采取的行动引起的仲裁索赔作出回应。

In the United States, Methanex owns a methanol production facility located in Fortier, Louisiana（"Fortier"）. In March 1999, Methanex was a joint venture partner in Fortier with Cytec Methanol Inc. （"Cytec"）whereby Methanex held 70% of the shares of Fortier, with the remaining 30% being held by Cytec. Methanex has subsequently acquired Cytec's interest in Fortier and Methanex now indirectly owns 100% of the shares of Fortier. Due to market conditions, Fortier temporarily shut down its operations in early 1999 and continues to beidle as at the date hereof. As a result of the measure detailed herein together with similar measures being threatened elsewhere in the United States, the current oversupply in the methanolindustry will be extended in time thereby resulting in a further extension of the Fortier plant closure.

在美国，梅赛尼斯在路易斯安那州的福捷（"福捷"）拥有甲醇生产设施。1999 年 3 月，梅赛尼斯与氰特甲醇公司（"氰特"）在福捷成立了合资公司，其中梅赛尼斯持有福捷 70% 的股份，其余 30% 由氰特持有。梅赛尼斯随后收购了氰特对福捷的股权，而梅赛尼斯现在间接持有福捷 100% 的股份。由于市场情况，福捷于 1999 年初暂时关闭了业务，截至目前仍处于闲置状态。由于本文详述的措施以及在美国其他地方受到威胁的类似措施，甲醇行业目前的供过于求的情况将不断地延长，从而进一步延长关闭工厂的时间。

Approximately 40% of Methanex US' sales of methanol in the United States are to third parties who use methanol for the production of MTBE. In 1998, Methanex US sold 797,412 tonnes of methanol in the United States. Approximately 132,000 tonnes were sold directly to California refineries for MTBE production. The balance of the methanol sales was torefineries, other MTBE manufacturers and other consumers located throughout the United States. In 1998, an estimated 860,000 tonnes of MTBE, representing approximately twenty percent of California MTBE requirement, was supplied to California from United States Gulf Coast producers.

梅赛尼斯在美国销售的甲醇中，约 40% 是向使用甲醇生产 MTBE 的第三方销售的。1998 年，梅赛尼斯美国在美国销售了 797412 吨甲醇。约 13.2 万吨直接出售给加利福尼亚炼油厂用于 MTBE 生产。其他的甲醇销售给了炼油厂、其他 MTBE 制造商和位于美国各地的其他消费者。1998 年，美国墨西哥湾生产商向加利福尼亚州供应了约 86 万吨 MTBE，约占加利福尼亚州 MTBE 需求量的 20%。

In 1990, Congress enacted Clean Air Act Amendments（the "CAAA"）, calling for new air quality standards and setting limitations on motor vehicle missions to meet the air-quality objectives in areas of the country which suffered significant air pollution, principally larger metropolitan centers. In particular, the CAAA sought to reduce carbon monoxide emissions, volatile organic compound emissions, and toxic air pollutants from vehicles by addin goxygenates (among other requirements) to gasoline (reformulated gasoline, hereafter "RFG") . The CAAA required a minimum 2% oxygen by weight standard in RFG. To meet the oxygenate requirements, petroleum refiners are permitted to blend in to gasoline a number of oxygenates including MTBE, fuel ethanol, ethyl tertiary-butyl ether ("ETBE") and tertiary amyl methyl ether ("TAME") .

1990 年, 国会颁布了《清洁空气法修正案》(简称 "CAAA"), 要求制定新的空气质量标准, 并对机动车辆的使命进行限制, 以实现该国空气污染严重地区 (主要是大城市中心) 的空气质量目标。特别是, CAAA 通过增加汽油 (精炼汽油, 以下简称 "RFG") 中的氧化剂 (除其他要求外) 来试图减少一氧化碳排放、挥发性有机化合物排放和车辆的有毒空气污染物。CAAA 要求在 RFG 中至少有 2% 的氧气重量标准。为了满足氧化剂的要求, 允许石油精炼厂将许多氧化剂, 包括 MTBE、燃料乙醇、乙基叔丁基醚 ("ETBE") 和叔戊基甲基醚 ("TAME") 混合到汽油中。

On March 25, 1999 the Governor issued an Executive Order (the "Executive Order") whereinhe stated that "the findings and recommendations of the UC report, the public testimony andthe regulatory agencies are that, while MTBE has provided California with clean air benefits, because of leaking underground fuel storage tanks MTBE poses an environmental threat to groundwater and drinking water". On this basis, the Governor certified that "on balance, there is significant risk to the environment from using MTBE in gasoline in California". The Executive Order, (among other things), called for the California Energy Commission in consultation with the California Air Resources Board, to develop a timetable for the removal of MTBE from gasoline at the earliest possible date, but not later than December 31, 2002.

1999 年 3 月 25 日, 州长发布了一项行政命令 ("行政命令"), 他表示, "加利福尼亚大学的报告、公开证词和监管机构的调查结果和建议是, 虽然 MTBE 已经向加利福尼亚州提供了清洁空气的好处, 但地下燃料储存罐泄漏 MTBE 对地下水和饮用水构成环境威胁"。在此基础上, 州长证明, "总的来说, 在加利福尼亚州在汽油中使用 MTBE 会对环境造成重大风险"。行政命令 (除其他事项外) 要求加利福尼亚能源委员会与加利福尼亚空气资源委员会协商, 制定一个在最早可能的日期, 但不迟于 2002 年 12 月 31 日从汽油中去除 MTBE 的时间表。

The ban on MTBE has caused and will cause losses including, inter alia:

i. loss to Methanex, Methanex US and Fortier of a substantial portion of their customer base, goodwill and market for methanol in California and elsewhere.

ii. losses to Methanex, Methanex US and Fortier as a result of the decline in the global price of methanol.

iii. loss of return to Methanex, Methanex US and Fortier on capital investments they have made in developing and serving the MTBE market.

iv. loss to Methanex due to the increased cost of capital.

v. loss to Methanex of a substantial amount of its investment in Methanex US and Fortier.

禁止 MTBE 已经造成并将造成损失，其中包括：

1. 梅赛尼斯、梅赛尼斯美国公司和福捷公司在加州和其他地方的甲醇客户群、商誉和市场的大部分损失。

2. 甲醇全球价格下跌导致梅赛尼斯、梅赛尼斯美国和福捷公司亏损。

3. 在开发和服务 MTBE 市场方面，对梅赛尼斯、梅赛尼斯美国和福捷的资本投资的回报损失。

4. 因资本成本增加造成的梅赛尼斯损失。

5. 梅赛尼斯在梅赛尼斯美国和福捷的大量投资损失。

Methanex claims：

a）Damages under the provisions of Article 1116 for breach of Articles 1105 and 1110 of the NAFTA in the amount of US＄970,000,000.00.

b）Its costs of this arbitration including without limitation, expert and attorney fees and disbursements plus any Canadian Goods and Services tax payable thereon.

c）Interest on the sums claimed in subparagraphs（a）and（b）until paid.

梅赛尼斯索赔：

a）因违反《北美自由贸易协定》第 1105 条和第 1110 条而导致第 1116 条规定的损失为 9.7 亿美元。

b）仲裁费用，包括但不限于专家和律师费用和支出，加上应缴纳的加拿大商品和服务税。

c）第（a）项和（b）项所述金额的利息，直至支付为止。

The Tribunal was formed on 18th May 2000 to decide Methanex' claim. From the outset, the USA challenged the Tribunal's jurisdiction to decide Methanex's claim and alternatively disputed Methanex's claim on the merits. After several written submissions, procedural sessions and a jurisdictional hearing in July 2001 followed by further written submissions, the Tribunal decided, by its Partial Award of 7th August 2002, that there was no jurisdiction under Chapter 11 to decide Methanex's claim as formulated in its Original Statement of Claim. By permission from the Tribunal, Methanex significantly amended its claim in November 2002 in the form of a "Second Amended Statement of Claim". In all subsequent submissions, the USA maintained its challenge to the Tribunal's jurisdiction and its denial of Methanex's amended claim on the merits.

仲裁庭于 2000 年 5 月 18 日成立，以处理梅赛尼斯的索赔主张。美国从一开始就质疑仲裁庭对于裁决梅赛尼斯方主张的管辖权，并对梅赛尼斯索赔的法律依据提出异议。经过数次书面陈述和2001年7月的程序性会议和管辖权听证会以及进一步的书面陈述后，仲裁庭在2002年8月7日的部分裁决中决定，根据第11章，仲裁庭没有管辖权来决定梅赛尼斯在其仲裁申请书中提出的主张。经仲裁庭许可，梅赛尼斯于2002年11月以"第二次修订的仲裁申请书"形式，对其索赔主张作出重大修改。在随后提交的所有文件中，美国继续对该仲裁庭的管辖权提出异议，并否认梅赛尼斯修正后的主张。

仲裁结果（Award）

For the reasons set out above, the tribunal awards as follows:

1. Jurisdiction: The Tribunal decides, pursuant to Article 21 of the Uncitral Arbitration Rules and Article 1101 NAFTA, that it has no jurisdiction to determine the claims advanced by Methanex in its Second Amended Statement of Claim.

2. Merits: Assuming that the Tribunal had jurisdiction to determine the claims advanced by Methanex in its Second Amended Statement of Claim, the Tribunal decides, pursuant to Article 21 (4) of the Uncitral Arbitration Rules and Articles 1102, 1105 and 1110 NAFTA, to dismiss on their merits all claims there advanced by Methanex.

3. Legal Costs: The Tribunal decides, pursuant to Articles 38 (e) and 40 (2) of the Uncitral Arbitration Rules, that Methanex shall pay to or to the order of the USA the sum of US $2,989,423.76 within 30 days of the date of this award in respect of the USA's legal costs incurred in these arbitration proceedings.

4. Arbitration Costs: The Tribunal decides, pursuant to Articles 38 (a), (b), (c) & (f), 39 (1) and 40 (1) of the Uncitral Arbitration Rules, that Methanex shall bear in full the other costs of the arbitration, requiring Methanex to indemnify the USA within 30 days of the date of this award in the further sum of US $1,071,539.21.

Made by the Tribunal on [3 August] 2005.

Place of Arbitration: The International Centre for Settlement of Investment Disputes, The World Bank, Washington D. C., USA.

本仲裁庭裁决如下：

1. 管辖权：仲裁庭认为，根据《联合国国际贸易法委员会仲裁规则》第21条和《北美自由贸易协定》第1101条，它无管辖权决定梅赛尼斯在其第二次修订的索赔书中提出的主张。

2. 实体问题：假设仲裁庭有权确定梅赛尼斯在其第二次修订的索赔书中提出的主

张，仲裁庭根据《联合国国际贸易法委员会仲裁规则》第 21 条第（4）款和《北美自由贸易协定》第 1102、1105 和 1110 条作出决定，驳回梅赛尼斯提出的所有索赔；

3. 法律费用：仲裁庭根据《联合国国际贸易法委员会仲裁规则》第 38 条（e）款和第 40 条（2）款决定，梅赛尼斯应在本裁决 30 天内向美国支付美国在仲裁程序中产生的法律费用 2989423.76 美元。

4. 仲裁费用：仲裁庭根据《联合国国际贸易法委员会仲裁规则》第 38 条（a）款、（b）款、（c）款和（f）款，39 条（1）款和 40 条（1）款决定，梅赛尼斯应承担本次仲裁的其他费用，要求梅赛尼斯在本裁决之日起 30 天内，支付美国另外一笔1071539.21 美元款项。

仲裁庭于 2005 年 8 月 3 日做出。

裁决地点：美国华盛顿特区世界银行国际投资争端解决中心。

裁决原因（Reasons for the Award）

1. Jurisdictional Issues（管辖问题）

As previously indicated, although many of the relevant factual issues and much of the legal materials overlap to a material extent, it is nonetheless convenient to consider in turn Methanex's case separately under NAFTA Articles 1101, 1102, 1105 and 1110.

如前所述，尽管许多相关事实问题和法律材料在很大程度上是重合的，但对梅赛尼斯案件分别根据《北美自由贸易协定》第 1101 条、1102 条、1105 条和 1110 条进行考虑无疑是便利的。

（1）Article 1102 NAFTA

Article 1102（3）NAFTA provides as follows：

"3. The treatment accorded by a Party under paragraphs 1 and 2 means, with respect to a state or province, treatment no less favorable than the most favorable treatment accorded, in like circumstances, by that state or province to investors, and to investments of investors, of the Party of which it forms a part. "

Methanex contends that this paragraph governs its claim in the present case.

《北美自由贸易协定》第 1102 条（3）款规定如下：

"3. 一方根据第 1 款和第 2 款给予的待遇，就作为成员方一部分的一个州或省而言，是指不低于该州或省在类似情况下给予投资者及其投资最优惠的待遇。"

梅赛尼斯主张本段适用于其在本案中的主张。

In the Tribunal's view, this is an entirely plausible reading of the provision：if a component state or province differentiates, as a matter of domestic law or policy, between members of a domestic class, which class happens to serve as the comparator for an Article 1102 claim, the investor or investment of another party is entitled to the most favourable treatment accorded to some members of the domestic class. The Tribunal need not enter into Methanex's citation of WTO cases, however, because Article 1102 (3) simply does not resolve Methanex's difficulty. The California ban does not differentiate between foreign investors or investments and various MTBE producers in California or, if it is relevant, methanol feedstock producers in the United States. There is no more or less favourable treatment here. The treatment is uniform, for the ban applies to all MTBE manufacturers. Article 1102 (3) is not relevant to this case.

在仲裁庭看来，这是对该条款的一个完全合理的解读：如果一个组成部分的州或省根据国内法律或政策，对国内成员进行区分，而一个成员恰好是第 1102 条索赔的比较者，则另一方的投资者及其投资有权享受给予国内某些成员的最优惠待遇。不过，该法庭不必对梅赛尼斯援引的世贸组织案件进行调查，因为第 1102 条（3）款根本无法解决梅赛尼斯的困难。加州禁令没有区分外国投资者或投资与加州的各种 MTBE 生产商或美国的甲醇原料生产商（如果相关）。这里没有优惠多或少的待遇问题，待遇是一致的，因为禁令适用于所有 MTBE 制造商。第 1102 条（3）款与本案无关。

（2）Article 1105 NAFTA

Methanex submits that the US measures were intended to discriminate against foreign investors and their investments and that intentional discrimination is, by definition, inequitable. Thus it is claimed that the USA's breach of Article 1102 NAFTA establishes a breach of Article 1105 as well.

梅赛尼斯提出美国的保护措施旨在歧视外国投资者及其投资，并且正如字面所述，故意歧视是不公正的行为。因此，它声称美国在违反《北美自由贸易协定》第 1102 条的同时同样构成了对 1105 条的违反。

Article 1105 NAFTA provides:

"1. Each Party shall accord to investments of investors of another Party treatment in accordance with international law, including fair and equitable treatment and full protection and security.

2. Without prejudice to paragraph 1 and notwithstanding Article 1108 (7) (b), each Party shall accord to investors of another Party, and to investments of investors of another Party, non-discriminatory treatment with respect to measures it adopts or maintains relating to losses suffered by investments in its territory owing to armed conflict or civil strife.

3. Paragraph 2 does not apply to existing measures relating to subsidies or grants that would be inconsistent with Article 1102 but for Article 1108 (7) (b)."

《北美自由贸易协定》第 1105 条规定：

"1. 各方应根据国际法给予另一方投资者的投资待遇，包括公平和公正的待遇以及充分的保护和保障。

2. 在不影响第 1 款的情况下，尽管有第 1108 条（7）款（b）项的规定，每一方应向另一方的投资者和另一方的投资者的投资，就其采取或维持的在与其领土上的武装冲突或内乱而造成的投资损失有关的措施方面给予非歧视性待遇。

3. 第 2 款不适用于补贴或赠款有关的与第 1102 条不一致但适用第 1108 条（7）款（b）项的现有措施。"

Even assuming that Methanex had established discrimination under Article 1102, (which the Tribunal has found it did not) and ignoring, for the moment, the FTC's interpretation-the plain and natural meaning of the text of Article 1105 does not support the contention that the "minimum standard of treatment" precludes governmental differentiations as between nationals and aliens. Article 1105 (1) does not mention discrimination; and Article 1105 (2), which does mention it, makes clear that discrimination is not included in the previous paragraph. By prohibiting discrimination between nationals and aliens with respect to measures relating to losses suffered by investments owing to armed conflict or civil strife, the second paragraph imports that the preceding paragraph did not prohibit-in all other circumstances-differentiations between nationals and aliens that might otherwise be deemed legally discriminatory: inclusio unius est exclusio alterius. The textual meaning is reinforced by Article 1105 (3), which makes clear that the exception in paragraph 2 is, indeed, an exception.

Thus, even if Methanex had succeeded in establishing that it had suffered a discrimination for its claim under Article 1102, it would not be admissible for it, as a matter of textual interpretation, to establish a claim under Article 1105.

即使假设梅赛尼斯已经根据第 1102 条确立了歧视（仲裁庭认为没有），并且暂时忽略了联邦贸易委员会的解释——第 1105 条文本的朴素和自然含义不支持"最低标准待遇"不允许政府区分国民和外国人的观点，第 1105 条（1）款未提及歧视；第 1105 条（2）款虽然提及歧视但明确指出歧视并不被包含在上列条款中。通过禁止在与武装冲突或内乱造成的投资损失有关的措施上对国民和外国人实行歧视，第二款引入了这样的意思，即前款规定在任何其他情况下并不禁止区别对待国民和外国人，这种歧视应被视为是合法的：明示其一即排斥其他。第 1105 条（3）款加强了文本含义，明确了第（2）款中的例外事实上就是例外。

所以，即使梅赛尼斯根据第 1102 条成功证明了它遭到了歧视，因为文本解释问题，根据第 1105 条提出索赔也是不可接受的。

（3）Article 1110 NAFTA

Methanex claims that a substantial portion of its investments, including its share of the California and wider US oxygenate markets, was taken by a discriminatory measure and handed to the US domestic ethanol industry. It submits that this was "tantamount... to expropriation" within Article 111 （1）. It also submits that the various exceptions listed in Article 1110 have been met, i. e. the US measures were not intended to serve a public purpose, were not in accordance with due process of law and Article 1105, and that no compensation has been paid.

梅赛尼斯声称，其大部分投资，包括其在加利福尼亚和美国氧气市场的份额，都因为歧视性保护措施被征收并交给了美国本土的乙醇行业。它认为这是第 111 条（1）款中"相当于征收"。它还提出，第 1110 条所列的各种例外情况已得到满足，即美国措施并非旨在为公共目的服务，不符合正当法律程序和第 1105 条，且未支付赔偿金。

The Tribunal concludes that the California ban was made for a public purpose, was non-discriminatory and was accomplished with due process. Hence, Methanex's central claim under Article 1110 （1）of expropriation under one of the three forms of action in that provision fails. From the standpoint of international law, the California ban was a lawful regulation and not an expropriation.

仲裁庭认为，加利福尼亚禁令是为了公共利益，通过正当程序颁布的，并且是非歧视性的。所以，梅赛尼斯根据第 1110 条第（1）款中规定的关于征收的三种不同的行为形式提出的中心诉求是无效的。从国际法的角度来看，加利福尼亚禁令是一个法律性规章而不是征收性规章。

（4）Article 1101 NAFTA

Having concluded on the evidential record that no illicit pretext underlay California's conduct and that Methanex has failed to establish that the US measures were intended to harm foreign methanol producers （including Methanex）or benefit domestic ethanol producers （including ADM）, it follows on the facts of this case that there is no legally significant connection between the US measures, Methanex and its investments. As such, the US measures do not "relate to" Methanex or its investments as required by Article 1101 （1）. Accordingly, the USA succeeds on its jurisdictional challenge under Article 1101, as regards Methanex's claim pleaded in its Second Amended Statement of Claim; and the Tribunal concludes that it lacks jurisdiction to determine Methanex's substantive claims alleged under NAFTA Articles 1102, 1105 and 1110.

根据证据记录得出这一结论：没有非法的托词隐藏在加利福尼亚的行为背后，因此梅赛尼斯无法证明美国的保护措施是旨在损害外国甲醇生产商（包括梅赛尼斯）或使国内乙醇生产商（包括 ADM）受益，随之而来的另一个事实结论是在美国保护措施和梅赛尼斯及其投资之间没有明显的法律联系。因此，美国的保护措施与梅赛尼斯及其投资之间没有第 1101 条第（1）款所规定的联系。所以，就梅赛尼斯在其第二次修订的索赔声明中提出的索赔而言，美国在第 1101 条的管辖权争议中取得了成功。法庭因此得出结论，其缺乏对梅赛尼斯根据《北美自由贸易协定》第 1102 条、第 1105 条和第 1110 条提出的诉讼请求的管辖权。

案件影响（Impact of the Case）

1994 年生效的 NAFTA 包含的富有特色的争议解决机制，尤其是投资者诉东道国仲裁机制（ISDS），并处理了几十件投资者针对三个成员国的投资争议仲裁案件。本案仲裁程序长达 5 年，仲裁庭用不同方法从不同角度驳回了作为申请人梅赛尼斯的所有仲裁请求，其裁决结果打破了国际投资仲裁"偏向"外国投资者的观点。仲裁庭援引了在 Clayton/Bilcon v. Canada 一案中确立的先例，认为《北美自由贸易协定》第 1105 条中记载的"公平公正待遇标准"并不意味着投资者权益高于东道国自身的经济与社会利益。在解释公平公正待遇标准时，应当考虑东道国的具体国情，即使投资者可以合理期待东道国履行国际条约下的义务，投资者也无权要求每个东道国提供的投资环境具有同等的稳定性；投资者在考虑投资前，即应通过尽职调查了解东道国投资环境。在美国禁止使用 MTBE 有其保护环境的公共利益考量的情况下，投资者受损并不能据此而要求索赔。本案裁决是从仲裁庭没有管辖权给出的结论，但实质上是驳回了申请人的实体仲裁请求。

本案审理过程中，仲裁庭收到了两份提交非争议方意见的申请，其一是国际可持续发展研究所（International Institute for Sustainable Development）作为法庭之友的申请，其二是地球正义（Earth Justice），代表蓝水网络（Bluewater Network）、环境改善协会（Communities for a Better Environment）和国际环境法中心（Center for International Environmental Law）作为非争议方的申请。在当时，NAFTA 和 UNCITRAL 仲裁规则均无任何条文明示地确认或否认第三方主体的此种权利。仲裁庭就仲裁庭在何种情形下可接受法庭之友意见书提出了三项检验要素：法庭之友意见书对解决实体争议的帮助、争议的公共利益、法庭之友意见书对当事方公平待遇的影响。仲裁庭对这三项要素逐一进行了检验，并最终接受了法律之友意见书的递交。美国和梅赛克斯对仲裁庭接受这些法庭之友的意见均未提出异议。仲裁庭的这一做法受到了美国联邦贸易委员会的欢迎。其在 2004 年 7 月 16 日的一份联合声明中表示："我们很高兴，我们在 2003 年 10 月会议期间采取的透明度举措已经开始改善投资章节投资者——国家争端解决机制的运作。今年早些时候，仲裁庭第一次接受非争议方的书面意见，并通过了我们在 2003 年 10 月 7 日蒙特利尔举行的会议之后所建议处理此类意见的程序。"可见，法庭之友通过参与国际司法程序，可以发挥提供事实方面的信息、提供法律等专业协助、加强程序公正，正确、及时解决国际争端、促进国际法发展等积极的作用。

思考问题（Questions）

1. 北美自由贸易协定的投资仲裁为何在 ICSID 进行？其适用的仲裁规则是如何确定的？

2. 向本案提交法庭之友意见的组织是何性质？在本案中其意见发挥了什么作用？

案例六　科夫公司和特梅诺公司诉美国案

Canfor Corporation v. United States of America and Terminal Forest Products Ltd. v. United States of America（2006）（In the Consolidated Arbitration Pursuant to Article 1126 of NAFTA）

选读理由（Selected Reason）

本案在《北美自由贸易协定》（NAFTA）投资仲裁实践中，是一桩较特殊和经典的案例。美国对从加拿大进口的软木材征收反补贴税和采取反倾销措施，属于典型的贸易争端，但申请人加拿大科夫公司与特梅诺公司却最终提起了投资仲裁程序，且就部分内容获得了仲裁庭在管辖权方面的支持。这一案件反映了 NAFTA 体制下，贸易与投资之间的特殊关系。本案案情虽不复杂，但仲裁庭娴熟地运用了有关条约的解释规则，对法律条文的含义得到进一步澄清具有重要作用。

仲裁申请情况（The Request for Arbitration）

Canfor is a British Columbia company carrying on business world-wide in the forest products industry. Canadian Forest Products Ltd. （"CFP"）is a British Columbia company and is a wholly ownedsubsidiary of Canfor. Canfor USA is a Washington corporation and is a wholly ownedsubsidiary of CFP. Canfor, directly or through its subsidiaries, employs approximately 5,760 people in its forest products and affiliated operations. The Canfor Group's （ie., Canfor and its subsidiaries, including CFP, Canfor USA, and Canfor Wood Products）major products are softwood lumber, pulp, specialty kraft paper, newsprint, plywood, hardboard and logs. These products are exported from Canada, primarily to the United States, Europe, and the Far East. The Canfor Group is the largest producer in Canada, and the largest exporter to the United States, of softwood lumber.

科夫是一家在世界范围内从事森林产品行业业务的不列颠哥伦比亚公司。加拿大森林产品有限公司（简称"CFP"）是不列颠哥伦比亚省的一家公司，是科夫的全资子公司。Canfor USA 是一家华盛顿公司，是 CFP 的全资子公司。科夫直接或通过其子公司，在其林业产品和附属业务中雇用了约 5760 名员工。科夫集团（即科夫及其子公司，包括 CFP、Canfor USA 和 Canfor Wood Products）的主要产品是软木木材、纸浆、特种牛皮纸、新闻纸、胶合板、硬纸板和原木。这些产品主要从加拿大出口到美国、欧洲和远东。科夫集团是加拿大最大的软木木材生产商，也是最大的对美国的软木木材出口商。

In 2000, approximately 68% of the Canfor Group's total softwood lumber production was imported into the United States by Canfor Wood Products, the importer of record, which has been liable for bonds and cash deposits and which will be liable for any duties ultimately assessed, as more fully set out below. The softwood lumber which is imported into the United States is re-manufactured, marketed and distributed through the Canfor Group's US-basedreload centres, vendor managed inventory facilitiesand re-manufacturing facility. Virtually all softwood lumber imported by Canfor Wood Products into the United States is shipped by rail and truck. To facilitate transporting its products to and throughout the United States the CanforGroup has leased a fleet of approximately 587 railcars.

Accordingly, Canfor is an investor of a Party as defined in NAFTA Article 1139, and by virtue of the facts set out above, has investments to the territory of the United States as contemplated by NAFTA Article 1101 and defined in NAFTA Article 1139.

2000 年，科夫集团软木木材总产量的约 68% 进口到美国是通过科夫木材产品公司进行的。科夫木材产品公司木材产品作为备案的进口商，负责持有债券和现金以用于支付最终被估算需缴纳的任何关税，具体在下文有更全面的阐述。进口到美国的软木木材通过科夫集团在美国的重新装载中心、供应商库存管理设施和再加工工厂进行再制造、销售和分销。实际上，所有由科夫木材产品公司进口到美国的软木木材都是通过铁路和卡车运输的。为了便于将其产品运输到整个美国，科夫集团租赁了约有 587 辆轨道车的车队。

因此，科夫是《北美自由贸易协定》第 1139 条规定的一方的投资者，根据上述事实，按照《北美自由贸易协定》第 1101 条的规定和《北美自由贸易协定》第 1139 条的规定，向美国领土进行投资。

Canfor brings this claim in connection with the Government of the United States' violations of NAFTA Articles 1102, 1103, 1105 and 1110 arising out of and in connection with conduct of the Government of the United States, including the DOC and ITC, in relation to the investigations of the Canadian softwood lumber industry, and more particularly, including the investigations carried out in response to the Petitions which resulted in the DOC's Preliminary Countervailing Duty Determination ("PD-CVD") and Preliminary Critical Circumstances Determination ("PD-CC") both issued by the DOC on August 9, 2001, the DOC's Preliminary Anti-Dumping Determination ("PD-ADD") issued by the DOC on October 30, 2001, the DOC's Final Countervailing Duty Determination ("FD-CVD") and Final Anti-Dumping Determination ("FD-ADD") both issued by the DOC on March 26, 2002, and the ITC's May 2002 Final Determination ("ITC-FD") that the United States softwood lumber industry was threatened with material injury by reason of imports from Canada of softwood lumber.

科夫针对美国政府违反《北美自由贸易协定》第 1102 条、第 1103 条、第 1105 条和第 1110 条提出了这一索赔，这些违反行为是由美国政府（包括美国商务部和美国国际贸易委员会）开展的对加拿大软木木材行业的调查引发的并与这些调查行为有关，尤其是，包括应申请而进行的调查从而形成的 2001 年 8 月 9 日美国商务部初步反补贴裁定和初步危急情况裁定，2001 年 10 月 30 日发布美国商务部初步反倾销裁定，2002 年 3 月 26 日美国商务部最终反补贴裁定和最终反倾销裁定，以及 2002 年 5 月美国国际贸易委员会确定美国软木木材行业因从加拿大进口的软木木材而受到实质损害威胁的最终决定。

The present claim arises from the unfair, inequitable and discriminatory treatment of the Canadian softwood lumber industry, including Canfor, or more particularly Canfor andits subsidiaries, by the Government of the United States. A review of the treatment receivedby the Canadian softwood lumber industry over the past 20 years demonstrates a pattern of conduct designed to ensure a predetermined, politically motivated and results-driven outcome to the investigations resulting to the PD-CVD, PD-CC, PD-ADD, FD-CVD, FDADD and the ITC-FD. That context includes three prior softwood lumber investigations by the DOC (hereafter, Lumber Ⅰ, Lumber Ⅱ and Lumber Ⅲ) as well as legislative changes to the countervailing duty law explicitly designed to ensure that softwood lumber from Canada would be found to be subsidized.

本索赔源于美国政府对加拿大软木木材行业（包括科夫，尤其是科夫及其子公司）的不公平、不公正和歧视待遇。加拿大软木木材工业在过去 20 年中所受到的待遇，表明了一种旨在确保预先确定的、政治上有动机的和结果驱动的结果为目标的行为模式，从而得出了美国商务部初步反补贴裁定、初步危急情况裁定、初步反倾销裁定、最终反补贴裁定和最终反倾销裁定，以及美国国际贸易委员会最终决定。这一背景还包括美国商务部之前的三次软木木材调查（以下简称"木材Ⅰ"、"木材Ⅱ"和"木材

Ⅲ"），以及明确设计用来确保证明加拿大软木木材得到了补贴的反补贴法的立法变更。

The claims filed against the United States by Canfor Corporation（"Canfor"），Tembec Inc.，Tembec Investments Inc. and Tembec Industries Inc.（collectively referred to as "Tembec"），and Terminal Forest Products Ltd.（"Terminal"），all Canadian producers of softwood lumber，concern a number of countervailing duty and antidumping measures adopted by the United States relating to Canadian softwood lumber products.

此案对美国所提出的索赔，是科夫公司（简称"科夫"）、天柏股份有限公司、天柏投资公司、天柏工业公司（统称为"天柏"），以及特梅诺林产品有限公司（"特梅诺"）这些所有的加拿大软木木材生产商共同对美国对加拿大软木木材产品采取的若干反补贴和反倾销措施所提出的。

After filing a Notice of Intent on 5 November 2001，Canfor，a forest-products company incorporated in British Columbia，Canada，filed on 9 July 2002 a Notice of Arbitration under Chapter Eleven of the NAFTA and the UNCITRAL Arbitration Rules against the United States. The Notice of Arbitration also served as a Statement of Claim. Canfor alleges that the United States adopted in May 2002 certain countervailing duty and antidumping measures on Canadian imports of softwood lumber to the United States，in breach of the NAFTA Articles 1102（National Treatment），1103（Most-Favored-Nation Treatment），1105（Minimum Standard of Treatment），and 1110（Expropriation）. Canfor also claims damages for losses caused by the allegedly illegal Continued Dumping and Subsidy Offset Act of 2000（"Byrd Amendment"），enacted into United States law in 2000，which provides that duties assessed pursuant to countervailing duty or antidumping orders shall be distributed annually to affected U. S. domestic producers. Canfor seeks damages of not less than US $ 250 million and an award of costs.

在 2001 年 11 月 5 日提交意向书后，科夫公司，其作为一家在加拿大不列颠哥伦比亚注册成立的森林产品公司，于 2002 年 7 月 9 日根据《北美自由贸易协定》第 11 章和《联合国贸易法委员会仲裁规则》提交了一份针对美国政府的仲裁通知。仲裁通知同时也是一份仲裁索赔起诉状。科夫公司称，2002 年 5 月，美国违反《北美自由贸易协定》第 1102 条（国民待遇）、1103 条（最惠国待遇）、1105 条（最低待遇标准）和 1110 条（征收），对美国从加拿大进口的软木产品采取了某些反补贴和反倾销措施。科夫公司还要求赔偿据称是非法的伯德修正案所造成的损失，该修正案于 2000 年颁布成为美国法律，其规定，经评估根据反补贴或反倾销命令获得的关税应每年分配给受影响的美国国内生产商。科夫公司要求美国赔偿至少 2.5 亿美元并承担裁决费用。

Having filed a Notice of Intent on 12 June 2003，Terminal，a forest products corporation organized under the laws of British Columbia，Canada，filed on 31 March 2004 a Notice of Arbitration under Chapter Eleven of the NAFTA and the Uncitral Arbitration Rules against the

United States on measures also challenged in the Canfor and Tembec arbitrations. Terminal seeks damages of at least US $ 90 million. Since filing its Notice of Arbitration, Terminal has not taken further steps to prosecute its claim. Terminal's Notice of Arbitration does not serve as a Statement of Claim, considering that Terminal stated in its Notice that it "will more fully articulate its basis for the claim in its Statement of Claim when filed".

根据不列颠哥伦比亚省法律组建的特梅诺森林产品公司于 2003 年 6 月 12 日提交了意向书，并于 2004 年 3 月 31 日根据《北美自由贸易协定》第 11 章和《联合国贸易法委员会仲裁规则》对美国提交了一份仲裁通知，其中涉及了科夫公司和天柏公司在仲裁中同样提出质疑的措施。特梅诺公司主张不少于 9000 万美元的损害赔偿。自提交仲裁通知以来，特梅诺公司没有采取进一步措施提出赔偿要求。特梅诺公司的仲裁通知不作为仲裁索赔起诉状，因为特梅诺公司在通知中指出其"将在提交起诉状时更充分地阐明索赔的依据"。

仲裁结果（Award）

The tribunal awards as follows:

1. Determines that Article 1901 (3) of the NAFTA establishes that the United States did not consent to arbitrate under Chapter Eleven the claims of Canfor and Terminal filed in Canfor Corporation v. United States of America and in Terminal Forest Products Ltd. v. The United States of America, respectively, except to the extent that they concern the Byrd Amendment;

2. Declares to lack jurisdiction over the claims of Canfor and Terminal filed in Canfor Corporation v. United States of America and in Terminal Forest Products Ltd. v. The United States of America, respectively, except to the extent that they concern the Byrd Amendment;

3. Reserves the decision on the costs of the present phase of the proceedings to a subsequent order, decision or arbitral award.

Made in Washington, D. C.

6 June, 2006

本仲裁庭裁决如下:

1. 确定第 1901 条（3）款可以支持美国不同意对仲裁申请人科夫和特梅诺根据《北美自由贸易协定》第 11 章在科夫公司诉美国和特梅诺森林产品有限公司诉美国案件中分别提出的诉求进行仲裁，除非在一定程度上他们与《2000 年持续倾销和补贴抵消法》有关;

2. 认定对仲裁申请人科夫公司诉美国和特梅诺森林产品有限公司诉美国案中分别

提出的索赔请求没有管辖权，除非在一定程度上他们与《2000 年持续倾销和补贴抵消法》有关。

3. 将本阶段仲裁费用的决定交由后面的命令、决定或仲裁裁决来决定。

裁决于华盛顿特区

2006 年 6 月 6 日

裁决原因（Reasons for the Award）

The first article of Chapter Nineteen of the NAFTA is captioned："General Provisions." Article 1901（1）sets forth the field of application of Chapter Nineteen. Article 1901（2）provides that Annex 1901. 2 governs the establishment of the panels referred to in Articles 1903 and 1904. Article 1901（3）then states："Except for Article 2203（Entry into Force），no provision of any other Chapter of this Agreement shall be construed as imposing obligations on a Party with respect to the Party's antidumping law or countervailing duty law."

In conclusion, the phrase "the Party's antidumping law or countervailing duty law," in Article 1901（3）, in the Tribunal's judgment, encompasses a very broad spectrum of matters, a conclusion that is particularly justified by the use of the phrasal preposition "with respect to" in Article 1901（3）and of the non-exhaustive verb "include" in the Article 1902（1）definition that the Tribunal has previously determined to apply to the meaning of that phrase in Article 1901（3）.

《北美自由贸易协定》第 19 章第 1 条的标题是："一般规定。" 1901 条（1）款规定了第 19 章的适用范围。1901 条（2）款规定，附件 1901. 2 应适用于按照 1903 条和 1904 条规定设立专家组事宜。1901 条（3）款规定："除第 2203 条（生效条款）外，本协议任何其他章节的任何条款均不得被解释为给任一方成员设置有关于其反倾销法或反补贴法方面的义务。"

总之，第 1901 条（3）款中的 "成员的反倾销法律或反补贴税法" 这一短语，依仲裁庭裁决，包括一个非常宽泛的内容，本结论是由第 1901 条（3）款中具体使用的介词短语 "有关于" 和第 1902 条（1）款定义中使用的未穷举的动词 "包括" 所判断形成的。仲裁庭此前已经决定使用第 1901 条（3）款中这一短语的含义。

The ordinary meaning of Article 1901（3）of the NAFTA establishes that the United States did not consent to arbitrate the claims of Canfor and Terminal under Chapter Eleven. The United States argues that the "ordinary meaning" and effect of this provision are clear：the United States has no obligations under the NAFTA with respect to its antidumping and countervailing duty laws except those specified in Chapter Nineteen and Article 2203. According to the United States, Chapter Nineteen sets forth a unique, self-contained mechanism for dealing with sensitive and complex antidumping and countervailing duty claims. The Parties to NAFTA intended for matters arising under a Party's antidumping and countervailing duty laws to be addressed exclusively under Chapter Nineteen.

The United States contends that the claims of Canfor and Terminal are based entirely on obligations found in Chapter Eleven. The claims, however, are based on obligations "with respect to [U.S.] antidumping and countervailing duty law." Their allegations are based on Commerce's and the ITC's interpretation of U.S. antidumping and countervailing duty laws and regulations, and in particular on the methodologies and procedures that Commerce used in calculating the duties at issue. In the view of the United States, these are precisely the type of claims that are-and in fact were-submitted to, and decided by, binational panels constituted under Chapter Nineteen.

《北美自由贸易协定》第 1901 条（3）款的通常含义决定了美国不同意根据第 11 章仲裁科夫和特梅诺的索赔。美国辩称，这一规定的"通常含义"和效力是明确的：美国在《北美自由贸易协定》下，除第 19 章和第 2203 条的规定以外，没有在反倾销和反补贴法方面的义务。在美国来看，第 19 章提出了一种独特的、自足的机制，用于处理敏感的、复杂的反倾销和反补贴方面的索赔。《北美自由贸易协定》的缔约方打算用第 19 章解决成员在反倾销和反补贴方面的问题。

美国认为，科夫和特梅诺的索赔完全基于第 11 章中的义务。然而，这些索赔是基于"与美国有关的反倾销和反补贴法"而提出的，它们的指控是针对商务部和国际贸易委员会对美国反倾销和反补贴法和条例的解释，特别是商务部计算争议关税的方法和程序。在美国看来，这些正是——事实上也是——应提交给根据第 19 章组成的双边专家组并由其做出决定的索赔类型。

As a final point, the Tribunal wishes to emphasize that, under well-known principles of international law, every provision of an international agreement must have meaning, because it is presumed that the State Parties that negotiated and concluded that agreement intended each of its provisions to have an effect. Accordingly, because the language of Article 1902 (2) (b) and Article 1902 (2) (c) is so plain that, for interpretive purposes, there is no occasion for recourse to supplementary sources of evidence under the terms of the Vienna Convention on the Law of Treaties, the Tribunal must perforce give effect to those two subparagraphs. To do otherwise would be to deny fundamental tenets of international law, which, pursuant to Article 1131 (1) of the NAFTA, are governing in this case. Consequently, the Tribunal has no choice but to follow strictly the clear demands of Articles 1902 (2) (b) and 1902 (2) (c). Furthermore, the conduct of the United States that was contemporaneous with, or proximate to, enactment of the Byrd Amendment is supportive of this conclusion, because it leads to the presumption that apparently the United States did not itself consider the Byrd Amendment to constitute a part of its antidumping or countervailing duty law. That observation brings the Tribunal to examine Claimants' contentions regarding relevant United States' conduct.

作为最后一点，仲裁庭希望强调，根据国际法众所周知的原则，国际条约的每一条款都必须具有含义，因为谈判和缔结该条约的缔约国被假定为打算使其每一条款都具有效力。因此，由于第 1902 条（2）款（b）项和第 1902 条（2）款（c）项的措词非常清楚，为了便于解释，根据《维也纳条约法公约》规定，没有必要求助于补充证据来源，因此仲裁庭必须使这两款具有效力，否则，将违背根据《北美自由贸易协定》第 1131 条（1）款应在此情况下适用的国际法的基本原则。因此，仲裁庭别无选择，只能严格遵守第 1902 条（2）款（b）项和 1902 条（2）款（c）项的明确要求。此外，美国在颁布《2000 年持续倾销和补贴抵消法》的同时或前后的时间的行为也支持这一结论，因为这导致了一个假设，即显然美国本身并不认为《2000 年持续倾销和补贴抵消法》构成其反倾销或反补贴法的一部分。这一点也促使仲裁庭审查申请人对美国相关行为提出的主张。

While the differences between proceedings under Chapters Eleven and Nineteen are noticeable, it must be borne in mind that Canfor's and Terminal's claims concern the conduct of Commerce, the ITC and other government officials prior to, during and subsequent to preliminary and final antidumping and countervailing duty determinations, including review by Article 1904 binational panels. To a large extent, it appears that the claims of Canfor and Terminal in the present case are based on the same factual matrix as the various Article 1904 binational panel review proceedings, in which they are permitted to participate, albeit that these claims are presented in the present proceedings from the angle of allegedly reprehensible conduct rather than of allegedly deficient preliminary or final determinations. Viewed from that perspective, the Article 1904 proceedings and the present Chapter Eleven proceedings are concurrent or parallel (with the attendant problems that this creates), even though the applicable law and available remedies differ.

虽然根据第 11 章和第 19 章进行的程序之间的差异是显而易见的，但必须记住，科夫和特梅诺的索赔涉及商务部、国际贸易委员会和其他政府官员在初步和最终反倾销和反补贴裁定之前、期间和之后的行为，包括通过第 1904 条"双边专家组"进行审查。在很大程度上，本案中科夫和特梅诺的权利要求似乎是基于与各种 1904 条双边专家组审理程序相同的事实背景，基于该些事实他们被允许参与其中，当然这些权利要求在本案中更多的是从主张其应受到谴责的事实角度呈现出来的，而不是主张这些初步或最终裁定有缺陷。从这一角度来看，1904 条程序和现在的第十一章程序是同时进行的或平行进行的（与由此产生的附带问题相同），即使适用法律和可用的补救措施不同。

For all these reasons, the Tribunal concludes with respect to the first question that the Byrd Amendment is not antidumping or countervailing duty law within the meaning of that term under Article 1901 （3） of the NAFTA, because （i） assuming that it pertains to U. S. antidumping and countervailing duty law, the United States failed to bring that subsequent statutory amendment into the definition of "antidumping law and countervailing duty law" of Article 1902 （1）, and （ii） the contemporaneous and proximate conduct of the United States indicates that it did not consider the Byrd Amendment to pertain to its antidumping and countervailing duty law. As previously noted, the Tribunal is of the view that such a conclusion is reinforced by the general rule of interpretation of treaties that restrictions and exceptions are construed narrowly.

基于所有这些原因，仲裁庭就第一个问题得出结论，即《2000 年持续倾销和补贴抵消法》不是《北美自由贸易协定》第 1901 条（3）款所指的反倾销或反补贴税法，因为（1）假设该修正案属于美国反倾销和反补贴法，美国未能将在其之后的法规修订内容纳入第 1902 条（1）款中"反倾销法和反补贴税法"的定义中；（2）美国的同期和近期行为表明，它不认为《2000 年持续倾销和补贴抵消法》与反倾销和反补贴法有关。如前所述，仲裁庭认为，这样的结论得到了条约解释原则的加强，即限制和例外条款的解释范围很窄。

In particular, in the Tribunal's judgment, the Claimants have made aprima facie showing that, while not constituting antidumping or countervailing duty law within the meaning of Article 1901 （3）, the Byrd Amendment may ultimately be proven to have conferred financial benefits on United States investors or investments in competition with the claimant Canadian investors that are demonstrably contrary to the national treatment provisions of Article 1102.

特别是，仲裁庭裁决，申请人已初步表明，虽然《2000 年持续倾销和补贴抵消法》不构成第 1901 条（3）款所指的反倾销或反补贴税法，但他们最终可能能够证明该法案已赋予与提出索赔的加拿大投资者相竞争的美国投资者或投资一定的经济利益，这明显违背了第 1102 条的国民待遇规定。

案件影响（Impact of the Case）

随着全球化进程的发展，国际贸易和国际投资之间两者关系越来越紧密，已经呈现出明显的融合趋势，不断促进全球经济发展。但各国制定的贸易政策和投资政策通常各自独立，缺乏相互协调，既阻碍国际贸易的发展，也影响了外资利用的效果。为加强投资政策和贸易政策的相互协调，通过国际协定将投资措施和贸易联系起来已成为较为普遍的做法。世界贸易组织 TRIMs 协议和北美自由贸易协议（NAFTA）就是典型的例子。TRIMs 主要规范与贸易有关的投资措施，而 NAFTA 则在区域性的层面上，对贸易和投资问题同时加以规制，即推动贸易和投资的自由化。

本案仲裁申请人以外国投资者的身份提出适用投资者与国家之间的争端解决程序向美国政府索赔，仲裁申请人面临的困境是其在美国投资的企业不断被美国采取反倾销和反补贴措施，大量的税负使其利益受损。仲裁申请人一方面寻求反补贴反倾销领域的政府间争议解决的努力，另一方面试图启动 NAFTA 第 11 章的投资争端解决机制。本案经典之处在于，仲裁庭认可了仲裁申请人加拿大公司的投资者地位，重点分析了 NAFTA 第 1901 条（3）款的规定，认为仲裁申请人对美国政府部门的反倾销反补贴过程中形成的各种裁定的不同意见，只能由第 19 章专门为反倾销反补贴争议设置的争议解决程序来解决，而不宜在 11 章之下另行启动一个平行程序。但是，仲裁庭笔锋一转，指出 2000 年美国所颁布的《持续倾销和补贴抵消法》规定把所收取的"双反"税金直接返还给美国本国的软木经销商，而不返还给外国投资的软木经销商，这明显涉嫌违反国民待遇。仲裁庭对这些问题给出了初步裁定，阐明了仲裁庭有权管辖返还税款问题的意见，认为这不是反倾销反补贴问题。这样实际上使投资争端管辖的"手臂"实质地延长到了"双反"的后院。

较为遗憾的是，因为本案争议问题背景的历史复杂性，在本案初步问题的裁决作出后不久，2006 年 9 月 12 日，在本案悬而未决的同时，美国和加拿大签署了《软木木材协议》，以解决对软木木材征收关税的潜在争议。该协议包括理赔的内容，本案申请人科夫和特梅诺分别致函仲裁庭终止了本案审理，据相关材料披露关联案件中的天柏公司获得了 2.42 亿美元的赔款，本案最终未对美国的做法是否违背投资领域的国民待遇作出裁决。

思考问题（Questions）

1. NAFTA 第 11 章和第 19 章争端解决程序的机制有何不同？

2. 你认为美国给国内生产者分发"双反"税的做法违背国民待遇义务吗？

案例七　谢业深诉秘鲁案

Tza Yap Shum v. Republic of Peru
（ICSID Case No. ARB/07/6）

选读理由（Selected Reason）

香港居民谢业深（Mr. Tza Yap Shum）援引 1994 年《中国—秘鲁双边投资条约》，以秘鲁政府为被申请人，未经东道国同意，径自单方向 ICSID 申请仲裁，声称秘鲁政府对他在秘鲁境内设立的一家鱼粉公司采取了征收措施。涉讼双方争议首先聚焦于 ICSID 仲裁庭对本案是否具有管辖权。对这一问题的回答主要取决于：（1）1994 年《中国—秘鲁 BIT》可否直接适用于"一国两制"下的中国香港特别行政区；（2）外国投资商可否不顾有关 BIT 中仲裁条款的限制，不经东道国同意，单方把一切投资争端都提交 ICSID 仲裁。本案仲裁庭于 2009 年 6 月 19 日作出裁定，确认该庭对本案具有管辖权。但该管辖权裁定并不符合国际公约、国际协定、中国法律以及香港基本法。

2006 年 9 月 29 日，Tza Yap Shum（谢业深）向总部设在华盛顿特区的"解决投资争端国际中心"提交了仲裁申请书，声称秘鲁共和国当局征收了他在秘鲁境内开设的一家鱼粉公司，即 TSG 有限公司（以下简称"TSG"公司），为此向秘鲁政府索赔 200 万美元。申请人谢业深在中国福建出生，后取得香港永久居民身份，在维京群岛注册了一家公司，到秘鲁进行投资，持有鱼粉生产企业 TSG 的 90% 股份。2004 年，秘鲁税务局在国内采取一系列措施，同年 9 月对 TSG 公司的税收审计情况签署报告，12 月通知 TSG 公司欠税 1200 万新索尔，并冻结了该公司的银行账户。2005 年 1 月税务局对 TSG 公司实施了"税收抵押扣押令"，至 3 月仍拒绝撤销该扣押令。谢业深认为，税务局对 TSG 公司采取的税收征管措施构成征收行为。因此，在 2006 年谢业深向 ICSID 提交仲裁申请书，2007 年 2 月 12 日，ICSID 秘书处对该案进行了登记，并于同年 10 月 1 日设立仲裁庭。仲裁庭于 2009 年 6 月 19 日作出仲裁裁决。本案的争议焦点之一是东道国作出的临时措施，包括冻结银行账户等，是否构成对谢业深投资的间接征收。

仲裁申请情况 (The Request for Arbitration)

Tza Yap Shum ("Tza"), a Chinese national commenced this arbitration against the Republic of Peru ("Peru"), claiming violations of the BIT that affected his investment in TSG del Perú S. A. C. "TSG", a Peruvian company involved in the purchase and exportation of fishmeal, primarily for Asian markets. Tza is a 90% indirect shareholder of TSG, having made an investment of US $ 400,000.

谢业深，一名中国公民，开始对秘鲁共和国（"秘鲁"）进行仲裁，声称违反了影响他对 TSG del PerúS. A. C 的投资的双边投资条约。"TSG"，一家秘鲁公司，主要为亚洲市场购买和出口鱼粉。Tza 是 TSG 90% 的间接股东，投资 40 万美元。

TSG commenced its operations in 2002 and between 2002 and 2004 was among the 12 largest exporters of fishmeal in Peru, with sales greater than US $ 20 million per year. TSG's business model consisted of contracting with, and financing, fishing vessels for the purchase of raw materials. Such raw material would be delivered directly by fishing vessels to third-party transforming plants, with which TSG contracted for the production of fishmeal. The produced fishmeal was warehoused at the third-party plants until ready for export. Thus, TSG never handled any products directly and served primarily as a coordinating and financing agent. TSG's comparative advantage in the industry consisted of access to financing from Tza's network of personal relationships with businesses and individuals. While TSG did not obtain financing from Peruvian banks, it used Peruvian banks to conduct its transactions, including the receipt of loans from abroad, the execution letters of credits from buyers abroad, and generally keeping track of its payments, costs, and accounts receivables.

TSG 于 2002 年开始运作，2002 年至 2004 年期间是秘鲁 12 个最大的鱼粉出口商之一，每年销售额超过 2000 万美元。TSG 的商业模式包括与渔船签订合同并为其融资，以购买原材料。这些原材料将由渔船直接交付给第三方转化厂，TSG 与其签订了生产鱼粉的合同。生产的鱼粉被存放在第三方工厂，直到准备出口。因此，TSG 从不直接处理任何产品，主要充当协调和融资代理。TSG 在该行业的相对优势包括从 Tza 与企业和个人的个人关系网络获得融资。虽然 TSG 没有从秘鲁银行获得资金，但它使用秘鲁银行进行交易，包括从国外接收贷款、执行国外买家的信用证，以及一般跟踪其付款、费用和应收账款。

In 2004, Peru's taxing authority, the Superintendencia Nacional de Administración Tributaria ("SUNAT"), commenced an audit of TSG, which was conducted with the company's cooperation. The audit appeared to be routine in nature and stemmed from TSG's requests in the prior two years of refunds of certain amounts paid in connection with sales taxes. During the audit, SUNAT concluded that TSG's books did not adequately reflect values for the raw material used in the production of fishmeal. SUNAT therefore, pursuant to the Peruvian tax code, utilized a "presumed basis" in its analysis rather than a basis based on TSG's books and records. Based upon the presumed basis, SUNAT concluded that TSG had underreported sales volumes. SUNAT, therefore, imposed back taxes and fines totaling approximately 10 million Peruvian solares ("S/.").

2004 年，秘鲁的税务主管部门国家税务管理局（"税务局"）开始对 TSG 进行审计，该审计是在公司的合作下进行的。审计似乎是例行的，并源于 TSG 在前两年要求退还与销售税有关的某些款项。在审计期间，税务局得出结论，TSG 的账簿没有充分反映鱼粉生产所用原材料的价值。因此税务局根据秘鲁税法使用了"推定基础"而不是基于 TSG 的账簿和记录进行分析。根据推定基础，税务局得出结论，TSG 未全部报告销售额。因此，税务局征收了总计约 1000 万秘鲁索尔的税收和罚款。

Shortly after the audit, SUNAT also imposed interim measures which had the effect of attaching certain limited assets of TSG and directing all Peruvian banks to retain any funds passing through them in connection with TSG's transactions. SUNAT is permitted under Peruvian law to impose interim measures to ensure the payment of tax debts in "exceptional circumstances", namely when the debtor has been uncooperative (by for example, failing to disclose material information) or when efforts to obtain payment of the tax debt would otherwise be unsuccessful. The report prepared by TSG's SUNAT auditor in support of the request for interim measures premised the request on TSG's "irregular behavior." The only behavior cited was SUNAT's determination that TSG's books had failed to accurately reflect the company's total sales volume. A second report was subsequently submitted by TSG's SUNAT auditor, which also premised the request on the failure to accurately reflect sales volumes and only modified the specific subsection of the Tax Code upon which the auditor based the request. Neither report provided specific support for the auditor's conclusions. Furthermore, SUNAT's executing division in charge of imposing interim measures (la División de Control de la Deuda y Cobranza) did not make any requests for additional information from the auditor before imposing the requested measures.

审计后不久，税务局还实施了临时措施，对 TSG 的资产予以某些限制，并指示所有秘鲁银行保留 TSG 通过他们进行交易的资金。秘鲁法律允许税务局采取临时措施，以确保在"特殊情况"下支付税款债务，即当债务人不合作（例如，未能披露重大信息）或当获得税款债务的努力因其他原因不成功。税务局负责 TSG 项目的审计师所准备的报告支持申请临时措施是以该申请建立在 TSG 的"不正常行为"前提基础上的。税务局的决定所引用的唯一行为是 TSG 的账簿未能准确反映公司的总销售额。随后，TSG 的税务局审计员提交了第二份报告，该报告也以未能准确反映销售额为前提，并仅修改了审计员根据提出该请求所依据的税法的具体部分。两份报告都没有为审计结论提供具体的支持。此外，税务局负责实施临时措施的执行部门（债务控制和收回司）在实施所要求的措施之前没有向审计员提出任何额外信息要求。

TSG challenged both SUNAT's audit determinations and its imposition of interim measures via administrative and judicial procedures available under Peruvian law. TSG commenced an administrative procedure requesting SUNAT to lift the interim measures on the basis that SU-NAT had not adequately justified such measures. SUNAT rejected TSG's application, but reduced its calculation of back taxes. TSG also challenged SUNAT's decision before the Fiscal Tribunal, which affirmed the interim measures but further reduced the amount of back taxes to approximately S/. 3. 1 million and ordered SUNAT to recalculate certain additional amounts.

TSG 对税务局的审计决定及其通过秘鲁法律规定的行政和司法程序实施临时措施提出质疑。TSG 启动了一项行政程序，要求税务局取消临时措施，理由是税务局没有充分说明采取这些措施的理由。税务局拒绝了 TSG 的申请，但减少了对欠税的计算。TSG 还向财政仲裁庭对税务局的决定提出质疑，该裁决确认了临时措施，但进一步将欠税额减至约 310 万索尔，并命令税务局重新计算某些额外数额。

Following the imposition of SUNAT's interim measures, TSG was unable to utilize Peruvian banks for its transactions. TSG's sales subsequently decreased dramatically and ultimately, TSG commenced a debt restructuring proceeding in March 2005, which had the effect of suspending the interim measures and permitted TSG to continue operating.

The Claimant Tza, the 90% shareholder of TSG, thereafter commenced an ICSID arbitration claiming that SUNAT's audit determinations and interim measures constituted an unjustified indirect expropriation of its investment, in violation of the BIT. Tza sought over S/. 57 million based on the projected cash flow of TSG, in addition to S/. 15 million for moral damages, plus interest (at a rate of 11%) and fees and costs. Total damages demanded therefore approximated US $ 25 million.

在税务局采取临时措施后，TSG 无法利用秘鲁银行进行交易。随后，TSG 的销售额大幅下降，最终，TSG 于 2005 年 3 月开始了债务重组程序，这导致临时措施暂停，并允许 TSG 继续运营。

申请人谢是 TSG 90% 的股东，此后开始了 ICSID 仲裁，声称税务局的审计决定和临时措施构成了违反双边投资条约的对其投资的无理间接征用。谢根据预测的 TSG 现金流量计算寻求超过 5700 万索尔的赔偿，另外要求 1500 万索尔用于精神损害赔偿，外加利息（利率为 11%）以及费用和成本。因此，所要求的损害赔偿总额约为 2500 万美元。

仲裁结果（Award）

On 19 June 2009, the Arbitral Tribunal issued a Decision on Jurisdiction and Competence in which it determined that Tza's interest in TSG constituted an investment for purposes of the BIT and that the Tribunal was competent to determine Claimant's expropriation claims.

Final Award on Merits rendered on 7 July 2011, under the Agreement between the Government of the Republic of Peru and the Government of the People's Republic of China for the Reciprocal Promotion and Protection of Investment (the "BIT") and in accordance with the ICSID Convention.

In its Final Award on the Merits, the Tribunal found that SUNAT's imposition of interim measures constituted an arbitrary taking and thus an indirect expropriation of Tza's investment. However, the Tribunal declined to adopt Tza's measure of damages, instead basing its calculation of compensation on the adjusted book value of TSG and awarding US \$ 786,306.24, plus interest (at U. S. Treasury Bond rates). The Tribunal further ordered each party to split costs evenly.

2009 年 6 月 19 日，仲裁庭发布了一项关于管辖权的决定，该决定确定谢在 TSG 中的权益构成了双边投资协定项下的投资，并且仲裁庭有权确定申请人的征收索赔。

根据秘鲁共和国政府和中华人民共和国政府关于相互促进和保护投资的协定（"BIT"），并根据 ICSID 公约，于 2011 年 7 月 7 日作出的最终实体裁决。

在最终裁决中，仲裁庭认为，税务局的临时措施构成了一种任意的行为，从而间接没收了谢的投资。然而，仲裁庭拒绝采用谢的损害赔偿标准，而是根据调整后的 TSG 账面价值计算赔偿金，并裁决 786306.24 美元，加上利息（按照美国国债利率）。仲裁庭进一步命令各方平均分摊费用。

裁决原因（Reasons for the Award）

The Tribunal found that the audit of TSG appeared to have been routine in light of TSG's request in prior years for large refunds on sales taxes. In light of the deference given to a State's regulatory and administrative powers, nothing in the conduct of SUNAT in conducting the audit constituted an expropriation. At the same time, the Tribunal also noted that TSG's challenges of SUNAT's determinations were not frivolous.

仲裁庭认为，鉴于 TSG 在过去几年中要求对销售税进行大额退款，对 TSG 的审计应该是常规的。鉴于对国家监管和行政权力的尊重，国家税务总局在进行审计时没有任何行为构成征用。与此同时，仲裁庭还指出，TSG 对 SUNAT 的挑战并非是任意的。

The Tribunal determined that the interim measures imposed by SUNAT were arbitrary in nature and constituted an expropriation for the following reasons:

The Tribunal found that the interim measures, which were legally binding on all affected banks, prevented TSG from continuing to transact with such banks. Given that TSG's business model used Peruvian banks to conduct its transactions, the interim measures presented a severe and substantial impact on TSG's business. The Tribunal found that, based on the information SUNAT obtained during its audit concerning how TSG was financed and operated, SUNAT should have known that interim measures were a "strike at the heart of the operative capacity of TSG." The Tribunal also noted that as a result of the interim measures, TSG's sales fell from an average of S/. 80 million for the 2005 – 2006 period to S/. 3. 4 million for 2005 – 2006.

仲裁庭裁定，国家税务总局实施的临时措施属于任意性质，构成征收，原因如下：

仲裁庭认为，对所有受影响的银行具有法律约束力的临时措施阻止了 TSG 继续与这些银行进行交易。鉴于 TSG 的商业模式是使用秘鲁银行进行交易，临时措施对 TSG 的业务产生了严重的影响。仲裁庭认为，根据税务局在审计 TSG 如何获得资金和运作方面获得的信息，税务局应该知道临时措施是"TSG 运作能力的核心"。仲裁庭还指出，由于采取了临时措施，TSG 的销售额下降。

Thus, the Tribunal distinguished the present case from the circumstances in LG&E Energy Corp. v. Republic of Argentina, where it was held that the decrease in an investment's capacity and income generation, by itself, does not constitute expropriation.

因此，仲裁庭将本案与 LG&E 能源公司诉阿根廷共和国的情况区分开来，后者认为，投资能力和创收的减少本身并不构成征用。

The Tribunal dismissed Peru's argument that the interim measures could no constitute an expropriation because they were ultimately suspended by TSG's restructuring proceedings. The Tribunal noted that SUNAT's interim measures were imposed for a period of one year and subsequently extended to be in effect for an additional two years. While the restructuring proceeding had the effect, under Peruvian law of suspending SUNAT's interim measures and allowing TSG to continue to operate through Peruvian banks, the Tribunal noted that the TSG could only resume normal operations once the restructuring proceedings concluded in June 2006. The

Tribunal further noted that the restructuring proceedings were commenced at TSG's own initiative and were a reasonable and necessary response by TSG under the circumstances to mitigate its damages. The Tribunal determined that Peru could not rely on TSG's own efforts to justify or minimize the impact of SUNAT's actions.

仲裁庭驳回了秘鲁的论点，即临时措施不能构成征用，因为它们最终被 TSG 的重组程序暂停。仲裁庭指出，SUNAT 的临时措施实施了一年，随后又延长了两年。虽然重组程序具有效力，但根据秘鲁法律暂停税务局的临时措施并允许 TSG 继续通过秘鲁银行运营，仲裁庭指出 TSG 只能在 2006 年 6 月重组程序结束后恢复正常运作。仲裁庭进一步注意到重组程序是由 TSG 自己主动开始的，并且是 TSG 根据情况作出的合理和必要的回应，以减轻其损害。仲裁庭裁定秘鲁不能依靠 TSG 自己的努力来证明或尽量减少税务局行动的影响。

The Tribunal recognized the deference given to a State's regulatory and administrative powers and noted the general rule that a State is not liable for any losses resulting from the good faith application of general taxes and regulations. However, the Tribunal also noted that this deference is bound by the principle of reasonableness and non-arbitrariness reflected in public international law, as well as Peruvian law and treaty practice.

仲裁庭承认对一国的监管和行政权力的尊重，并注意到一般规则，即一国不对因善意适用一般税收和法规而造成的任何损失负责。但是，仲裁庭还指出，这种尊重受到国际公法以及秘鲁法律和条约惯例所反映的合理性和非任意性原则的约束。

Here, the Tribunal determined that SUNAT failed to comply with its own internal guidelines and procedures which required inter alia (i) a more precise identification of assets to be attached via interim measures, (ii) a reasoned basis for the "exceptional" remedy of interim measures accompanied by detailed evidentiary support, and (iii) efforts to avoid interfering with the debtor's business operations. The Tribunal also noted that SUNAT's executing division failed to make relevant inquiries or requests for additional information from the auditor before imposing interim measures. As a result, the Tribunal found that SUNAT's actions were arbitrary in nature, resulting in unjustified losses on the part of TSG.

在这方面，仲裁庭裁定税务局未能遵守其内部准则和程序，这些准则和程序除其他外必须：（1）通过临时措施更准确地识别资产，（2）对"特殊"补救措施的合理依据。临时措施，附有详尽的证据支持，（3）努力避免干涉债务人的业务运作。仲裁庭亦注意到，在采取临时措施前，税务局的执行部门未能向审计师提出相关查询或要求提供额外资料。因此，仲裁庭认为，税务局的行为属于任意性质，导致 TSG 无理损失。

The Tribunal determined that while SUNAT's interim measures had a severe impact on the continued operations of TSG, they ultimately failed to be effective. The Tribunal noted that due in large part to the lack of precise identification of assets, such interim measures secured assets worth only US $ 172 out of the approximately US $ 4 million tax debt that resulted from the audit.

仲裁庭裁定，虽然税务局的临时措施对 TSG 的持续运作产生了严重影响，但它们最终未能生效。仲裁庭指出，由于缺乏对资产的准确识别，这种临时措施在审计产生的约 400 万美元税收债务中获得的资产仅为 172 美元。

The Tribunal recognized that TSG availed itself of administrative and judicial procedures to challenge the imposition of SUNAT's interim measures. However, the Tribunal held that such procedures did not amount to an adequate and effective legal recourse to SUNAT's decision. The administrative and judicial bodies that reviewed the interim measures failed to address and analyze sufficiently TSG's claims and, instead, adopted SUNAT's positions without a reasoned basis. The Tribunal found that TSG therefore had access only to formal, rather than substantive, legal recourse.

仲裁庭确认 TSG 利用了行政和司法程序来质疑税务局的临时措施。但是，仲裁庭认为，这种程序并不构成对税务局决定的充分和有效的法律程序。审查临时措施的行政和司法机构未能充分处理和分析 TSG 的主张，而是在没有合理依据的情况下采纳了税务局的立场。仲裁庭认为，TSG 只是获得了官方的但非实质性的法律救济程序。

Finally, the Tribunal rejected respondent's arguments that Tza had conducted himself in bad faith because of the manner in which he organized his investment in TSG and TSG's failure to use funds reimbursed by SUNAT to pay his tax debt rather than TSG's business loans. The Tribunal noted that neither the structure of Tza's investment (and his delegation of authority to others) nor TSG's decision to pay off its business debts (and thereby mitigate its damages) evidenced bad faith.

最后，仲裁庭驳回了被申请人的论点，即谢组织投资投入 TSG 的方法来看其是恶意的以及 TSG 未能使用税务局返还的资金来支付其税务债务而不是 TSG 的商业贷款。仲裁庭指出，谢的投资结构（以及他对其他人的授权）和 TSG 决定偿还其商业债务（从而减轻其损害赔偿）都没有被证明是恶意的。

The Tribunal also rejected the argument that TSG failed to mitigate its damages by failing to request certain other measures available to it under Peruvian law (e. g. requesting the executing division of SUNAT to substitute the interim measures or requesting waivers to make certain payments for the continued operation of TSG). The Tribunal found that it was doubtful that these additional measures would have been effective. It would therefore be unreasonable to expect TSG to exhaust these remedies. The Tribunal noted that TSG had mitigated its damages with the commencement of restructuring proceedings and that TSG's efforts to mitigate damages would be taken into account in the determination of damages.

仲裁庭还驳回了 TSG 未能根据秘鲁法律要求其提供某些其他措施来减轻其损害的论点（例如，要求税务局的执行部门取代临时措施或要求豁免为 TSG 继续运营支付某些费用）。仲裁庭认为，这些额外措施是否有效是值得怀疑的。因此，期望 TSG 用尽这些补救措施是不合理的。仲裁庭指出，TSG 已经通过重组程序的启动减轻了损失，并且在确定损害赔偿时将考虑 TSG 减轻损害的努力。

With respect to compensation, the Tribunal noted that standard that the measure of damages is the amount needed to place the Claimant in the same position he would have been without the expropriatory act. Both parties were in agreement that this amount should be based upon the value of TSG. However each party had different methods as to how to calculate the value of the company: Tza based his requested damages on the discounted cash flow of TSG, while Peru argued that the appropriate standard was the company's adjusted book value.

关于赔偿问题，仲裁庭指出，损害赔偿措施的标准是将申请人置于与没有征收行为的情况相同的位置所需的数额。双方同意这一数额应基于 TSG 的价值。然而，各方在如何计算公司价值方面有不同的方法：谢是基于其对 TSG 折现现金流量的要求赔偿，而秘鲁则认为公司调整后的账面价值是适当的标准。

The Tribunal rejected Tza's requested damages, which were based on the discounted cash flow of TSG. The Tribunal noted that TSG had been in operation for only two years during which its cash flow was negative. TSG was highly leveraged, operated in the high risk fishing industry and had already begun to lose market share in the industry when SUNAT imposed its interim measures. In light of this, the Tribunal adopted Respondent's position that proper compensation should be based on TSG's adjusted book value, resulting in awarded compensation of US $ 786,306.24.

仲裁庭驳回了谢要求的损害赔偿金，这些赔偿金是根据 TSG 的贴现现金流量计算的。仲裁庭指出，TSG 仅运作了两年，其间现金流为负数。TSG 高度杠杆化，在高风险渔业中运营，并且在税务局实施临时措施时已经开始失去该行业的市场份额。鉴于此，仲裁庭采用了被申请人的立场，即适当的赔偿应基于 TSG 的调整后的账面价值，从而计算出 786306.24 美元的赔偿金额。

The Tribunal rejected wholesale Claimant's request for moral damages. Relying on Lemire v. Ukrain (ICSID Case No. ARB/06/18), the Tribunal found that none of the conduct outlined in that case as justify moral damages (i. e. (i) physical harm or threat of harm to the investor, (ii) State action resulting in a deterioration of physical or mental health or harm to reputation, and (iii) severe and substantial causes and effects of expropriation) existed here.

仲裁庭驳回了申请人的大额精神损害赔偿请求。仲裁庭依据勒米尔诉乌克兰案

（ICSID 案件号 ARB／06/18），认为在本案中不存在有权获得道德损害赔偿的任何行为〔即（1）对投资者的人身伤害或威胁，（2）存在导致身心健康恶化或声誉受损的国家行为，（3）征收的严重、实质性原因和影响〕。

Finally, the Tribunal also rejected Claimant's requested interest rate of 11%. This rate was based on the rates used by TSG for its financing, and thus incorporated a risk factor that the Tribunal determined was no longer applicable post-expropriation. Instead, the Tribunal adopted respondent's position that the appropriate interest rate should approximate the rate of return had the damages awarded been re-invested for a favorable return. The Tribunal therefore ruled that the interest rate on damages would be tied to the average monthly rate on 10-year U. S. treasury bonds. At the date of the Award, the interest awarded was US $ 227,201. 30.

最后，仲裁庭还驳回了索赔人要求的 11% 的利率。这一比率是根据 TSG 用于融资的费率计算的，因此属于仲裁庭确定的征收后不再适用的风险因素。相反，仲裁庭采纳了被申请人的立场，即如果赔偿金被重新投入以获得有利的回报，则适当的利率应接近回报率。因此，仲裁庭裁定损害赔偿率与 10 年期美国国债的平均月利率挂钩。在裁决之日，裁决的利息为 227201. 30 美元。

裁决撤销或执行情况（Annulment or Enforcement of the Award）

On 3 November 2011, the Republic of Peru (or the "Applicant") filed a timely application for annulment of the Decision on Jurisdiction and Competence rendered on 19 June 2009 ("the Decision on Jurisdiction and Competence"), or, alternatively, of the Award rendered on 7 July 2011 ("the Award") in ICSID Case No. ARB/07/6 in favor of Mr. Tza Yap Shum, a Chinese national, by an Arbitral Tribunal composed of Mr. Judd L. Kessler (President), Professor Juan Fernández Armesto and Mr. Hernando Otero (Co-Arbitrators) ("the Application for Annulment"). The Application for Annulment was filed in accordance with Article 52 of the Convention on the Settlement of Investment Disputes between States and National of Other States ("the ICSID Convention"), and Rule 50 of the ICSID Rules of Procedure for Arbitration Proceedings ("the ICSID Arbitration Rules").

2011 年 11 月 3 日，秘鲁共和国（或"申请人"）及时提出申请，要求撤销 2009 年 6 月 19 日作出的仲裁机构和仲裁庭管辖权决定（"管辖权决定"），或者取消 2011 年 7 月 7 日在 ICSID 案例号 ARB/07/6 中，由 Judd L. Kessler 先生（主席）、Juan Fernández Armesto 教授和 Hernando Otero 先生（共同仲裁人）组成的仲裁庭做出的支持中国公民谢业深先生作出的裁决（"裁决"）（以下简称"撤销申请"）。撤销申请是根据《解决国家与其他国家国民之间投资争端公约》（"ICSID 公约"）第52 条和《ICSID 仲裁程序规则》（"ICSID 仲裁规则"）第50 条提出的。

The Application for Annulment is based on the grounds enumerated in Article 52 （1）（b）, （d） and （e） of the ICSID Convention, namely that the Arbitral Tribunal （i） manifestly exceeded its powers, （ii） seriously departed from a fundamental rule of procedure and （iii） failed to state reasons on which the Decision on Jurisdiction and Competence or the Awardare based. In the Application for Annulment, the Republic of Peru requested annulment of the Decision on Jurisdiction and Competence "in its entirety" with the consequent annulment of the Award "in its entirety," or in the alternative, in the event that the Committee did not grant the annulment of the Decision on Jurisdiction and Competence, the Republic of Peru asked for independent annulment of the Award in its entirety. The Republic of Peru later made clear that it was only seeking "partial annulment of the Decision on Jurisdiction with respect to the Tribunal's conclusion that all of Claimant's expropriation claims were within the scope of Article 8 （3） of the BIT. "

撤销申请是基于 ICSID 公约第52 条（1）款（b）项、（d）项和（e）项列举的理由，即仲裁庭（1）明显超出其权力，（2）严重违反基本程序规则，（3）未能说明做出管辖权决定的原因及裁决依据。在撤销申请中，秘鲁共和国要求"全部"撤销对管辖权决定，并随后"全部"撤销裁决，或者在委员会未批准撤销管辖权决定的情况下，秘鲁共和国要求完全独立撤销裁决。秘鲁共和国后来明确表示，它只寻求"部分撤销关于仲裁庭在管辖权决定中的结论，即申请人的征收索赔在双边投资协定第8 条（3）款的范围内"。

In accordance with article 52, paragraph 5, of the Washington Convention, Peru applies for a stay of enforcement of the award at the same time as it applies for withdrawal until the ad hoc committee decides on the application for withdrawal.

On March 20, 2012, Taz Yap Shum applied for the termination of the suspension of arbitral awards or for Peru to issue a guarantee to guarantee the performance of debts. Later Peru undertook to pay unconditionally within 30 days of the award if the final award did not revoke the previous award. On April 21, 2012, Taz Yap Shum said at the first meeting that he would no longer request the suspension of arbitral awards, so the suspension period lasted until the date of the final award.

依据《华盛顿公约》第52 条第5 款的规定，秘鲁在申请撤裁时，同时申请暂停执行仲裁裁决，直至特设委员会对撤裁申请作出决定。

2012 年3 月20 日，谢业深申请终止暂停执行仲裁裁决，或请求秘鲁出具担保，保证履行债务。后秘鲁承诺若最后裁决不撤销之前的裁决，则在裁决后30 天内无条件支付赔偿金额。2012 年 4 月 21 日，谢业深在第一次会议中表示不再要求终止暂停执行仲裁裁决，故暂停期间直至最终裁决作出之日。

The challenge to the Decision on Jurisdiction and Competence hinges upon the interpretation by the Arbitral Tribunal of the dispute settlement clause at Article 8 of the Peru-China BIT, which reads in pertinent part:

3. If a dispute involving the amount of compensation for expropriation cannot be settled within six months after resort to negotiations as specified in Paragraph 1 of this Article, it may be submitted at the request of either party to the international arbitration of the International Center for Settlement of Investment Disputes (ICSID), established by the Convention on the Settlement of Investment Disputes between States and Nationals of other States, signed in Washington D. C. on March 18, 1965. Any disputes concerning other matters between an investor of either Contracting Party and the other Contracting Party may be submitted to the Center if the parties to the dispute so agree. The provisions of this Paragraph shall not apply if the investor concerned has resorted to the procedure specified in Paragraph 2 of this Article.

对管辖权决定的质疑取决于仲裁庭对秘鲁中国双边投资协定第 8 条争议解决条款的解释，该条款在相关部分：

3. 如涉及征收补偿款额的争议，在诉诸本条第一款的程序后六个月内仍未能解决，可应任何一方的要求，将争议提交根据 1965 年 3 月 18 日在华盛顿签署的《关于解决国家和他国国民之间投资争端公约》设立的 "解决投资争端国际中心" 进行仲裁。缔约一方的投资者和缔约另一方之间有关其他事项的争议，经双方同意，可提交该中心。如有关投资者诉诸了本条第二款所规定的程序，本款规定不应适用。

The Committee is of the opinion that the Arbitral Tribunal committed no manifest excess of powers in its interpretation of Article 8 and in finding that the word "involving" is ambiguous. On their face, the words of the first sentence of Article 8 (3) of the Peru-China BIT which read "[i] f a dispute involving the amount of compensation for expropriation cannot be settled within six months after resort tonegotiations [...]" do not include the question of the legality of expropriation, but equally do not refer to disputes exclusively limited to the amount of compensation. Out of context, the meaning of the phrase is not textually obvious. The Arbitral Tribunal interpreted the expression "dispute involving the amount of compensation for expropriation" in the overall context of Article 8.

The Arbitral Tribunal went through an interpretative process mandated by the VCLT. It looked at the ordinary meaning of the word "involving", considered the context of Article 8 (3) and then looked at subsidiary sources. It is not for the Committee to replace the Arbitral Tribunal's judgment by its own. A body that had appellate jurisdiction might well find fault as a matter of law with some aspects of the Arbitral Tribunal's application of the VCLT, but an ad hoc committee does not have such powers. The Republic of Peru's request for annulment on the basis of manifest excess of powers is accordingly dismissed.

委员会认为，仲裁庭在解释第 8 条和认定"涉及"一词不明确时，没有明显越权。从表面上看，《秘鲁—中国双边投资协定》第 8 条（3）款第一句中的"涉及征收补偿金额的争端，在诉诸谈判后的六个月内不能解决……"不包括征收的合法性问题，但同样不仅限于赔偿金额的争议。从上下文来看，这个短语的意思在文本上并不明显。仲裁庭在第 8 条的总体背景下解释了"涉及征收补偿金额的争议"一词。

仲裁庭使用了《维也纳条约法公约》规定的解释程序。它着眼于"涉及"一词的一般含义，考虑到第 8 条（3）款的上下文，然后着眼于附属来源。委员会不应自行取代仲裁庭的判决。一个拥有上诉管辖权的机构很可能会在仲裁庭对《维也纳条约法公约》适用的某些方面将过失视为法律问题，但一个特设委员会没有这种权力。秘鲁共和国基于明显的越权要求撤销的请求也因此被驳回。

For the reasons given above, the ad hoc Committee decides that:

● The Republic of Peru's Application for Annulment is dismissed in its entirety.

● The Republic of Peru shall bear 80% of all the costs of the proceedings incurred in connection with the Annulment proceeding and Mr. Tza Yap Shum 20% of the said costs.

● Each Party shall bear its own Party costs incurred in connection with the Annulment proceeding.

● Pursuant to Article 52 (5) of the ICSID Convention and ICSID Arbitration Rule 54 (3), the stay of enforcement of the Award is terminated.

由于上述原因，特设委员会决定：

1. 秘鲁共和国的撤销申请被全部驳回。

2. 秘鲁共和国应承担与撤销程序有关的全部程序费用的 80%，谢业深先生应承担上述费用的 20%。

3. 各方应承担与撤销程序有关的各方自己发生的费用。

4. 按照 ICSID 公约第 52 条（5）款和 ICSID 仲裁规则 54 条（3）款，裁决执行的暂停结束。

案件影响（Impact of the Case）

本案涉及中国与秘鲁双边投资协定条款的适用和解释问题。中秘 BIT 第 1.2 条对"投资者"的定义是"在中华人民共和国方面，系指：（一）依照中华人民共和国法律拥有其国籍的自然人；……"事实上，中秘 BIT 是 1994 年香港回归之前签订的，并不适用于香港，BIT 中的中方投资者也并不包括香港居民。再者，香港回归后，中国实行一国两制，香港作为特别行政区具有高度自治权，具有独立的对外签订 BIT 的缔约权。根据《中英联合声明》、中国《宪法》和《香港特别行政区基本法》等的相关规定，中秘 BIT 并不适用于香港居民，因此谢业深不能依据中秘 BIT 取得"投资者"身份，也就不能援引该 BIT 在 ICSID 起诉秘鲁了。遗憾的是，仲裁庭仅从中秘 BIT 对投资者的定义的字面意义出发，认定谢业深是中国公民，因此"没必要确定中秘 BIT 是否适用于香港地区"，也"不予分析"。这需要我们予以批判。

在条款解释问题上，本案涉及"涉及征收补偿款额的争议"是否包括"涉及征收的争议"问题。我国在 1998 年之前签订的 BIT 均采用了"严格限制国际仲裁"条款。即一、当事人双方首先通过协商解决，二、6 个月内双方解决不了提交东道国法院解决，三、只有涉及与征收补偿有关的争议才允许当事人双方不经对方同意即可提交 IC-SID 解决，对于涉及征收补偿以外的争议当事人一方经过另一方的书面同意才可以将争议提交 ICSID。在本案中，秘鲁坚持认为，中秘 BIT 第 8 条（3）款"涉及征收补偿款额的争议"仅指关于征收补偿额之争议，不包括关于征收的争议。为支持该解释，秘鲁还特意提交了当年亲自参加谈判的中、秘双方代表的证言，以此证明当时双方政府的立场是只将征收补偿数额的争议提交 ICSID。然而，仲裁庭最终还是接受了申请人的解释，将"涉及征收补偿款额"解释为，除补偿额之外，还包括与征收有关的其他重要事项，并认为，对"涉及征收补偿款额"的这一"最宽泛的解释"恰巧就是"最恰当"的解释。仲裁庭还援引《维也纳条约法公约》解释"涉及征收补偿款额"这一用语。该条约第 31 条规定："条约应依其用语按其上下文并参照条约之目的及宗旨所具有之通常意义，善意解释之。"仲裁庭认为，对"涉及"的通常意义和善意解释是"包括"而不是"限于"或"排他地"。

思考问题（Questions）

1. 如 BIT 中对 ICSID 管辖采用"全面同意式"条款，如何在 ICSID 争端解决中维护我国作为投资东道国的利益？

2. ICSID 的特设委员会撤销裁决程序是否打破了国际仲裁的一裁终局制？

案例八 埃尔帕索诉阿根廷案

ELPaso Energy International Companyv.
The Argentine Republic（2006）
（ICSID Case No. ARB/03/15）

选读理由（Selected Reason）

埃尔帕索是一家美国公司，在 20 世纪 90 年代收购了五家从事石油勘探开采以及电力业的阿根廷公司的股份。从 2001 年起，阿根廷政府采取了一系列措施应对经济危机和货币贬值，其中包括取消比索和美元间一对一的汇率；将某些外汇支付义务转为以比索支付；冻结电价；将所有的物价和关税都根据一对一的方式用比索表示；即使政府单方面修改合同，配电公司也不得中止履行合同。埃尔帕索认为这些措施影响了其商业活动，损害了其投资所享有的权利，违反了 1991 年阿根廷—美国双边投资协定，于 2003 年向 ICSID 提起仲裁。本案涉及保护伞条款且本案仲裁庭对保护伞条款作出的解释具有突破性，在国际公约中具有重要的指导作用。

仲裁申请情况（The Request for Arbitration）

On 6 June 2003, the International Centre for Settlement of Investment Disputes（hereinafter the "Centre"）received a request for arbitration（hereinafter the "Request"）submitted by El Paso Energy International Company（hereinafter "El Paso" or "the Claimant"）, a company organised under the laws of the State of Delaware（United States of America）against the Republic of Argentina（ hereinafter "Argentina" "the Respondent" "the respondent State" "the respondent Government" or "GOA"）.

2003 年 6 月 6 日，国际投资争端解决中心（以下简称"中心"）收到埃尔帕索能源国际公司（以下简称"埃尔帕索"或"申请人"），一家依特拉华州的法律（美国）设立的，提交的针对与阿根廷共和国（以下简称"阿根廷""被申请人""被申请人国""被申请人政府"或"阿政府"）的仲裁请求（以下简称"请求"），

As indicated by its name, the Claimant is an energy company. It alleges that, up until 2003, it owned indirect and non-controlling shareholdings in a number of Argentinian entities: Compañías Asociadas Petroleras (CAPSA) and CAPEX SA (El Paso contends that it held a 45% indirect interest in CAPSA which, in turn, owned 60.36% of the shares of CAPEX); Central Costanera SA (Costanera), in which El Paso claims to have acquired a 12.335% indirect interest; and Gasoducto del Pacífico SA (Pacifico), in which its indirect interest was said to amount to approximately 13.4% (preferred shares), and 11.8% (ordinary shares) respectively. These four entities have been collectively referred to, in the present proceedings, as the "Argentinian companies." El Paso further alleged an indirect controlling interest (99.92%) in SERVICIOS El Paso, another entity incorporated in Argentina, and a 61.6% interest in the Triunion Energy Company.

如其名称所示，申请人是一家能源公司。它声称，在 2003 年之前，它间接或非控股地持有数个阿根廷公司的股权：石油伙伴公司（CAPSA）和 CAPEX SA（埃尔帕索主张它持有 CAPSA 45% 的间接权益，而 CAPSA 则持有 60.36% 的 CAPEX 股份）；中央海岸公司（Costanera）埃尔帕索称享有其 12.335% 的间接权益；以及太平洋天然气管道公司（Pacifico），埃尔帕索称对其享有的间接权益分别约为 13.4% 优先股和 11.8% 普通股。在本程序中，这四个实体被统称为"阿根廷公司"。埃尔帕索还声称，在阿根廷另一家公司埃尔帕索服务公司间接控股 99.92%，在三联能源公司（Triunion）拥有 61.6% 的股权。

The respondent State argued, however, that these direct and indirect interests had not been proved by the Claimant. The latter had, shortly after filing its Reply, submitted an amended version of paragraphs 314 – 326 of that document to the Arbitral Tribunal. According to the respondent State, a comparison between the amended text and the original one yielded serious discrepancies.

然而，被申请人政府辩称，这些直接和间接利益没有得到申请人的证实。申请人在提交答复后不久，向仲裁庭提交了该文件第 314—326 段的修订本。根据被申请人的情况，修订文本与原文本之间的比较产生了严重的差异。

In April 1997, El Paso acquired, through KLT Power Inc., an indirect non-controlling shareholding of 12.335% in Costanera. The latter, a local company engaged in the generation and sale of electricity, with a total capacity of 2311 megawatt-hour (MWh), is the largest thermal generator in Argentina. It owns approximately 10% of the installed generation capacity in the country, with a plant that includes two state-of-the-art combined cycle units located in the city of Buenos Aires.

1997 年 4 月，埃尔帕索通过 KLT 能源公司获得了在中央海岸公司的间接非控股持股 12.335%。后者是一家从事发电和销售的当地公司，总发电量为 2311 兆瓦时（MWh），是阿根廷最大的热力发电厂。它拥有全国 10% 的发电装机容量，在布宜诺斯艾利斯有一座包括两个最先进的联合循环机组的工厂。

In January 1998, El Paso acquired an indirect non-controlling interest in Pacifico, which owns and operates a natural gas pipeline linking Argentina to the Chilean city of Cochabamba. That interest amounted to 13.4% of the preferred shares and 11.8% of the ordinary shares of Pacifico.

1998 年 1 月，埃尔帕索收购了太平洋天然气管道公司的非控股股权。太平洋公司拥有并运营着一条连接阿根廷和智利城市科恰班巴的天然气管道。该权益占太平洋公司优先股的 13.4% 和普通股的 11.8%。

Further observations are in order regarding Servicios, Costanera and Pacifico. Servicios was established by El Paso as an Argentinian subsidiary in March 1998 and entered thereafter into an agreement with an Argentinian branch of the Bank of Boston to lease a gas processing plant located on the Agua de Cajón field in Neuquén Province. Pursuant to a ten-year gas processing agreement with CAPEX, SERVICIOS transformed gas produced at CAPEX's facilities into liquid petroleum gas (LPG) by-products that were sold by CAPEX.

对埃尔帕索服务公司、中央海岸公司和太平洋公司进行了进一步的观察。埃尔帕索服务公司是由埃尔帕索于 1998 年 3 月作为阿根廷子公司成立的，此后与波士顿银行的阿根廷分行达成协议，租用位于内乌肯省卡洪气田的天然气加工厂。根据与 CAPEX 签订的 10 年天然气处理协议，埃尔帕索服务公司将 CAPEX 设施生产的天然气转化为由 CAPEX 销售的液化石油气副产品。

CAPSA produces oil and, via CAPEX, generates electric power in Argentina; it also markets propane, butane and gasoline. From December 2001 onward, the GOA took a series of measures which, according to the Claimant, caused considerable harm to the latter, breached undertakings assumed by the respondent State when the investments were made, rendered the investments worthless, particularly those in CAPSA and CAPEX, and prevented these companies from functioning independently. These measures were alleged to be in violation of provisions of the 1991 BIT, i. e. those on expropriation, on discriminatory treatment, on fair and equitable treatment, and on full protection and security.

CAPSA 生产石油，并通过 CAPEX 在阿根廷发电；它还销售丙烷、丁烷和汽油。从

2001 年 12 月起，阿根廷政府采取了一系列措施，根据申请人的说法，这些措施对后者造成了相当大的损害，违反了被申请人政府在进行投资时所做的承诺，使投资，特别是在 CAPSA 和 CAPEX 中的投资变得毫无价值，还阻止这些公司独立运作。这些措施被指控违反了 1991 年 BIT 的规定，即关于征收、歧视待遇、公平和公正待遇以及全面保护和安全的规定。

The years between 1991 and 1998 were good for Argentina. They brought a growth of the GDP averaging close to 6% and an important influx of capital. When deterioration began to set in, the International Monetary Fund (IMF) identified both external and internal causes therefore, including a sharp rise of the public debt from 1999 onward. This led to solvency problems which were aggravated by the rise of the US dollar and the drop of capital flows to developing market economies. Despite exceptional financial assistance by the IMF, confidence was not restored.

Argentina's crisis of 2001 – 2002 resulted in a massive default regarding the public debt on the domestic as well as the international level. The real gross domestic product decreased by about 10% in 2002, the cumulative decline since 1998 amounting to 20%; and inflation rose to approximately 10% in April 2002, but eventually reached 40% for that entire year. More generally, due to the over-valuation of the peso and the deterioration in the economy's competitiveness, the Buenos Aires stock market lost more than 60% between 1998 and 2002; conversely, unemployment rose to over 20% in 2002. Fifty four percent of the urban population now lived on the "poverty level," while the population on an "indigence level" reached 25%; private consumption dropped by 20%. So alarming was the situation that the United Nations General Assembly resolved to reduce Argentina's membership dues on account of the crisis, which was the first case in history.

1991 年到 1998 年这段时间阿根廷发展得很好。他们的国内生产总值平均增长率接近 6%，并带来了重要的资本流入。当经济开始恶化时，国际货币基金组织（IMF）发现了外部和内部原因，包括 1999 年以来公共债务的急剧上升。这导致了偿付能力问题，这些问题因美元升值和流向发展中国家市场经济体的资本流下降而加剧。尽管国际货币基金组织提供了特殊的财政援助，但信心并未恢复。

阿根廷 2001—2002 年的危机导致国内和国际公共债务大规模违约。2002 年实际国内生产总值下降了 10% 左右，1998 年以来累计下降了 20%，2002 年 4 月通货膨胀率上升到 10% 左右，但最终达到了全年的 40%。更普遍的是，由于比索估值过高和经济竞争力下降，布宜诺斯艾利斯股市在 1998 年至 2002 年间下跌了 60% 以上；相反，2002 年失业率上升至 20% 以上。54% 的城市人口现在生活在"贫困线"上，而贫困人口达到了 25%，私人消费下降了 20%。由于这场危机如此令人担忧，联合国大会决定减少阿根廷的会费，这是历史上第一例。

The specific measures complained of by El Paso were adopted by Argentina in the context described above and were aimed at overcoming the crisis. Most of them were related, in one way or another, to the convertibility regime and its demise.

A first measure consisted in freezing bank deposits and introducing foreign exchange controls. This was achieved, initially, by Decree No. 1570 of 1 December 2001, followed by the Public Emergency Law No. 25, 561 of 6 January 2002 and by implementing measures. The Public Emergency Law: (i) abolished the parity of the US dollar and the peso; (ii) converted US dollar obligations into pesos at the rate of 1:1, a measure known as "pesification"; (iii) effected the conversion, on that basis, of dollar-denominated tariffs into pesos; (iv) eliminated adjustment clauses established in US dollars or other foreign currencies as well as indexation clauses or mechanisms for public service contracts, including tariffs for the distribution of electricity and natural gas; (v) required electricity and gas companies to continue to perform their public contracts; and (vi) authorised the GOA to impose withholdings on hydrocarbon exports.

These measures, according to the Claimant, turned the electric power sector into a strictly regulated industry operating with price caps and other requirements which made it difficult to earn a profit and even to retrieve investments.

阿根廷在上述背景下采取了埃尔帕索所抱怨的旨在克服危机的具体措施，他们中的大多数通过某种方式与可自由兑换制度及其终止有关。

第一项措施是冻结银行存款和实行外汇管制。这一目标最初是通过 2001 年 12 月 1 日第 1570 号法令、2002 年 1 月 6 日第 25561 号《公共紧急状态法》和实施措施实现的。《公共紧急状态法》①废除了美元与比索的平价；②以 1:1 的比例将美元债务转换成比索，这是一种称为"比索化"的措施；③在此基础上实现了美元计价关税转换成比索；④取消了美元或其他外币兑换协议中的调整条款以及公共服务合同中的指数化条款或机制，包括电力和天然气分销的关税；⑤要求电力和天然气公司继续履行其公共合同；⑥授权阿政府对碳氢化合物出口征收预扣税。

根据申请人的说法，这些措施将电力行业变成了一个严格管制的行业，其运营有价格上限和其他要求，这使得很难赚取利润，甚至很难收回投资。

It is alleged that, from 1997 to 2001, El Paso invested US $ 336 million in the Argentinian companies, and that its parent company guaranteed around US $ 24 million of Servicios' lease obligations. El Paso sold its interest in the companies' shares in two sales, one in June 2003 – in CAPSA (consequently in CAPEX) and in Servicios-another in October 2003-in Costanera.

According to El Paso, the sale of its investment in the Argentinian companies was due to the destruction of their value by the measures of the GOA and theirlack of prospects. The respondent State pointed out, however, that the sale was a consequence, not of its own conduct, but of a decision made by El Paso to concentrate on its core business world-wide in order to improve its liquidity, which had suffered through inadequate policies pursued by the Claimant.

据称，从 1997 年至 2001 年，埃尔帕索向阿根廷公司投资 3.36 亿美元，其母公司担保埃尔帕索服务公司约 2400 万美元的租赁义务。埃尔帕索出售了两家公司的股份，一次是在 2003 年 6 月出售在 CAPSA（后来是 CAPEX）和埃尔帕索服务公司的股份，另一次是在 2003 年 10 月出售在 Costanera 的股份。

根据埃尔帕索的说法，出售其对阿根廷公司的投资是由于阿政府的措施破坏了它们的价值，而且它们缺乏前景。然而，被申请人政府指出，出售是一种后果，而不是其自身行为，是埃尔帕索为集中在其全球核心业务以提高其流动性而做出的决定，是由于申请人所采取的政策不充分而造成的。

Claimant respectfully requests an award granting it the following relief:

1. A finding and declaration that the Argentine Republic violated the BIT.

2. An order that the Argentine Republic compensate Claimant for all damages it has suffered, plus interest compounded quarterly until the date of payment.

3. An order that the Argentine Republic pay the costs of these proceedings, including the Tribunal's fees and expenses, the cost of Claimant's legal representation, and other costs.

申请人尊重地要求授予其以下救济的裁决：

1. 确认并宣告阿根廷共和国违反 BIT。

2. 命令阿根廷共和国向申请人赔偿其所遭受的所有损害，加上每季复利直至付款日期。

3. 命令阿根廷共和国支付诉讼费用，包括仲裁庭的费用和开支、申请人的律师代理费和其他费用。

仲裁结果（Award）

For the foregoing reasons, the Tribunal decides as follows:

A）Argentina breached Article II (2) (a) of the BIT by failing to accord fair and equitable treatment to El Paso's investment.

B）Argentina's defence of necessity to El Paso's claims is rejected.

C）Within 30（thirty）days of the date of dispatch to the Parties of this Award, Argentina shall pay to El Paso compensation in the sum of US＄43.03 million, increased by semi-annually compounded interest on that amount at the rate of LIBOR plus 2% from January 1, 2002 until the date of payment in full of this Award.

D）The Parties shall bear all their own legal costs and expenses, without recourse to each other.

E）The Parties shall bear equally the costs and expenses of the Tribunal and ICSID.

All other claims by either Party are rejected.

基于上述原因，仲裁庭裁决如下：

一、阿根廷没有对埃尔帕索的投资给予公平和公正的待遇，从而违反了 BIT 第 Ⅱ（2）款（a）项。

二、阿根廷对埃尔帕索索赔必要性的辩护被驳回。

三、在本裁决各方发出通知之日起 30 天内，阿根廷应向埃尔帕索赔偿 4303 万美元，从 2002 年 1 月 1 日起至支付该笔款项之日止，按 LIBOR 加 2% 的利率每半年增加一次复利。

四、双方应自行承担一切法律成本和费用，不得相互追索。

五、各方应平等承担仲裁庭和解决投资争端国际中心的费用和开支。

任何一方的所有其他索赔均被拒绝。

裁决原因（Reasons for the Award）

It is well known that in order to qualify for protection under the ICSID/BIT mechanism, an investment has to satisfy the requirements of the definition of an investment both under the Washington Convention and the BIT. Although there is no definition of an "investment" in the ICSID Convention, case-law has emerged to allow for determination of what constitutes an investment. One of the central purposes of ICSID arbitration is the protection of foreign investments.

The Tribunal has come to the clear conclusion that the investment protected by the BIT was constituted by the shares in the Argentinian companies that belonged to El Paso. The Claimant in fact has itself admitted this conclusion of the Tribunal, if one looks at its Memorial, where it is stated that "［i］n summary, El Paso owned certain investments in Argentina, which include indirect noncontrolling shareholdings in CAPSA, CAPEX and Costanera and an indirect controlling shareholding in SERVICIOS." The overall conclusion related to the definition of the protected investment could be: what is protected are "the shares, all the shares, but only the shares."

众所周知，为了符合 ICSID/BIT 机制下的保护条件，投资必须满足华盛顿公约和 BIT 下投资定义的要求。尽管 ICSID 公约中没有对"投资"的定义，但判例法已经出现允许对构成投资做决定。ICSID 仲裁的核心目的之一是保护外国投资。

仲裁庭得出了一个明确的结论，即受 BIT 保护的投资是由属于埃尔帕索的阿根廷公司的股份构成的。事实上，申请人已经承认了仲裁庭的这一结论，如果有人看了它的法律意见，其中指出"总的来说，埃尔帕索在阿根廷拥有某些投资，包括间接非控股的 CAPSA，CAPEX 和 Costanera 的股权以及对埃尔帕索服务公司的间接控股股权"。与受保护投资定义相关的总体结论是：受保护的是"股权，所有股权，但只有股权"。

According to the Claimant, "[a]n investor will never invest if it expects that the rules of the game will be completely altered in a manner it cannot predict." It asserts that there were commitments by the GOA that it would not be affected by a new crisis in that country because all the main parameters were either in dollars or linked to the dollar: the electricity Spot Price was connected with the US PPI, adjusted bi-annually (a kind of de facto dollarisation); the VPCs were declared in dollars bi-annually; and the capacity payments were in dollars. According to El Paso, as a foreign company investing money in Argentina's economy, it relied on the overall setting of the legal framework, which was clearly aimed at protecting the foreign investor from a devaluation of the dollar. These features were of the utmost importance due to the economic history of Argentina.

根据申请人的说法，"如果投资者预期游戏规则将以其无法预测的方式完全改变，他们将永远不会进行投资。"它声称，阿政府承诺不会受到该国新危机的影响，因为所有的主要标准货币单位为美元或与美元挂钩：电力现货价格与美国生产者价格指数挂钩，每两年调整一次（实际上是美元化）；可变生产成本每两年宣布一次，容量付款使用美元。据埃尔帕索说，作为一家投资阿根廷经济的外国公司，它依赖于法律框架的整体设置，这显然是为了保护外国投资者不受美元贬值的影响。由于阿根廷的经济历史，这些特征极为重要。

The fact that the contracts were in US dollars could also be viewed as a special commitment towards the companies in which El Paso invested, and the pesification as entailing a violation of freely agreed terms and conditions.

Although they may be seen in isolation as reasonable measures to cope with a difficult economic situation, the measures examined can be viewed as cumulative steps which individually do not qualify as violations of FET, as pointed out earlier by the Tribunal, but which amount to a violation if their cumulative effect is considered. It is quite possible to hold that Argentina could pesify, put a cap on the Spot Price, etc., but that a combination of all these measures completely altered the overall framework.

合同以美元计价的事实也可以被视为对埃尔帕索投资的公司的特殊承诺，而这种比索化做法将导致违反自由商定的条款和条件。

尽管可以孤立地将其视为应对困难经济形势的合理措施，但正如仲裁庭早些时候指出的，所审查的措施可以被视为累积步骤，单独不符合违反 FET 的条件，但如果其考虑累积效应，则会构成违反。很有可能认为阿根廷可以比索化，对现货价格设定上限等，但所有这些措施的结合完全改变了整体框架。

It cannot be denied that in the matter before this Tribunal the cumulative effect of the measures was a total alteration of the entire legal setup for foreign investments, and that all the different elements and guarantees just mentioned can be analysed as a special commitment of Argentina that such a total alteration would not take place. As stated by the tribunal in LG&E Capital Corp. and LG&E International Inc. v. Argentine Republic, when evaluating the same events, "here, the Tribunal is of the opinion that Argentina went too far by completely dismantling the very legal framework constructed to attract investors."

The Tribunal, taking an all-encompassing view of consequences of the measures complained of by El Paso, including the contribution of these measures to its decision to sell its investments in Argentina, concludes that, by their cumulative effect, they amount to a breach of the fair and equitable treatment standard.

不可否认，在本仲裁庭审理的案件中，这些措施的累积效应是对整个外国投资法律制度的彻底改变，而且，刚才提到的所有不同要素和担保都可以作为阿根廷的一项特别承诺加以分析，即不会发生完全的改变。正如 LG&E 诉阿根廷仲裁庭在评估同一事件时所说，"在这里，仲裁庭认为阿根廷完全废除了为吸引投资者而构建的法律框架，这做得太过火了"。

仲裁庭对埃尔帕索所抱怨的措施的后果，包括这些措施对其决定出售其在阿根廷的投资的促成作用，采取了全面的看法并得出结论，根据这些措施的累积效应，它们构成违反公平和公正待遇标准。

The so-called umbrella clause contained in Article Ⅱ (2) (c) provides as follows: "Each Party shall observe any obligation it may have entered into with regard to investments."

According to the Claimant, the Respondent violated the BIT by failing to observe its obligations under Article Ⅱ (2) (c). In particular, the breach of some contractual rights of the Argentinian companies was complained of under that provision. The Claimant asserted that under Article Ⅱ (2) (c) Argentina had assumed an obligation, inter alia:

"To respect the terms of the Concessions that provide fiscal stability and not impose in the future either Export Withholdings nor discriminatory taxes.

To respect the right of power generators and hydrocarbon producers, like CAPSA, CAPEX and COSTANERA, to freely sell their production and agree on the terms governing its sale, including price and currency...

To respect the license agreements with gas distribution companies and power distributors to pass through to their tariffs the market price of the gas and electricity they acquire from gas producers and power generators. "

These are all contractual rights belonging to the Argentinian companies, CAPSA, CAPEX and Costanera.

The Respondent's answer can be summarised as follows: According to Argentina, the umbrella clause only applies to investment agreements entered into with foreign investors, not to hydrocarbon concessions granted by the State to national companies. In other words, there are no contractual commitments directly between the Claimant and Argentina, as any such commitments were made to CAPSA and CAPEX via the concessions and are not protected rights under the BIT.

第二条第（2）款（c）项中的所谓"保护伞"条款规定："各方应遵守其在投资方面可能已经确定的任何义务。"

根据申请人的说法，被申请人未遵守其在第二条第（2）款（c）项下的义务而违反了 BIT。特别是，阿根廷公司的某些合同权利遭到了违反该条款的指控。申请人声称，根据第二条第（2）款（c）项，阿根廷承担了一项义务，除其他外：

"尊重提供财政稳定的特许条款，将来不征收出口预扣税或歧视性税收。

尊重发电商和碳氢化合物生产商（如 CAPSA、CAPEX 和 Costanera）自由销售其产品的权利，并就其销售条款（包括价格和货币）达成一致。……

遵守与天然气配送公司和电力分销商签订的许可协议，将其从天然气生产商和发电商处获得的天然气和电力的市场价格转移到其电价中。"

这些都是属于阿根廷公司、CAPSA、CAPEX 和 Costanera 的合同权利。

被申请人的回答概括如下：根据阿根廷的规定，保护伞条款仅适用于与外国投资者签订的投资协议，而不适用于国家授予国家公司的碳氢化合物特许权。换言之，申请人和阿根廷之间没有直接的合同承诺，因为任何此类承诺都是通过特许权对 CAPSA 和 CAPEX 作出的，不是受 BIT 保护的权利。

The Tribunal has already decided that El Paso has no contract claim based on contracts or licenses and that there is no investment agreement entered into by El Paso. As a consequence, the question of their elevation to the level of a treaty claim does not arise.

The Tribunal wishes to add that this position finds support in the Annulment Decision in the CMS Gas Transmission Company v. Argentine Republic. The ad hoc Committee criticised the tribunal's findings concerning the violation of the umbrella clause, stating that it was "impossible for the reader to follow the reasoning on this point," and therefore annulled this part of the decision for failure to state reasons. At the same time, it tried to reconstruct the possible reasoning of the Tribunal and, while doing so, gave some hints as to what could, in its view, be the possible meaning of an umbrella clause or, to be more precise, as to what could not be the meaning of an umbrella clause. Thus, two points were made clear by the ad hoc Committee. First, according to that Committee, the umbrella clause, if it had any meaning——a question on which it did not take a position——could only concern consensual obligations and not general obligations. Second, the ad hoc Committee also made it clear that, in its view, a contractual obligation towards a non-protected investor cannot be transformed by the magic of the so-called umbrella clause into a treaty obligation towards a protected investor.

It is evident that the Tribunal cannot find any violation of a right pertaining to El Paso under the so-called umbrella clause, for the reason that the so-called umbrella clause cannot not elevate any contract claims to the status of treaty claims as El Paso cannot claim a contractual right of its own in this case.

仲裁庭已经决定，埃尔帕索没有基于合同或许可证的合同索赔，也没有埃尔帕索签订的投资协议。其结果是，它们被提升到条约要求水平的问题没有出现。

仲裁庭希望补充一点，这一立场在 CMS 案件的撤销决定中得到支持。特设委员会批评了仲裁庭关于违反保护伞条款的调查结果，指出"读者不可能明白这一点的推理"，因此取消了这部分决定，因为没有说明原因。同时，它试图重建仲裁庭的可能推理，并在这样做的同时，就其认为什么可能是保护伞条款的可能含义，或者更确切地说，是什么不可能是伞条款的含义给出了一些提示。因此，特设委员会明确了两点。第一，根据该委员会的说法，如果保护伞条款有任何意义——一个它没有立场的问题——它只能涉及双方同意的义务，而不是一般义务。第二，特设委员会还明确表示，在其看来，对非受保护投资者的合同义务不能通过所谓的保护伞条款的魔力转化为对受保护投资者的条约义务。

很明显，根据所谓的保护伞条款，仲裁庭不能发现任何违反与埃尔帕索有关的权利的行为，因为所谓的保护伞条款不能将任何合同索赔提升到条约索赔的地位，因为在本案中埃尔帕索不能主张其所拥有的合同权利。

It cannot be denied that the general economic situation was taken into account by El Paso when deciding the sale in question. However, contrary to what is mentioned by Argentina, there is no contribution by the Claimant to a loss it suffered due to its own conduct, in the absence of wilful or negligent action by the Claimant. The Tribunal does not view the sale by the

Claimant of its investment in the Argentinian companies as a wilful or negligent action, "i. e. an action which manifests a lack of due care on the part of the victim of the breach for his or her own property or right." The Tribunal has examined the relationship between the sale of El Paso's shares in the Argentinian companies and the GOA measures in the context of determining whether such measures may be considered a violation of the FET standard, concluding that the measures were the prevailing cause of the sale. The Tribunal concludes that a causal connection exists between the GOA measures and the Claimant's damage.

不能否认，埃尔帕索在决定出售问题时考虑了一般经济情况。但是，与阿根廷所述的情况相反，申请人不存在故意或疏忽行为，其自身行为没有促成其遭受的损失。仲裁庭不认为申请人出售其对阿根廷公司的投资是一种故意或疏忽的行为，"即一种表明受害人对自己的财产或权利缺乏应有的照顾的行为。"为了确定此类措施是否被视为违反公平公正待遇标准，仲裁庭已经审查了埃尔帕索出售其在阿根廷公司股份与阿政府措施之间的关系，认为这些措施是出售的主要原因。仲裁庭认为，阿根廷政府的措施与申请人的损害之间存在因果关系。

裁决撤销或执行情况（Annulment or Enforcement of the Award）

On February 28, 2012, ICSID received from Argentina an application for annulment and request for stay of enforcement of the Award (the "Application" and the "Request for Stay," respectively).

Argentina divided the claim on jurisdictional issues into various issues: 1. Manifest excess of powers; 2. Failure to provide reasons for the decision; 3. Risk of double recovery in indirect claims; 4. Argentine law does not recognize these types of claims; 5. General international law does not allow indirect actions to be taken in this case.

The Committee considers that in this case there was no violation of due process or the right of defense, as fundamental rules of procedure. Argentina had the opportunity to defend itself and to express its point of view on the effect of the measures that it adopted during the crisis, and on the general legal framework. For this reason the Committee will reject Argentina's application for annulment, based on this and its other arguments.

2012 年 2 月 28 日，ICSID 从阿根廷收到撤销申请和中止执行裁决的请求（分别为"申请"和"中止请求"）。

阿根廷将管辖权问题的主张分为多个问题：①明显越权的；②未说明裁决理由；③间接索赔获得双倍赔偿的风险；④阿根廷法律不承认这类索赔；⑤一般国际法不允

许在这种情况下采取间接行动。

委员会认为，本案没有违反正当程序或侵害作为程序基本规则的抗辩权，阿根廷有机会为自己辩护，并就其在危机期间采取的措施的效果和一般法律框架表达其观点。因此，委员会将根据这一点及其其他论点，驳回阿根廷的撤销申请。

案件影响（Impact of the Case）

保护伞条款是指双边投资协定（"BIT"）项下所约定的，缔约国保证遵守其对另一缔约国投资者所作出承诺的条款。保护伞条款使得投资者基于东道国违反合同义务而提起国际仲裁成为可能，虽然其极大地加重了东道国一方义务，但却是缔约国吸引投资而常设的一类条款。由于 BITs 中保护伞条款可能威胁东道国的司法主权，全球范围内签订的双边投资协定中包含保护伞条款的协定仅占 40%，尚未大范围地被国际社会所接纳。

根据各仲裁庭对"保护伞条款"不同的解释方法，仲裁庭大体上可分为三大阵营——限制解释阵营、扩大解释阵营以及中立解释阵营。限制解释——只有在缔约双方于 BIT 中明确约定，任何合同违约都应当视为对 BIT 的违反的情况下，才能适用保护伞条款将合同违约升级为对 BIT 的违反。扩大解释——认为设计保护伞条款目的是使得投资合同国际化，因此可将合同义务直接升级为 BIT 项下的义务。中立解释——包含"保护伞条款"的 BIT 仅对投资者以及作为主权国家的东道国之间所签署的投资合同的违反具有管辖权，但若国家并非以主权国家的角色签署投资协议之时，基于违反合同的请求则不能升级为 BIT 项下的条约请求。本案裁决认定申请人与阿根廷未达成投资协议，而只是作为阿根廷的国内公司与政府有许可权合同，不受"保护伞"条款的保护。这种解释方式下，对于一般的商业性合同，保护伞条款并没有将合同约定提升到国家条约从而可以直接诉诸国际投资争端解决机构，投资者还可根据普合同中争端解决条款寻求救济，在这种情况下，东道国亦不享有主权豁免。

思考问题（Questions）

1. 如何认识保护伞条款存在之必要性？
2. 在阿根廷的比索化危机中，外国投资者的汇率损失能否获得政府赔偿？

案例九　铁路发展公司诉危地马拉案

Railroad Development Corporation v. Republic of Guatemala（2012）（ICSID Case No. ARB/07/23）

选读理由（Selected Reason）

本案是 ICSID 中关于《中美洲自贸协定》之下"最低待遇标准"的第一案。在 2007 年 6 月 14 日，美国铁路发展公司就危地马拉共和国关于投资争端向"国际投资争端解决中心"提起仲裁，ICSID 在受理该案件之后作出了仲裁裁决。该仲裁裁决认为危地马拉政府违反了《多米尼加—中美洲—美国自由贸易协定》（简称《中美洲自贸协定》）第 10 条第 5 款规定的"最低待遇标准"，并裁定危地马拉向美国铁路发展公司支付损失。该案不仅涉及 ICSID 的管辖权限问题，还涉及对国际最低待遇标准的理解和适用问题，因此，本案极具参考性。

仲裁申请情况（The Request for Arbitration）

On June 14, 2007, Railroad Development Corporation（"RDC" or "Claimant"）filed before the International Centre for Settlement of Investment Disputes（"ICSID" or the "Centre"）a Request for Arbitration against the Republic of Guatemala（"Respondent', "Guatemala" or the "Government"）on its own behalf and on behalf of Compañía Desarrolladora Ferroviaria, S. A., a Guatemalan company which does business as Ferrovías Guatemala（"FVG"）and is majority-owned and controlled by RDC. The Request was brought under the Dominican Republic-Central America-United States of America（United States）Free Trade Agreement（"CAFTA" or the "Treaty"）. ICSID registered the Request for Arbitration on August 20, 2007.

2007年6月14日，铁路发展公司（"RDC"或"申请人"）代表自己及铁路开发商有限公司，一家在危地马拉经营危地马拉铁路且由铁路发展公司控股和控制的危地马拉公司（"FVG"），向国际投资争端解决中心（"ICSID"或"中心"）提交了针对危地马拉共和国（"被申请人"，"危地马拉"或"政府"）的仲裁请求。这项请求是根据《多米尼加共和国—中美洲—美利坚合众国（美国）自由贸易协定》（《中美洲自贸协定》或"协定"）提出的。ICSID于2007年8月20日登记了该仲裁请求。

RDC is a privately-owned railway investment and management company which in 1997 won, through international public bidding, the use of the infrastructure and other rail assets to provide railway services in Guatemala (the "Usufruct"). Only two bids were submitted and RDC's bid was the only one considered responsive by Respondent. RDC's bid consisted of a staged plan to rebuild the rail system, which had been closed since March 1996, with an investment program of about ten million U. S. dollars. Although the bidding conditions did not include rolling stock, RDC included in its bid a rehabilitation plan for the rolling stock that would be required for the operation of the railroad (Section 4.2, "Rehabilitation Plan for Locomotives and Freight Cars"). The Usufruct that was awarded to RDC consisted of a 50-year right to rebuild and operate the Guatemalan rail system and did not include rolling stock. On November 25, 1997, FVG signed the Usufruct Contract of Right of Way (the "Usufruct Contract", "Contract 402" or "Deed 402") with Ferrocarriles de Guatemala ("FEGUA"), a state-owned company established in 1969 which is responsible for providing certain railway transport services and managing the rail equipment and real estate assets. The Usufruct and the Usufruct Contract were ratified by the Congress of Guatemala by Decree 27 – 98, published in the Official Gazette on April 23, 1998, and came into force on May 23, 1998.

铁路发展公司是一家私人拥有的铁路投资和管理公司，1997年通过国际公开招标赢得了在危地马拉利用基础设施和其他铁路资产提供铁路服务的权利（"用益权"）。只有两个投标被提交，铁路发展公司的投标是唯一一个被申请人认为具有响应性的投标。铁路发展公司的投标包括重建铁路系统的分阶段计划，该铁路系统自1996年3月关闭，已投资约为1000万美元。尽管投标条件不包括机车车辆，但铁路发展公司在其投标中包括了铁路运营所需的机车车辆修复计划（第4.2节，"机车和货车修复计划"）。授予铁路发展公司的用益权包括重建和运营危地马拉铁路系统的50年权利，不包括机车车辆。1997年11月25日，FVG与1969年成立的国有的负责提供某些铁路运输服务并管理铁路设备和房地产资产的危地马拉铁路公司（"FEGUA"）签署了《用益权通行权合同》（"用益权合同""合同402"或"契约402"）。危地马拉国会于1998年4月23日通过第27—98号法令批准了用益权和用益权合同，并于1998年5月23日生效。

The Usufruct covers a 497 – mile narrow gauge railroad and includes the right to develop alternative uses for the right of way, such as pipelines, electricity transmission, fiber optics and commercial and institutional development. In return for the right-of-way Usufruct, RDC (through FVG) agreed to make certain payments to FEGUA.

In November 1997 Guatemala invited bids for the use of the FEGUA rail equipment in onerous usufruct. On December 11, 1997, FVG submitted its bid and won the rail usufruct on December 16, 1997. FEGUA and FVG signed Usufruct Contract No. 41, dated March 23, 1999 ("Contract No. 41"), which granted FVG "the use, enjoyment, repair and maintenance of railway equipment owned by FEGUA for the purposes of rendering railway transportation services." This contract never went into force because it was never approved by acuerdo-gubernativo. Such approval is required under Guatemalan Administrative Law and Clause 6.4 of the bidding conditions for Contract No. 41. No explanation was offered to the Tribunal of why the government approval was not given.

Since Contract No. 41 had not entered into force, FVG and FEGUA entered into Contract No. 143 on August 28, 2003. The circumstances and effect of Contract No. 143 are a matter of controversy between the parties and the Tribunal simply registers the fact that FVG and FEGUA signed this contract and modified it in October 2003 by deed No. 158 ("Contract 143/158").

用益权涵盖一条 497 英里窄轨铁路，并包括开发替代通行权用途的权利，如管道、电力传输、光纤以及商业和机构发展。作为对用益权的回报，铁路发展公司（通过 FVG）同意向危地马拉铁路公司支付某些款项。

1997 年 11 月，危地马拉邀请投标人以有偿使用权使用危地马拉铁路公司的铁路设备。1997 年 12 月 11 日，FVG 提交了投标，并于 1997 年 12 月 16 日赢得了铁路使用权。危地马拉铁路公司和 FVG 于 1999 年 3 月 23 日签署了第 41 号用益权合同（"第 41 号合同"），授予 FVG "使用、享用、维修和维护危地马拉铁路公司拥有的用于提供铁路运输服务的铁路设备"。这份合同从未生效，因为它从未得到政府首脑的批准。危地马拉行政法和第 41 号合同投标条件第 6.4 条要求获得此类批准。没有向仲裁庭解释为什么政府没有批准。

由于第 41 号合同尚未生效，FVG 和危地马拉铁路公司于 2003 年 8 月 28 日签订了第 143 号合同。第 143 号合同的情况和效力是双方之间的争议，仲裁庭只是记录了 FVG 和危地马拉铁路公司签署了该合同，并于 2003 年 10 月通过第 158 号契约（"第 143 / 158 号合同"）对其进行了修改。

FVG restored commercial service between El Chile and Guatemala City on April 15, 1999. In December 1999, commercial service was restored between Guatemala City and the Atlantic ports of Puerto Barrios and Puerto Santo Tomás. Tonnage gradually increased until

2005 but declined in 2006.

On June 26, 2005, FVG initiated two domestic arbitration cases against FEGUA for breach of contract. The Claimant alleged that Guatemala through FEGUA failed to remove squatters from the rail right of way and to make agreed payments to the Trust Fund. The Claimant further alleged that, in anticipation of FVG's filings, FEGUA requested the Attorney General to investigate the circumstances surrounding the award of the Usufruct and to issue an opinion on the validity of Deed 143 and Deed 158. The Attorney General issued Opinion No. 205 – 2005 on August 1, 2005 ("Lesivo Opinion"), and recommended that Guatemala declare Contract 143/158 void as not in the interest of the country. As translated by the Claimant, the Lesivo Opinion stated:

"Lesion was caused in this case because there is a violation to rules and procedures that should have been applied in order to execute the agreement in due form and with legal validity. The relevant contract breaks the Government Contracting Law and other laws that govern the process to grant FEGUA's property in usufruct.

"There is pecuniary lesion by executing an Onerous Usufruct Contract to grant the State's property in usufruct to be exploited by a private entity, in exchange of one point twenty-five percent (1.25%) of the gross income as a result of rendering transportation services."

FVG 于 1999 年 4 月 15 日恢复了智利和危地马拉城之间的商业服务。1999 年 12 月，危地马拉城与大西洋港口巴里奥斯港和圣托马斯港之间恢复了商业服务。运输吨位逐渐增加，直到 2005 年，但在 2006 年有所下降。

2005 年 6 月 26 日，FVG 对危地马拉铁路公司提起了两起违约国内仲裁案件。申请人说，危地马拉通过危地马拉铁路公司没有将擅自占用者从铁路通行权上移走，也没有向信托基金支付商定的款项。申请人还称，在 FVG 提交文件之前，危地马拉铁路公司要求总检察长调查授予用益权的情况，并就第 143 号和第 158 号契约的有效性发表意见。总检察长于 2005 年 8 月 1 日发布了第 205—2005 号意见（"损害意见"），并建议危地马拉宣布第 143／158 号合同无效，因为这不符合国家利益。申请人翻译的损害意见称：

"本案中造成损害的原因是违反了本应适用的规则和程序，以便以适当的形式和法律效力执行协议。相关合同违反了《政府合同法》和规范授予 FEGUA 用益权程序的其他法律。

"通过执行一项有偿用益权合同，以提供运输服务所得总收入的 1.25 ％作为交换，将国家的用益权财产授予私人实体使用，这是一种经济损害。"

On January 13, 2006, FEGUA issued Opinion 05 – 2006, in agreement with the Attorney General's opinion, arguing that Contract 143/158 was not awarded as a result of a public bid.

Claimant and FVG made numerous attempts to reach an understanding. Claimant met the President of the Republic, Mr. Oscar Berger, on March 7, 2006. The President set up a high level commission to work with RDC and FVG, on which FEGUA was represented. This commission met a number of times but after about three months the meetings were suspended. It is the contention of the Claimant that, in parallel, the Government was preparing a resolution to declare the usufruct of the rolling stock injurious to the interests of the State. Such a resolution ("Lesivo Resolution" or "Lesivo Declaration") was adopted by the Government on August 11, 2006 and published on August 25, 2006.

2006 年 1 月 13 日，危地马拉铁路公司发表了第 05—2006 号意见，同意总检察长的意见，认为第 143/158 号合同不是公开投标的结果。

申请人和 FVG 多次试图达成谅解。申请人于 2006 年 3 月 7 日会见了共和国总统奥斯卡·伯杰先生。总统设立了一个高级别委员会，与铁路发展公司和 FVG 合作，危地马拉铁路公司派代表参加了该委员会。该委员会举行了多次会议，但大约三个月后会议暂停。申请人辩称，与此同时，政府正在起草一项决议，宣布铁路车辆的使用权损害国家利益。政府于 2006 年 8 月 11 日通过了这样一项决议（"损害决议"或"损害宣言"），并于 2006 年 8 月 25 日公布。

Claimant requests that the Tribunal determine:

a. That Claimant is an "investor of a Party" protected by CAFTA.

b. That Claimant's "covered investments" under CAFTA include (i) income generated under the Usufruct, (ii) investment capital and loans committed by RDC to FVG under the Usufruct, and (iii) the value of FVG as the business enterprise operating the Usufruct.

c. That the Lesivo Resolution and subsequent conduct of the Republic of Guatemala pursuant to the Resolution described here in constitute an indirect expropriation of Claimant's rights in the Usufruct, in violation of CAFTA Article 10. 7. 1.

d. That through these measures, the Republic of Guatemala violated the minimum standard of treatment of CAFTA Article 10. 5 by failing to provide, in accordance with customary international law, fair and equitable treatment and full protection and security to Claimant's covered investments.

e. That the Republic of Guatemala has violated the national treatment standard of CAFTA Article 10. 3.

f. That the Republic of Guatemala shall pay Claimant $64,035,859 in damages plus compound pre-award interest at the average interest ratepaid by Guatemala on its private commercial debt.

g. That that the Tribunal, pursuant to its power under CAFTA Article 10.26, award Claimant its costs and attorneys' fees incurred in prosecuting its CAFTA claims.

申请人要求仲裁庭裁定：

a. 该申请人是受《中美洲自贸协定》保护的"一方投资者"。

b. 申请人在《中美洲自贸协定》项下的"涵盖的投资"包括：（i）用益权项下产生的收入，（ii）铁路发展公司根据用益权向 FVG 承诺的投资资本和贷款，（iii）FVG 作为经营用益权的企业的价值。

c. 根据本协议所述决议，危地马拉共和国的损害决议和随后的行为构成了违反《中美洲自贸协定》第 10 条 7 款 1 项的间接征用申请人在用益权中的权利。

d. 危地马拉共和国通过这些措施，未能按照国际习惯法，为申请人的受保投资提供公平、公正的待遇和充分的保护和担保，从而违反了中美洲自贸协定第 10 条 5 款的最低待遇标准。

e. 危地马拉共和国违反了中美洲自贸协定第 10 条 3 款的国民待遇标准。

f. 危地马拉共和国应按照危地马拉对其私人商业债务支付的平均利率，向申请人支付 64035859 美元的损害赔偿金加上裁决前的复利。

g. 仲裁庭根据其在《中美洲自贸协定》第 10 条 26 款下的权力，裁决给申请人提起中美洲自贸协定的索赔所产生的费用和律师费。

仲裁结果（Award）

The tribunal awards as follows:

1. That Respondent breached the minimum standard of treatment under Article 10.5 ofCAFTA in respect of Claimant's investment.

2. That Respondent shall pay Claimant: a) $6,576,861 on account of its investment in Phases I and II; b) $1,350,429 for operating the railroad for another year after the Lesivo Declaration which permitted an orderly closure of the railroad service; and c) 82% (the percentage of shares in FVG held by Claimant) of $4,121,281.62 ($3,379,450.93) – the NPV of the existing real estate leases measured over their remaining life as of the date of Lesivo-minus 82% of rents paid to FVG under such leases post-Lesivo and until payment by Respondent of the compensation here awarded. Because the Tribunal cannot determine at this time when Respondent will pay the award, there will be a need for a final calculation of this amount.

3. That, on payment of the awarded compensation, Claimant shall forfeit and renounce

all its rights under the Usufruct Contracts and transfer to Respondent Claimant's shares in FVG.

4. That the awarded amount of compensation shall carry compound interest at a rate equivalent to six-month LIBOR plus two percentage points as from the date of the Lesivo Declaration to the date of payment.

5. That Respondent shall be responsible for the administrative expenses of ICSID and fees and expenses of the Tribunal related to the two jurisdictional phases. As calculated by the ICSID Secretariat, such fees and expenses amount to ＄384,854.01. Since each party has advanced 50% of the amounts requested by the ICSID Secretariat to finance these proceedings, Respondent shall pay Claimant ＄192,427.00. Such amount shall carry interest at the rate set forth in sub-paragraph 4 above.

6. That each party shall be responsible for 50% of the remainder of administrative expenses of ICSID and of the fees and expenses of the Tribunal.

7. That each party shall be responsible for its own counsel fees and expenses.

8. That all other claims are dismissed.

Donein Washington, D. C.

本仲裁庭裁决如下：

1. 对于申请人美国铁路发展公司的投资，被申请人危地马拉违反了中美洲自贸协定第 10 条第 5 项规定的最低待遇标准。

2. 被申请人危地马拉应向申请人美国铁路发展公司支付：（1）6576861 美元，为其在第一和第二阶段的投资；（2）1350429 美元，用于在 Lesivo 允许有秩序地关闭铁路服务后再运营一年；（3）4121281.62 美元的 82%（申请人持有的 FVG 股份的百分比），即 3379450.93 美元——自损害决议作出起计算剩余使用寿命内的现有不动产租赁的净现值——减去根据此类租赁在损害决议之后向 FVG 支付的租金的 82%，直至被申请人支付本裁决作出后的补偿。由于仲裁庭目前无法确定被申请人何时支付赔偿金，因此需要对这一金额进行最终计算。

3. 在支付裁定赔偿后，申请人美国铁路发展公司将丧失并放弃其在用益权合同下的所有权利，并将在 FVG 的股份转让给被申请人危地马拉。

4. 裁定赔偿额应包含复利，利率相当于 6 个月伦敦银行同业拆借利率加上两个百分点，从损害声明之日计至付款日。

5. 被申请人危地马拉应负责 ICSID 的行政费用以及与两个管辖阶段相关的仲裁庭费用。根据 ICSID 秘书处的计算，此类费用和开支为 384854.01 美元。由于每一方预付了 ICSID 秘书处要求的 50% 的金额来资助这些诉讼，被申请人危地马拉应向申请人美国铁路发展公司支付 192427.00 美元。该金额应按上文第 4 项规定的利率计息。

6. 每一方应承担 ICSID 剩余行政费用的 50% 以及仲裁庭的费用和开支。

7. 各方自行承担律师费。

8. 驳回其他索赔。

裁决于华盛顿

裁决原因 （Reasons for the Award）

National Treatment

The Tribunal turns to the allegation that Respondent breached Article 10.3 of CAFTA. The Tribunal has already concluded that Claimant has not shown that the purpose of the Lesivo Resolution was to favor Mr. Campollo. It is on this premise that Claimant has in great measure based its allegation under Article 10.3. As noted by the Tribunal, more than five years after the Lesivo Resolution, Claimant continues to have its contractual rights to the right-of-way and to remain in possession of the railway equipment. This by itself is sufficient basis for rejecting Claimants' allegation that Respondent treated Claimant differently from Mr. Campollo. Furthermore, the Tribunal considers that Respondent has failed to show that Claimant and Mr. Campollo are foreign and domestic investors in "like circumstances." According to Claimant, both are competitors in the same economic sector since they have been competing to invest and operate the railroad and in leasing and developing the railroad's assets. Claimant supports this statement by citing the fact that Mr. Campollo has certain interests in the sugar industry in the Dominican Republic, and operates a railroad there purely for the transportation of the produce of his estate. In the Tribunal's view, the obvious difference in scale between the railroad for the exclusive exploitation of the sugar plantation of Mr. Campollo in the Dominican Republic and the railway operation of Claimant in Guatemala defeats the "like circumstances" argument.

Claimant contends that, in any case, "even absent the complicity between the Government and Mr. Campollo, Guatemala discriminated against RDC when it sought to coerce RDC into surrendering unrestored rail segments in favor of 'other [interested] investors' in exchange for the Government abandoning the Lesivo Resolution." (Memorial, para. 165) The Tribunal will address the substance of this contention under the minimum standard of treatment. As to the expression "other investors", without further substantiation (which Claimant has failed to provide), it is too vague to state a separate basis of claim. The Tribunal is in no position to determine who these investors are and whether they are in "like circumstances", nor has the Tribunal been presented with evidence of the identity of these investors.

To conclude, the Tribunal finds that the allegation of breach by Respondent of its obligations under Article 10.3 of CAFTA is without merit.

仲裁庭转向被申请人违反中美洲自贸协定第10条3款的指控。仲裁庭已经得出结论，申请人没有证明损害决议的目的是偏袒坎波略先生。正是在这一前提下，申请人在很大程度上根据第10条3款提出了指控。正如仲裁庭指出的那样，损害决议通过五年多之后，申请人继续享有其合同规定的通行权，并继续拥有铁路设备。这本身就足以驳回申请人的指控，即被申请人对申请人的待遇不同于坎波略先生。此外，仲裁庭认为，被申请人未能证明申请人和坎波略先生是"类似情况下"的外国和国内投资者。据申请人说，两者都是同一经济部门的竞争对手，因为它们一直在竞争投资和运营铁路以及租赁和开发铁路资产。申请人支持这一说法，称坎波略先生在多米尼加共和国的制糖业有一定的利益，在那里经营一条铁路纯粹是为了运输他的地产产品。仲裁庭认为，专门开发多米尼加共和国坎波略先生甘蔗种植园的铁路和危地马拉申请人的铁路运营之间的规模明显不同，推翻了"类似情况"的论点。

申请人争辩说，无论如何，"即使没有政府和坎波略先生之间的共谋，危地马拉也歧视铁路发展公司，因为它试图迫使铁路发展公司交出未归还的铁路段，以利于'其他感兴趣的'投资者，从而换取政府放弃损害决议。"仲裁庭将根据最低待遇标准处理这一争论的实质内容。至于"其他投资者"一词，在没有进一步证据的情况下（申请人没有提供证据），它过于模糊，无法单独说明索赔的依据。仲裁庭无法确定这些投资者是谁，他们是否处于"类似情况"，仲裁庭也没有收到这些投资者身份的证据。

最后，仲裁庭认为，被申请人违反中美洲自贸协定第10条3款规定的义务的指控是没有根据的。

The Claim of Indirect Expropriation

For convenience of reference, it will be useful to reproduce here therelevant provisions of CAFTA:

Article 10.7: Expropriation and Compensation.

No Party may expropriate or nationalize a covered investment either directly or indirectly through measures equivalent to expropriation or nationalization（"expropriation"）, except:

（a）For a public purpose.

（b）In a non-discriminatory manner.

（c）On payment of prompt, adequate, and effective compensation in accordance with paragraphs 2 through 4.

（d）In accordance with due process of law and Article 10.5.

为了便于参考，这里复制中美洲自贸协定的相关规定将有所帮助：

第10条7款：征用和补偿。

任何一方不得通过相当于征收或国有化（"征收"）的措施直接或间接征收或国有化所涵盖的投资，除非：

（a）为公共目的。

（b）以非歧视的方式。

（c）根据第 2—4 款支付及时、充分和有效的赔偿。

（d）符合正当程序的法律和第 10 条 5 款。

The Tribunal will first consider Respondent's argument that Claimant cannot claim expropriation of usufruct rights that FVG does not own. It will then proceed to analyze the nature of the Lesivo Declaration, its public purpose, whether the Government interfered with reasonable investment backed expectations and theireconomic impact on Claimant's investment. To the extent necessary, the Tribunal will complement the summary of the parties' arguments on specific matters.

The Tribunal notes that Article 2 of the Lesivo Declaration instructs and authorizes the Attorney General of the Nation "to undertake and execute all legal measures required in order to cease the binding force of the contract identified above [Contract 143/158] and hold the relevant parties legally accountable, if applicable. " The text shows that Respondent considered that Contract 143/158 was binding; otherwise there would have been no purpose in instructing the Attorney General in these terms. The Tribunal also notes that Respondent recognizes that this is the case in its Counter-Memorial: " […] because Claimant's alleged right to compensation is not yet ripe, because the Contencioso Administrativo court has not yet decided the matter and thus Contract 143/158 remains valid and in full force, Guatemala has not violated any duty to pay 'prompt, adequate and effective compensation. '" Respondent also states that the court may decide that Contract 143/158 is not Lesivo and leave it permanently in effect.

The Tribunal concludes that FVG's rights under Contract 143/158 are in effect and could be expropriated by Respondent. Whether the Lesivo Declaration expropriated them and the extent to which it affected Claimant's investment beyond Contract 143/158 are matters to which the Tribunal now turns.

仲裁庭将首先考虑被申请人的论点，即申请人不能要求没收 FVG 不拥有的用益权。然后，它将继续分析损害宣言的性质、其公共目的、政府是否干预了合理的投资支持预期及其对申请人投资的经济影响。在必要的情况下，仲裁庭将补充双方关于具体事项的论点摘要。

仲裁庭注意到，《损害宣言》第 2 条指示并授权国家总检察长"采取和执行所有必要的法律措施，以终止上述第 143／158 号合同的约束力"，并在适用的情况下追究相关各方的法律责任。该案文表明，被申请人认为第 143／158 号合同具有约束力；否则，用这些术语来指示司法部长是没有目的的。仲裁庭还注意到，被申请人承认其辩诉状中的情况是这样的："……因为申请人声称的赔偿权尚未成熟，因为争议行政法院尚未对此事做出裁决，因此第143 / 158 号合同仍然有效，完全有效，危地马拉没有违反任何支付及时、充分和有效赔偿的义务"被申请人还表示，仲裁庭可以裁定第143 / 158 号合同不是有损害的合同，并使其永久有效。

仲裁庭得出结论，FVG 在第143 / 158 号合同下的权利是有效的，可以被被申请人没收。损害声明是否没收了他们，以及在多大程度上影响了申请人在第143 / 158 号合同之外的投资，这是仲裁庭现在要处理的问题。

The Tribunal concludes that：(a) Lesivo is unrelated to the performance of either party under the contract declared Lesivo；(b) it leaves the rights of the parties unaffected；(c) it is a process that applies only to contracts with the State and its agencies；(d) a declaration of Lesivo may or may not be accepted by the Administrative Tribunal；(e) if the declaration is accepted, the defendant would have the possibility to appeal the decision to the Supreme Court；and (f) if the Lesivo declaration is confirmed, a Lesivo contract is void ab initio.

仲裁庭的结论是：(a) 损害声明与任何一方履行被声明有损害的合同无关；(b) 它使双方的权利不受影响；(c) 它是一个仅适用于与国家及其机构签订的合同的程序；(d) 损害声明可以或可以不被行政法庭接受；(e) 如果声明被接受，被告将有可能向最高法院上诉；(f) 如果损害声明被确认，则损害合同自始至终无效。

As to the circumstances here, the Tribunal would note：(a) that more than five years after the publication of the Lesivo Declaration, Contract 143/158 and Contract 402 remain in effect；(b) Claimant continues to be in possession of the railway equipment；(c) Claimant continues to receive rents associated with its real estate rights under Contract 402；and (d) such rents amount to 92% of revenues of FVG. For these reasons, the Tribunal concludes that the effect on Claimants' investment does not rise to the level of an indirect expropriation.

关于这里的情况，仲裁庭将注意到：(a) 在损害宣言公布后五年多，合同143/158 和合同402 仍然有效；(b) 申请人继续拥有铁路设备；(c) 申请人继续收取与402 号合同项下的不动产权利相关的租金；(d) 此类租金占 FVG 收入的92%。基于这些原因，仲裁庭得出结论，对申请人投资的影响不会上升到间接征收的水平。

Minimum Standard of Treatment

Claimant argues that Respondent did not treat it fairly and equitably, contrary to Article 10. 5 of CAFTA. Claimant refers to this standard of treatment as understood by arbitral tribunals in Waste Management Ⅱ (Waste Management, Inc. v. United Mexican States, ICSID Case No. ARB (AF) /00/3) and Tecmed (Técnicas Medioambientales S. A. v. United Mexican States, ICSID Case No. ARB (AF) /00/2) . According to Claimant, this standard requires the State to respect the reasonable expectations that were taken into account and reasonably relied upon by the foreign investor; in that regard the conduct of the State must be transparent, consistent, non-discriminatory and not based on unjustifiable or arbitrary distinctions. According to Claimant, this is an objective standard unrelated to whether the State has had any deliberate or malicious intention or manifested bad faith.

Claimant relates the breach of this standard to the Lesivo Resolution. Claimant contends that the Lesivo procedure does not define what makes a contract detrimental to the interests of the State and, therefore, the Government can declare such contract Lesivo for reasonsunsupported by the facts and within the control of the Government regardless of whether a contract is in truth harmful to the State's interests. According to Claimant, the Lesivo procedure does not afford due process since it does not allow the investor an opportunity to contest or respond to the Government's allegations before the declaration is issued. Claimant argues that as applied in this case the Lesivo procedure was "arbitrary, grossly unfair, unjust or idiosyncratic, [was] discriminatory [and] involve [d] a lack of due process leading to an outcome which offends judicial propriety".

申请人诉称，被申请人没有公平和公正地对待他，这违反了《中美洲自贸协定》第10条5款。申请人提到了第二废物管理案和泰克麦德公司案中仲裁庭所理解的这一处理标准。据申请人说，这一标准要求国家尊重外国投资者考虑并合理依赖的合理期望；在这方面，国家的行为必须透明、一致、非歧视性，而不是基于不合理或任意的区别。据申请人称，这是一个客观标准，与国家是否有任何蓄意或恶意意图或表现出恶意无关。

申请人将违反这一标准与损害决议联系起来。申请人争辩说，损害程序没有界定是什么导致合同损害国家利益，因此，政府可以出于没有事实支持的理由，在政府控制范围内宣布此类合同有损害，而不管合同是否事实上损害国家利益。据申请人称，损害程序没有提供正当程序，因为它不允许投资者在声明发表之前有机会对政府的指控提出质疑或作出回应。申请人辩称，在本案中，损害程序是"任意的、严重不公平的、不公正的或怪僻的，歧视性的并涉及缺乏正当程序，导致违反司法正当性的结果"。

Respondent stresses that under CAFTA the obligation of fair and equitable treatment requires only the minimum standard of treatment under customary international law and does not create additional substantive rights. Respondent asserts that Claimant carries the burden of proof that the standards of conduct it invokes as part of its fair and equitable treatment claim are indeed part of the minimum standard of treatment under customary international law. Furthermore, according to Respondent, Claimant may not rely on the definition of fair and equitable treatment provided by international tribunals that were not similarly bound by the minimum standard of treatment of customary international law.

Respondent argues that "Claimant has failed to demonstrate that the three alleged standards of treatment——non-arbitrariness, transparency and adherence to an investor's legitimate expectations-are elements of the minimum standard of treatment." According to Respondent, even if Claimant had succeeded in doing so, it still failed to demonstrate that Guatemala breached this standard. Respondent recalls that customary international law places a heavy burden upon a claimant to demonstrate that a State has breached an applicable standard of conduct and refers to the large amount of deference accorded by arbitral tribunals to respondent States in determining whether their action violates the fair and equitable treatment standard.

Respondent refers with approval to how the minimum standard of treatment was described by the arbitral tribunals in Waste Management Ⅱ, GAMI, Thunderbird and Geninand asserts that Claimant has completely failed to demonstrate that Guatemala's conduct fell short of the minimum standard of treatment required by customary international law.

被申请人强调，根据《中美洲自由贸易协定》，公平和公正待遇的义务只要求习惯国际法规定的最低待遇标准，并不创造额外的实质性权利。被申请人声称，申请人负有举证责任，证明其作为公正和公平待遇诉请内容的一部分援引的行为标准确实是习惯国际法规定的最低待遇标准的一部分。此外，被申请人认为，申请人不得依赖不受习惯国际法最低待遇标准类似约束的国际仲裁庭提供的公平和公正待遇的定义。

被申请人辩称，"申请人未能证明所称的三项待遇标准—非任意性、透明度和遵守投资者的合法期望—这是最低待遇标准的要素。"据被申请人称，即使申请人成功做到了这一点，它仍未能证明危地马拉违反了这一标准。被申请人回顾，习惯国际法给申请人带来了沉重的负担，要求其证明一国违反了适用的行为标准，并提到仲裁庭在确定被申请国的行为是否违反了公平和公正待遇标准时给予被申请国的大量尊重。

被申请人认可地提到废物管理Ⅱ、GAMI、Thunderbird 和 Geniun 案件仲裁庭如何描述最低待遇标准，并声称申请人完全没有证明危地马拉的行为没有达到习惯国际法要求的最低待遇标准。

In the Tribunal's view, the manner in which and the grounds on which Respondent applied the lesivo remedy in the circumstances of this case constituted a breach of the minimum standard of treatment in Article 10. 5 of CAFTA by being, in the words of Waste Management Ⅱ, "arbitrary, grossly unfair, [and] unjust." In particular the Tribunal stresses the following facts, which taken together demonstrate the arbitrary, grossly unfair, and unjust nature of lesivo in this case, including by evidencing that lesivo was in breach of representations made by Guatemala upon which Claimant reasonably relied: a) the Government declared lesivo Contract 143/158 for the use of railway equipment for which FEGUA received rents without protest；b）that contract had been concluded at the initiative of FEGU Abecause the Government itself failed，for unknown reasons，to ratify Contract after FVG had won it through public bidding；c）failure of Government ratification and lack of public bidding for the use under Contract 143/158 of the same equipment as under Contract 41，both under control of the Government，and which it had the power to remedy，were in part the justification to declare lesivo Contract 143/158；d）other grounds for lesivo referred to terms of Contract 41 that the Government itself had proposed and FVG and FEGUA had copied in Contract 143/158；e）the railway equipment in question had been used since the initiation of the rail service in 1998 with full knowledge of the Government and without which Claimant could not have performed its obligations under Contract 402；f）FEGUA certified that such obligations under Phase I and II of the railway rehabilitation had been performed satisfactorily by FVG，which had used the very same railway equipment，first under the exchanges of letters between FEGUA and FVG and later under Contract 143/158；g）the conditions proposed by the Government for not proceeding with lesivo were for the most part unrelated to the curing of lesivoand the Lesivo Declaration was used as a tactic to pressure Claimant to invest more，irrespective of its obligations under Contract 402，or forfeit its investment in favor of other unspecified investors.

仲裁庭认为，在本案的情况下，被申请人应用损害国家利益这一救济措施的方式和理由构成违反中美洲自贸协定第10条5款的最低处理标准，用废物管理Ⅱ案的话说，"任意、严重不公平和不公正。"特别是仲裁庭强调了以下事实，这些事实共同证明了在本案中，损害声明的武断、严重不公平和不公正性质，包括证明损害声明违反了危地马拉的表态，而这些表述是申请人所合理依赖的：a）政府宣布了143/158号合同的损害，但在该合同使用铁路设施而由危地马拉铁路公司收取租金而从未提出异议；b）41号合同是在危地马拉铁路公司的倡议下签订的，在FVG通过公开招标获得的该合同后因为政府自身因不明原因未能批准；c）政府未能批准41号合同，并且缺乏对143/158号合同项下与41号合同项下相同设备的使用的公开招标，这两项问题均受政府控制，并且政府有权进行补救，这在一定程度上可以裁量宣告143/158号合同有损害的正当性；d）损害声明的其他理由提到的第41号合同的条款是政府自己提议的，也是从FVG和危地马拉铁路公司的143/158合同中复制的；e）自1998年开始的铁路服务，政府是充分了解的，如果政府不知道，申请人不可能履行其在合同402号下的义务；f）危地马拉铁路公司证明，在铁路翻修的第一阶段和第二阶段中，FVG已圆满履行了此类义务，FVG使用了非常相同的铁路设备，这体现在危地马拉铁路公司和FVG之间的信件交换，以及后来143/158号合同中；g）政府提出的不继续推进执行损害声明的建议在很大程度上与损害声明的救济无关，并且损害声明被用作一种策略，迫使申请人增加投资，不考虑其在402号合同项下的义务，或者为了其他未指明的投资者而没收申请人的投资。

案件影响（Impact of the Case）

本案最主要的争议焦点有三方面：ICSID管辖权，间接征收以及国际最低待遇标准。有关ICSID管辖权方面，危地马拉认为ICSID对本案没有管辖权，针对危地马拉提出的观点，仲裁庭进行了反驳，最终认定ICSID具有管辖权。有关间接征收方面，RDC与危地马拉进行了两次辩论，针对危地马拉政府的行为是否构成间接征收，以及间接征收的界定，仲裁庭归纳总结铁路发展公司与危地马拉的主要观点，结合需要考虑的各种因素，最终认定危地马拉的行为不构成间接征收。有关国际最低待遇标准方面，铁路发展公司、危地马拉和仲裁庭针对危地马拉政府的行为是否符合国际最低待遇标准，从适用法律、案件事实以及最低待遇标准的认定三方面进行了辩论，最终，仲裁庭认为，在本案中，危地马拉适用"损害决议"的原因和方式，造成了对《中美洲自由贸易协定》第10条5款的最低待遇标准的违反。

对比以往案例，本案中对于ICSID管辖权的认定，是仲裁庭罕见的对《维也纳条约法》第28条做出的积极解释，虽然ICSID官方不支持遵循先例，但其又接受先例的指导意义，因此，在本案环境下，仲裁庭认定其在此环境下有管辖权，足可认定本案对于ICSID管辖权的扩大具有积极意义。间接征收也是本案的一大争议焦点，间接征收有三大认定标准："纯粹效果标准"、"目的标准"以及"效果兼目的标准"，在本案中仲裁庭采用了"纯粹效果标准"，其实这是最有利于投资者的，因此本案亦可以作为证实ICSID对间接征收的认定标准采取保护投资者的"纯粹效果标准"的先例。

本案是最低待遇标准在《中美洲自由贸易协定》中的第一案，因此仲裁庭在裁决时多援引先例，对于在本案后有关国际最低待遇标准抑或是公平公正待遇标准的案件，本案也可作为一个先例。先例的作用扩大化，可以说是ICSID仲裁的一个趋势。

思考问题（Questions）

1. 最低待遇标准除了公平公正待遇的内容以外，往往还和"充分保护和安全"义务有关，本裁决为何未展开分析？

2. 中美洲自由贸易协定的投资争端解决机制是如何设置的？

案例十　西方石油公司诉厄瓜多尔案

Occidental Petroleum Corporation Occidental Exploration and Production Company v. The Republic of Ecuador（ICSID Case No. ARB/06/11）

选读理由（Selected Reason）

西方石油公司诉厄瓜多尔政府案是一起典型的投资仲裁案件，展现了一项投资如何从合作走向争端，进而走上仲裁庭的过程，也展示了投资仲裁庭通常采取的法律解释方法、法律推理过程以及赔偿金计算方法。自 2006 年 7 月西方石油公司申请仲裁程序、2012 年 10 月厄瓜多尔申请撤销程序并于 2015 年 12 月形成部分撤销原裁决的决定，该案历经 9 年多时间审理。由于仲裁裁决作出的巨额赔偿在当时创造了历史纪录，本案引发了学界和实务界的广泛关注。并且，该案是 ICSID 专门委员会最新做出撤销决定的案件，其对撤销理由的解释和论证也值得进一步跟进。

仲裁申请情况（The Request for Arbitration）

On 17 May 2006, Occidental Petroleum Corporation（"OPC"）and Occidental Exploration and Production Company（"OEPC"）, two U. S. companies（together the "Claimants"）, filed with the International Centre for Settlement of Investment Disputes（ICSID）a Request for Arbitration under the Convention on the Settlement of Investment Disputes between States and Nationals of Other States（"ICSID Convention'）against the Republic of Ecuador（"Ecuador" or the "Respondent"）and Empresa Estatal Petróleos del Ecuador（"Petro Ecuador"）.

The parties' dispute concerns the termination [Caducidad] of a 1999 Participation Contract between OEPC and Petro Ecuador for the exploration and exploitation of hydrocarbons in Block 15 of the Ecuadorian Amazon region (the "Participation Contract").

2006 年 5 月 17 日，西方石油公司（OPC）、西方勘探和生产公司（OEPC）这两家美国公司（合称"申请方"）向国际投资争端解决中心（ICSID）提交了一份仲裁请求，根据《关于解决国家与其他国家国民之间投资争端公约》对厄瓜多尔共和国（"厄瓜多尔"或"被申请方"）和厄瓜多尔国家石油公司（"厄瓜多尔石油"）提起仲裁请求。

当事人的争议涉及一份 1999 年由西方勘探和生产公司和厄瓜多尔国家石油公司签署的在厄瓜多尔亚马逊地区"15 区块"进行石油勘探和开采的产品分成合同的终止事宜。

OEPC's presence in Ecuador began on 25 January 1985, when it entered into a services contract with the Corporación Estatal Petrolera Ecuatoriana (now Petroecuador). Pursuant to that contract, OEPC provided services related to the exploration and production of oil in Block 15 (the "Services Contract"). Under the terms of the Services Contract, OEPC provided 100% of the services required to produce oil in Block 15, ranging from identifying possible deposits through exploration to producing the oil out of the ground. If OEPC discovered oil, it was reimbursed for its costs and investments pursuant to various conditions and formulas in the contract. However, 100% of the crude oil produced belonged to Petroecuador. At the time the Services Contract was signed, Block 15 remained relatively unexplored. Hence, OEPC's initial focus in the block was on identifying possiblereserves for exploitation. After eight years of exploration, OEPC began production Block 15 in 1993. In May 1993, OEPC and Petroecuador also signed a unitized field from agreement for the joint operation of the Limoncocha field. That unitized field agreement was set to expire as soon as the Services Contract expired.

OEPC 于 1985 年 1 月 25 日开始在厄瓜多尔开展业务，当时它与厄瓜多尔国家石油公司（现为厄瓜多尔石油）签订了服务合同。根据该合同，OEPC 提供与 15 区石油勘探和生产相关的服务（"服务合同"）。根据服务合同的条款，OEPC 提供了生产 15 区石油所需的 100% 服务，范围从通过勘探确定可能的矿床到从地面开采石油。如果OEPC 发现了石油，则根据合同中的各种条件和公式对其成本和投资进行补偿。然而，生产的原油 100% 属于厄瓜多尔石油公司。在签订服务合同时，15 号区块仍相对未勘探。因此，OEPC 在该区块的最初重点是确定可能的开采储量。经过 8 年的勘探，OEPC 自 1993 年开始在 15 号区块生产石油。

In 1993, Ecuador amended its Hydrocarbons Law to allow the negotiation of "participation contracts." At its core, a participation contract is essentially a type of production sharing agreement: the State and contractors share in the production of crude oil, with all expenditures borne by the contractor. This contractual model gave producers a stake in the production that made exploration risks more palatable. Further, it guaranteed Ecuador a profit from its production share, since it no longer had any expenses associated with oil production.

1993 年，厄瓜多尔修订了其《碳氢化合物法》，允许谈判"分成合同"。分成合同的核心实质上是一种产品分享协议：国家和承包商共同分享原油生产，所有支出由承包商承担。这种合同模式使生产商在生产中获得了权益份额，从而使勘探风险更加容易接受。此外，由于厄瓜多尔不再有任何与石油生产相关的支出，因此它也能保证厄瓜多尔从其产品份额中获得利润。

OEPC and Ecuador began the negotiation of their participation contract in January 1997. The negotiations took nearly two years, and the Participation Contract was finally signed on 21 May 1999 (the previously-defined "Participation Contract"). According to Clause 1, the contracting parties were the "Republic of Ecuador, through [...] Petroecuador [...] [and] Occidental Exploration and Production Company, Ecuador Branch." Pursuant to Clause 6. 1 of the Participation Contract, OEPC had the right to develop and to exploit the Indillana Complex, known as the Base Area in the Contract, until 2012, and other fields from which production began after the signing of the Participation Contract, such as the Edén Yuturi and Yanaquincha fields and potentially the Paka Sur and Paka Norte fields, until 2019.

OEPC 和厄瓜多尔于 1997 年 1 月开始谈判分成合同。谈判历时近两年，分成合同最终于 1999 年 5 月 21 日签署（即之前定义的"分成合同"）。根据第 1 条，缔约方为"厄瓜多尔共和国，通过［……］厄瓜多尔石油公司［……］［和］西方勘探和生产公司厄瓜多尔分公司"。根据分成合同第 6.1 条，OEPC 有权发展和开发英迪拉纳杂岩地带，即合同中的基本地区，直到 2012 年，以及签署分成合同后开始生产的其他油田，如伊甸·尤里和扬卡扬查油田，以及可进一步洽谈的南帕卡省和北帕卡省油田，直到 2019 年。

The amount of OEPC's participation was determined on the basis of the equation described in the above-referred Clause 8. 1. That equation took into account several factors, including the field, the rate of production, and certain agreed-upon percentages. At the end of 2005, OEPC's participation was approximately 70% of the oil produced from Block 15. After payment of expenses, taxes and other assessments, however, between 1999 and 2006, OEPC allegedly received approximately 30% of total net profits.

OEPC 的分成量是根据上述第 8 条 1 款所述方程式确定的。该方程考虑了几个因素，包括油田、生产率和某些商定的百分比。在 2005 年底，OEPC 分成的石油约占 15 区石油产量的 70%。然而，在支付了费用、税款和其他核定费用后，1999 年至 2006 年期间，OEPC 据称获得了总净利润的约 30%。

Chapter 16 of the Participation Contract, entitled "Transfer and Assignment", sets forth these conditions in provisions which are at the heart of the parties' dispute in this arbitration. These provisions, which are considered in greater detail later in this Award, include the following:

16. 1 Transfer of this Participation Contract or assignment to third parties of the rights under the Participation Contract, must have the authorization of the Corresponding Ministry, in accordance with existing laws and regulations, especially the provisions contained in Art. 79 of the Hydrocarbons Law and Executive Decrees No. 809, 2713 and 1179.

分成合同的第 16 章，标题为"转让和让与"，规定了在本仲裁中双方争议的核心条款。这些条款在本裁决中将作更详细的考虑，包括以下内容：

第 16 章 1 节参与合同的转让或向第三方让予分成合同项下的权利，必须得到相应主管部门的授权，符合现行法律法规，特别是《碳氢化合物法》第 79 条的规定、第 809 号行政法令第 2713 条和 1179 条的规定。

At this juncture, the Tribunal also observes that these provisions of the Participation Contract refer to many of the provisions of Ecuador's HCL, in particular the following:

Chapter Ⅸ Caducidad, Sanctions and Transfers.

Art. 74. The Ministry of Energy and Mines may declare the Caducidad of contracts, if the contractor:

11. Transfers rights or enters into a private contract or agreement for the assignment of one or more of its rights, without the Ministry's authorization.

Art. 79. The transfer of a contract or the assignment to third parties of rights derived from a contract shall be null and void and shall have no validity whatsoever if there is no prior authorization from the Ministry of Energy and Mines, without prejudice to the declaration of Caducidad as provided for in this Law.

同时，仲裁庭还注意到分成合同的这些条款涉及厄瓜多尔《碳氢化合物法》的许多条款，特别是以下条款：

第 9 章 无效、处罚和转让。

第 74 条 如果承包商有下列情形之一的，能源和矿产部可以宣告合同无效：

11. 未经能源和矿产部的授权，转让合同的全部权利或签订一份私人合同或协议转让本合同项下的一项或多项权利。

第 79 条 如果没有得到能源和矿产部的事先批准，合同的转让或将合同项下的权利转让给第三方的行为是无效的，且不影响根据本法律的其他规定宣告无效。

In order to finance the expansion of its operations in Ecuador, OEPC sought an arrangement that could provide the necessary funds, as well as diversify and reduce its exposure. At the same time, Alberta Energy Corporation Ltd. ("AEC"), through the related entity AEC International ("AECI" or "AEC"), was looking to expand its investments in Ecuador. On 19 October 2000, the OEPC and AEC signed the Farmout Agreement (the "Farmout" or "Farmout Agreement"). The Farmout, an agreement governed by the laws of New York, provided for two phases. In the first phase of the transaction AEC purchased a 40% so-called "economic interest" in Block 15. Essentially, through contributions to OEPC's Block 15 investments, AEC purchased the right to 40% of OEPC's share of Block 15's production. In exchange for its economic interest in the production from Block 15, AEC agreed to pay 40% of all the capital and operating expenses in developing Block 15. AEC also agreed to pay approximately $180 million towards OEPC's historical development costs.

为了融资以扩张其在厄瓜多尔的业务，OEPC 寻求一种安排可以提供必要的资金，并使资金来源多样化和降低风险。与此同时，阿尔伯塔能源有限公司（"AEC"）通过相关实体 AEC 国际（"AECI"或"AEC"）寻求扩大其在厄瓜多尔的投资。2000 年 10 月 19 日，OEPC 和 AEC 签署了《分包协议》。分包合同是一项受纽约法律管辖的协议，分为两个阶段。在交易的第一阶段，AEC 购买了 15 区 40%的所谓"经济利益"。实际上，通过对 OEPC15 区的投资，AEC 购买了 OEPC 在 15 区生产中所占份额的 40%。作为对 15 区生产的经济利益的交换，AEC 同意支付开发 15 区所有资本和运营费用的 40%。AEC 还同意支付约 1.8 亿美元作为 OEPC 的历史开发成本。

On 25 October 2000, Mr. MacInnes wrote to Minister Terán regarding the previous day's meeting. Mr. MacInnes wrote that the Farmout was an "imminent transaction pursuant to which [OEPC] intends to transfer to [AEC] 40% of its economic interest in the Participation Contract." Mr. MacInnes also wrote that, following that first stage of the transaction, "OEPC will continue being the only 'Contractor' entity under the Contract for Block 15;" and that "once [AEC] has complied with its obligations contemplated in the transfer agreement, OEPC shall transfer to [AEC] the legal title corresponding to 40% of its interests [...] subject to the approvals that the Government of Ecuador may require at that time." The letter ended with a request to the Minister to "confirm [...] [the] consent with respect to the aforementioned transfer of economic interests in favor of [AEC]."

The evidence discloses that, by February 2004, AEC had made all payments due to OEPC under the Farmout. The day after Moores Rowland issued its audit report, on 15 July 2004, OEPC wrote to the new Minister of Energy and Mines, Mr. Eduardo López Robayo, "request [ing] the Ministry to approve the transfer by OEPC to AEC Ecuador of legal title to a 40% interest" in Block 15, as contemplated under the Farmout. In making this request,

OEPC referred to its letter of 25 October 2000, as well as Minister Terán's response of 17 January 2001. The approval sought by OEPC was not granted.

2000 年 10 月 25 日，麦金尼斯先生就前一天的会议给特恩部长写信。Macinnes 先生写道，转包是一项"即将发生的交易，根据该交易，OEPC 打算将其在参与合同中 40% 的经济利益转让给 AEC"。Macinnes 先生还写道，在交易的第一阶段之后，"OEPC 将继续是 15 区合同下唯一的'承包商'实体"，"而且"一旦 AEC 履行了其在转让协议中规定的义务，且在当时已获得厄瓜多尔政府可能要求的批准的情况下，OEPC 应向 AEC 转让其 40% 的权益对应的法定所有权。信末请求部长"同意上述以 AEC 为受益人的经济利益转让"。

证据表明，到 2004 年 2 月，AEC 已经支付了所有到期应付 OEPC 的转让款项。2004 年 7 月 15 日，Moores Rowland 发布审计报告的第二天，OEPC 写信给新的能源和矿业部长 Eduardo López Robayo 先生，"请求部批准 OEPC 向 AEC 转让 15 号区块 40% 权益的合法所有权"，正如分包合同计划的一样。在提出这一请求时，OEPC 提到了其 2000 年 10 月 25 日的信，以及特恩部长 2001 年 1 月 17 日的答复。但 OEPC 寻求的批准未获同意。

In August 2001, Ecuador's tax authority, the SRI, contrary to its established practice of refunding value added taxes ("VAT") to oil companies, refused to grant such refunds in the future and, retroactively, claimed refunds of the taxes already paid. OEPC interpreted this decision to be a violation of Ecuadorian tax laws and the Treaty Between the United States of America and the Republic of Ecuador Concerning the Encouragement and Reciprocal Protection of Investment ("the Treaty") and, in November 2002, filed an international arbitration claim against Ecuador to recover the VAT refunds. On 1 July 2004, the VAT Tribunal issued a \$75 million VAT Award in OEPC's favor, finding that Ecuador's conduct had been unfair and discriminatory. The VAT Award was sent to the parties on 12 July 2004, and was immediately made public. Ecuador challenged the award in the English courts. Its annulment application was rejected by the High Court on 2 March 2006 and that decision was confirmed by the Court of Appeal on 4 July 2007.

2001 年 8 月，厄瓜多尔税务局，即 SRI，违反其向石油公司退还增值税（"VAT"）的既定惯例，拒绝在未来发放此类退税，并追溯已缴纳税款的退税。OEPC 将这一决定解释为违犯了厄瓜多尔税法和《美国与厄瓜多尔关于鼓励和相互保护投资的协定》（"双边协定"），并于 2002 年 11 月向厄瓜多尔提出了一项国际仲裁索赔，要求收回增值税退税。2004 年 7 月 1 日，增值税仲裁庭发布了一项 7500 万美元的有利于 OEPC 的增值税裁决，认定厄瓜多尔的行为是不公平和歧视性的。增值税裁决于 2004 年 7 月 12 日发给缔约方，并立即公布。厄瓜多尔在英国法院对该裁决提出质疑。其撤销申请于

2006 年 3 月 2 日被高等法院驳回，上诉法院于 2007 年 7 月 4 日确认该决定。

On 15 May 2006, Minister Rodríguez issued the Caducidad Decree. The Decree terminated, with immediate effect, OEPC's Participation Contract and ordered OEPC to turn over to Petro Ecuador all its assets relating to Block 15. On 16 May 2006, State officials arrived at OEPC's offices in Quito and seized all of its property, including computers, files and other equipment, which were now said to be the property of the State. The next day, 17 May, other State officials, accompanied by the National Police, seized OEPC's oil fields in Block 15, including wells, drills, storage facilities and other oil exploration and production assets.

2006 年 5 月 15 日，罗德古兹部长颁布了《宣告无效法令》。该法令立即终止了 OEPC 的分成合同，并命令 OEPC 将其与区块 15 有关的所有资产移交给厄瓜多尔石油公司。2006 年 5 月 16 日，国家政府官员抵达位于基多的 OEPC 办公室，没收了其所有财产，包括电脑、文件和其他设备，这些现在被称为国家财产。第二天，5 月 17 日，其他政府官员在国家警察的陪同下，查获了 OEPC 第 15 区的油田，包括油井、钻头、储存设施和其他石油勘探和生产资产。

仲裁结果（Award）

For all of the foregoing reasons, and rejecting all submissions and contentions to the contrary, the Tribunal Declares, Awards and Orders as follows in respect of the issues arising for determination in these proceedings:

(i) Ecuador acted in breach of Article Ⅱ.3 (a) of the Treaty by failing to accord fair and equitable treatment to the Claimants' investment, and to accord the Claimants treatment no less than that required by international law;

(ii) Ecuador acted in breach of Article Ⅲ.1 of the Treaty by expropriating the Claimants' investment in Block 15 through a measure "tantamount to expropriation";

(iii) Ecuador issued the Caducidad Decree in breach of Ecuadorian law and customary international law;

(iv) OEPC breached Clause 16.1 of the Participation Contract by failing to secure the required ministerial authorization for the transfer of rights under the Farmout Agreement; as a result of this breach, the damages awarded to the Claimants will be reduced by a factor of 25% (see subparagraph (v));

(v) Claimants are awarded the amount of US $ 1,769,625,000 (US One billion, seven hundred sixty nine millions, six hundred twenty five thousand dollars), as calculated in paragraph 825 of this Award, for damages suffered as a result of the breaches set out above in sub-paragraphs (i), (ii) and (iii);

(vi) Ecuador is ordered to pay pre-award interest on the above amount at the rate of 4.188% per annum, compounded annually from 16 May 2006 until the date of this Award;

(vii) Ecuador is ordered to pay post-award interest from the date of this Award at the U. S. 6 month LIBOR rate, compounded on a monthly basis; and

(viii) Ecuador's counterclaims, except that counterclaim specified in subparagraph (iv) above, are dismissed; and

(ix) Each Party is ordered to bear its own costs of the proceedings and the Claimants and the Respondent are ordered and mandated each to pay half of ICSID's and the Tribunal's costs of and incidental to the proceedings.

In accordance with Article 48 (4) of the ICSID Convention, Arbitrator Stern dissents from the above majority and her statement of dissent is attached.

鉴于上述所有理由，并驳回所有与此相反的意见和争论，仲裁庭就在本仲裁程序中需裁决的争议问题宣布、裁决和命令如下：

（一）厄瓜多尔违反了双边协定第 2 条 3 款（a）项的规定，未能对申请人的投资给予公平和公正的待遇，并且未能给予申请人不低于国际法要求的待遇；

（二）厄瓜多尔违反了双边协定第 3 条 1 款的规定，通过"相当于征收"的措施征收了申请人在 15 区的投资；

（三）厄瓜多尔颁布《宣告无效法令》违反厄瓜多尔法律和国际习惯法；

（四）西方石油公司违反了参与合同第 16 条 1 款的规定，未能获得转让协议项下权利转让所需的部长授权；因此，授予申请人的损害赔偿将减少 25% ［见（五）项］；

（五）根据本裁决第 825 段的计算，对于因第（一）、（二）和（三）项所述违约行为而遭受的损害，申请人获得 1769625000 美元的赔偿金；

（六）厄瓜多尔被要求以 4.188% 的年利率支付上述金额在裁决作出前的利息，从 2006 年 5 月 16 日起至本仲裁作出之日止每年计取复利；

（七）厄瓜多尔被要求以美国 6 个月伦敦银行同业拆放利率（按月复利）支付裁决后利息；

（八）厄瓜多尔的反请求被驳回，但上文第（四）项规定的反请求除外；

（九）仲裁各方被责令承担各自的仲裁费用，申请人和被申请人被责令各自支付 ICSID 和仲裁庭的仲裁费用和附带费用的一半。

根据 ICSID 公约第 48 条（4）款，仲裁员 Stern 反对上述多数裁决意见，后附其反对声明。

裁决原因（Reasons for the Award）

The Proportionality of the Sanction for the Unauthorized Transfer of Rights under the Participation Contract

The Claimants have submitted that even if any of the alleged Termination Events had occurred, the Respondent would still have breached its obligations under the Treaty and the Participation Contract by imposing a sanction which in the circumstances was manifestly disproportionate. As to the Treaty, reliance was placed on Article Ⅱ.3（a）which obliges Ecuadorinter alia to accord investments fair and equitable treatment.

For the Respondent, Dr. Aguilar accepted that the principle of proportionality was an established feature of Ecuadorian law. During cross-examination, Dr. Aguilar also accepted the applicability of the principle of proportionality in fact situations such as the present one, where an administrative sanction is imposed following a violation of relevant domestic law.

the Tribunal observes that there is a growing body of arbitral law, particularly in the context of ICSID arbitrations, which holds that the principle of proportionality is applicable to potential breaches of bilateral investment treaty obligations. In the present case, the Treaty provides at Article Ⅱ.3（a）that investments shall at all times be accorded fair and equitable treatment, shall enjoy full protection and security and shall in no case be accorded treatment less than that required by international law. The obligation for fair and equitable treatment has on several occasions been interpreted to import an obligation of proportionality.

对未经批准转让分成合同项下权利进行处罚的比例问题

申请人主张，即使发生了任何所谓的终止事件，被申请人所实施的制裁措施也是明显不成比例的，违反了其在双边协定和分成合同项下的义务。双边协定第二条第3款（a）项的规定中，包括了厄瓜多尔有义务给予投资公平和公正待遇。

对于被申请人，阿吉拉尔博士承认比例原则是厄瓜多尔法律的一个既有特征。在交叉询问质证期间，阿吉拉尔博士还承认了比例原则在本案情形下的可适用性，本案涉及对违反国内法律的行为实施的一项行政处罚。

仲裁庭注意到，仲裁法越来越多，特别是在ICSID仲裁的情况下，认为比例原则适用于可能发生的违反双边投资协定义务的行为。在本案中，双边协定第二条3款（a）项规定，投资应始终得到公平和公正的待遇，应享有充分的保护和保障，在任何情况下，其待遇均不得低于国际法所要求的待遇。公平公正待遇义务在若干情况下被解释为符合比例的义务。

In summary, the Tribunal considers that the foregoing options existed as an alternative to Caducidad, namely:

i) insistence on payment of a transfer fee in the order of US $ 11. 8 million.

ii) improvements to the economic terms of the original contract.

iii) a negotiated settlement which could of course have covered any areas that the parties so desired, including payment of the transfer fee which had been avoided, renegotiation of thecontract and additional compensation.

It is apparent that the VAT Award had created anger and disappointment in Ecuadorian political circles. It is not appropriate in this Award to discuss the merits or demerits of the VAT Award. It is sufficient to note that it seems to have led to a good deal of ill-feeling against OEPC, as did the discovery that OEPC had transferred rights under the Participation Contract in violation of the laws of Ecuador.

综上所述,仲裁庭认为,被申请人有很多选择可作为宣告无效措施的替代方案:

1) 坚持要求支付 1180 万美元的转让费。

2) 对原分成合同的经济条款进行改进。

3) 协商解决方案,当然可以涵盖双方所希望的任何领域,包括支付本已避免支付的转让费、重新谈判合同和要求额外补偿。

很明显,增值税仲裁案的裁决在厄瓜多尔政界引起了愤怒和失望。在本案的裁决中讨论增值税裁决的优缺点是不适当的。值得注意的是,这似乎导致了被申请人对 OEPC 的强烈不满,被申请人发现 OEPC 违反厄瓜多尔法律转让了分成合同项下的权利时也同样如此。

It follows that even if OEPC, as the Tribunal found earlier, breached Clause 16. 1 of the Participation Contract and was guilty of an actionable violation of Article 74. 11 (or Articles 74. 12 or 74. 13), the Caducidad Decree was not a proportionate response in the particular circumstances, and the Tribunal so finds. The Caducidad Decree was accordingly issued in breach of Ecuadorian law, in breach of customary international law, and in violation of the Treaty. As to the latter, the Tribunal expressly finds that the Caducidad Decree constituted a failure by the Respondent to honour its Article II. 3 (a) obligation to accord fair and equitable treatment to the Claimants' investment, and to accord them treatment no less than that required by international law.

The Tribunal agrees with the Claimants. Having found in the previous Section of the present Award that the Caducidad Decree was issued in breach of Ecuadorian law, in breach of customary international law and in violation of the Respondent's Article II. 3 (a) obligation to accord fair and equitable treatment to the Claimants' investment, the Tribunal now has no hesitation in finding that, in the particular circumstances of this case which it has traversed earlier, the taking by the Respondent of the Claimants' investment by means of this administrative sanction was a measure "tantamount to expropriation" and thus in breach of Article Ⅲ. 1 of the Treaty.

由此可见，如仲裁庭先前认定的，即使 OEPC 违反了分成合同第 16 条 1 款，并违反了第 74 条 11 款（或第 74 条 12 款或 74 条 13 款）的可被起诉的犯罪的规定，但在特定情况下，该宣告无效的法令并不是与之相称的回应。因此，《宣告无效法令》是在违反厄瓜多尔法律、违反国际习惯法和违反双边协定的情况下颁布的，这也是仲裁庭所发现的。对于后者，仲裁庭明确认为，《宣告无效法令》构成被申请人未能履行其第二条 3 款（a）项规定的义务，即对申请人的投资给予公平和公正的待遇，并给予他们不低于国际法要求的待遇。

仲裁庭同意申请人的意见。在本裁决的前一节中，仲裁庭发现《宣告无效法令》的颁布违反了厄瓜多尔法律，违反了国际习惯法，违反了被申请人第二条 3 款（a）项对申请人投资给予公平和公正待遇的义务，现在，仲裁庭毫不犹豫地认为在本案早些时候经历的特殊情况下，被申请人对申请人投资采取的行政处罚措施是一项"相当于征收"的措施，因此违反了双边协定第三条 1 款。

The Fault of the Claimants Prior to the Caducidad Decree

Since OEPC did not seek nor obtain the required authorization, the Tribunal has found that it acted negligently and committed an unlawful act. The Claimants' fault prevented the Respondent from exercising, in a formal way, its sovereign right to vet and approve AEC as the transferee of those rights and, even more importantly on the facts of the present case, to vet any other unknown investor to which AEC could eventually transfer its rights.

The Tribunal agrees with the ICSID Annulment Committee in the MTD Equity case that "the role of the two parties contributing to the loss [is] [...] only with difficulty commensurable and the Tribunal [has] a corresponding margin of estimation."

However, the Tribunal must reach a decision and it has. Having considered and weighed all the arguments which the parties have presented to the Tribunal in respect of this issue, in particular the evidence and the authorities traversed in the present chapter, the Tribunal, in the exercise of its wide discretion, finds that, as a result of their material and significant wrongful act, the Claimants have contributed to the extent of 25% to the prejudice which they suffered when the Respondent issued the Caducidad Decree.

《宣告无效法令》颁布以前被申请人的过错

由于 OEPC 未寻求或未获得所需的批准，仲裁庭认为其行为疏忽，并实施了违法行为。申请人的过错妨碍了被申请人以正式方式行使其审查和批准 AEC 作为这些权利受让人的主权权利，更重要的是，就本案事实而言，还妨碍了被申请人审查 AEC 最终将其权益转让给任何其他未知投资者。

仲裁庭同意在 ICSID 撤销委员会 MTD 股份公司诉智利案件中的意见，"双方对所造成的损失的作用虽然很困难，但仍是可以测算的，仲裁庭在测算时相应地有出现误差的空间"。

但是，仲裁庭必须做出决定，而且已经做出了决定。经过审议并权衡了各方就此问题向仲裁庭提交的所有论据，特别是本章所述的证据和权威观点，仲裁庭行使其广泛的酌情决定权，认为由于其实质以及重大的错误行为，申请人在 25% 的范围内对被申请人发布《宣告无效法令》时遭受的不公平待遇负有责任。

Calculation of Damages

The Claimants submit that international law governs the proper remedy for the Respondent's Treaty breaches, and that the appropriate standard of reparation under international law is compensation for the losses suffered by the victim. Under international law, the Claimants add, Fair Market Value (FMV) is the appropriate measure of damages.

The Tribunal is of the view that, in this case, the standard economic approach tomeasuring the fair market value today of a stream of net revenues (i. e. , gross revenues minus attendant costs) that can be earned from the operation of a multi-year project such as OEPC's development of Block 15 is the calculation of the present value, as of 16 May 2006, of the net benefits, or "discounted cash flows". These net cash flows are appropriately determined by calculating the flow of benefits ("cash flows") that the Claimants would have reasonably been expected to earn in the "but for" state of the world in which the termination of the Participation Contract hypothetically did not occur relative to the actual cash flow that the Claimants will derive subsequent to the termination. The difference between these two cash flow streams (the "but for" state of the world with no termination less the actual state of the world with contract termination), discounted to the date of the actual contract termination, is the economically appropriate and reliable measure of the cumulative economic harm suffered by the Claimants as a consequence of the contract termination.

Using the economic model agreed by Professor Kalt and Mr. Johnston, the Tribunal, informed by all the findings that it has made in the present Section of its Award and assisted by Professor Kalt and Mr. Johnston's agreed calculations, determines that the Net Present Value of the discounted cash flows generated by the Block 15 OEPC production as of 16 May 2006 is US $ 2,359,500,000 (US Two billion, three hundred fifty nine millions and five hundred thousand dollars).

损害赔偿额的计算

申请人认为，被申请人违反协定的行为应适用国际法以正当的救济，国际法规定的适当赔偿标准是对受害人遭受的损失的赔偿。根据国际法，申请人补充说，公平市场价值（FMV）是适当的损害计算方式。

仲裁庭认为，在本案中，用标准的经济学方法来测算公平市场价值，可以通过计算 OEPC 在 15 区块上多年来运营项目净收入（即总收入减去相应的成本）来计算 2006 年 5 月 16 日时点上的净收益现值，或者称为"折现现金流"。这些净现金流是通过计算在假设分成合同的终止并非发生情况下申请人合理预期的收益流（"现金流"）来适当确定的，与申请人在分成合同被终止后所获得的实际现金流不同。这两种现金流之间的差额（假定的不终止合同状态减去合同终止时的实际状态），折现至实际合同终止之日，是对申请人因合同被终止所遭受的累积经济损害在经济上的适当和可靠的衡量。

根据 Kalt 教授和 Johnston 先生同意的经济模型，仲裁庭根据其在本节裁决中所做的所有调查结果，并在 Kalt 教授和 Johnston 先生同意的计算结果的协助下，确定 15 区 OEPC 生产在 2006 年 5 月 16 日产生的折现现金流的净现值为 2359500000 美元。

撤销裁决的决定（Decision on Annulment of The Award）

Referring to the the Convention on the Settlement of Investment Disputes between States and Nationals of Other States (the "ICSID Convention"), which states that the original arbitral tribunal clearly exceeded its competence, that there was a serious departure from the basic rules of procedure and that the award did not state the reasons on which it was based, and put forward three claims to the committee, including: (1) Annul the award in its entirety; (2) alternatively, partially annul the award as described in this Reply on Annulment at paragraphs 230, 285, 358, 391, 404, 494, 641, 652, 745, and 769; (3) claimants bear the entire costs of this annulment proceeding, including the ICSID costs and Ecuadorianlegal costs and other expenses.

厄瓜多尔援引了《解决国家与他国国民间投资争端公约》，认为原仲裁庭明显超越权限、存在严重背离基本程序规则的情形、裁决未陈述其所依据的理由，并向专门委员会提出三项主张，包括：（1）全部撤销原仲裁裁决；（2）部分撤销列于"本撤销决定"第 230、285、358、391、404、494、641、652、745 及 769 段中的原裁决内容；（3）在申请人西方石油公司承担本撤销程序的全部费用，包括 ICSID 的费用以及厄瓜多尔花费的法律费用和其他费用。

The Committee reached the following conclusions on the basic facts and applicable law. It considered that the implementation of the participation contracthad enabled the OEPC to retain only 60 percent of the original participation contractand that 40 percent of the ownership had been transferred to AEC/Andes, and that the transfer had never been approved by the Ecuadorian authorities. Although the participation contract stipulates that the transfer of rights under the contract without the approval of the government of Ecuador will lead to the automatic termination of the contract, the "invalidation decree" issued by the government of Ecuador will not lead to the automatic invalidation of 40% of the transfer of rights. Judicial decisions need to be passed through the courts, and no relevant procedure has been conducted in this case. In addition, although AEC/Andes is a party to the participation contract, it is not a party to this arbitration procedure. Therefore, this arbitration procedure does not have the right to directly adjudicate the participation contract invalid.

专门委员会根据基本事实和准据法问题得出下述结论。其认为"分包合同"的执行使得 OEPC 仅保留了原"分成合同"项下 60% 的权益，40% 的所有权已转让给 AEC/Andes，而这一转让从未取得厄瓜多尔当局的批准。虽然"分成合同"中规定未经厄政府批准而转让合同项下的权益会导致该合同的自动终止，但厄政府颁发的《宣告无效法令》并不能导致 40% 权益转让部分的自动无效。需要经过法院进行司法宣判，而本案中并未进行过相关程序。此外，AEC/Andes 虽是"分包合同"的一方当事人，但并不是本仲裁程序的当事人，本仲裁程序因此无权直接裁判"分包合同"无效。

In the case, the arbitral tribunal ruled that Ecuador should compensate OEPC for the amount equivalent to 100 percent of the investment of Block 15, but that 40 percent of that amount did not belong to OEPC, but was now owned by Chinese company Andes. Although OEPC is protected by BIT and is a party to the participation contract, Chinese company Andes is not protected by the United States and Ecuador BIT, and is not a party to the participation contract. The arbitral tribunal unduly extended its jurisdiction by granting to protected investors compensation for the benefits actually enjoyed by unprotected investors.

本案中，仲裁庭裁定厄瓜多尔应赔偿给 OEPC 等同于 15 号区块油田 100% 投资额的赔偿金额，但是其中的 40% 并不属于 OEPC，而现属于中国公司 Andes。虽然 OEPC 受美厄 BIT 的保护，且是"分成合同"的当事人，但中国公司 Andes 不受美厄 BIT 的保护，更不是"分成合同"的当事人。仲裁庭对受保护的投资者给予实际由不受保护的投资者所享有利益的赔偿额，不当地扩大了管辖权范围而超越了权限。

The Committee unanimously renders the following decision:

The Committee partially annuls the Award, on the ground of manifest excess of powers, to the extent that the Tribunal assumed jurisdiction with regard to the investment now beneficially owned by the Chinese investor Andes (and previously by the Bermudan company AEC), with the result that the proper compensation owed by Respondent to Claimants is US $ 1,061,775,000.

2. The rest of the Award remains unaffected.

3. All other grounds of respondent's application for annulment are rejected.

4. Each party shall bear one half of the ICSID costs, and its own litigation costs and expenses incurred with respect to this annulment proceeding.

5. The suspending enforcement of the Award is declared automatically terminated in accordance with Rule 54 (3) of the ICSID Arbitration Rules.

全体委员一致通过如下决定：

委员会以明显越权为由部分撤销原裁决结果，在某种程度上，原仲裁庭对目前由中国投资者安德斯（以前由百慕大 AEC 公司）所享有权益的投资不当地行使了管辖权。本决定的结果是被申请人应付申请人的正确赔偿金额应为1061775000 美元。

2. 原裁决其余内容不受影响。

3. 被申请人其他申请撤销裁决的理由均予以驳回。

4. 双方各自承担解决投资争端国际中心的一半费用和各自的诉讼费用以及与本撤销程序有关的开支。

5. 根据 ICSID 仲裁条款第 54 条（3）款，原裁决的暂缓执行被宣布自动终止

案件影响（Impact of the Case）

西方石油公司诉厄瓜多尔案是曾经的"史上第一大 ISDS 案件"。在对西方石油公司有利的仲裁裁决中，仲裁庭分几个层次进行论证：（一）厄宪法、厄美（国）投资保护协定（BIT）以及习惯国际法都确立了比例原则或者通过公平与公正待遇间接规定了比例原则；（二）对于未经批准擅自转让这种行为，厄法律虽然授权厄当局可以终止合同，但并未要求必须终止合同，换言之，厄当局拥有终止或不终止合同的裁量权；（三）在终止合同之外，厄当局拥有替代选项，例如修改合同以提高厄方的分成比例；（四）厄方终止合同给西方公司造成了高达几十亿美元的损失；（五）AEC 公司长期在厄从事石油勘探开发，拥有相应资质，受让分成合同的部分权利义务不会给厄方造成损失；（六）最后，厄方终止合同背后有明显的政治动机，包括为其在增值税纠纷案中的败诉进行报复，安抚国内反美情绪，等等。在计算赔偿额时，仲裁庭采用了现金流量折现法，即将 15 号油田未来预计将产生的全部净收益折现到分成合同被终止之日（2006 年 5 月 16 日）。根据争端双方顾问提交的联合报告，15 号油田的可开采储量为2.09 亿桶，据此计算出西方石油公司遭受的损失为 23.6 亿美元。由于该公司未经批准

而转让分成合同权益，也有过错，仲裁庭裁令厄瓜多尔承担 75% 的责任，赔偿 17.7 亿美元。

　　厄瓜多尔随即申请 ICSID 成立专门委员会以撤销仲裁裁决。历经近三年的审理，专门委员会最终驳回了厄瓜多尔的大部分撤销理由，但支持了厄瓜多尔要求部分撤销裁决的申请，将赔偿额降低 40%。仲裁庭的基本思路是：在"分成合同"项下的 40% 权益已经被转让给 AEC 公司的情况下，这部分投资损失只能由"受益所有人"（beneficial owner）AEC 公司（而不能由"名义上的所有人"西方石油公司）向厄瓜多尔求偿；该部分投资不受厄美 BIT 的保护，仲裁庭对其行使管辖权，明显超出了权限。2012 年 11 月 2 日，ICSID 专门委员会作出决定，部分撤销仲裁庭的裁决，将厄瓜多尔的赔偿义务降为原赔偿金额 17.7 亿美元的 60%，即 10.6 亿美元。

　　另外，加拿大能源公司已于 2005 年将 AEC 公司转让给了中石油和中石化合资设立的安第斯石油公司。2006 年 2 月，安第斯石油公司曾与西方石油公司达成协议，对于因终止"分成合同"而产生的损失，将由后者向厄瓜多尔求偿，所获赔偿的 40% 归属于安第斯。专门委员会做出的部分撤销原裁决的决定可能会对安第斯石油公司及中石油和中石化的利益产生较大影响。本案撤销程序中厄瓜多尔采取了平行诉讼策略，即先以"管辖权裁定"有误申请全部撤销原裁决，同时提出针对赔偿金额的"部分撤销"诉求。本案对我国政府或企业参与国际投资仲裁具有借鉴意义。

思考问题（Questions）

　　1. 石油勘探开采开发合作合同的"服务合同"模式与"产品分成合同"合作模式有何差异？

　　2. 仲裁庭裁决是否否认了《宣告失效法令》的效力？为何仲裁庭认为厄瓜多尔政府的《宣告失效法令》未导致"分包合同"无效？

案例十一　米库拉兄弟诉罗马尼亚案

Ioan Micula，Viorel Micula， S. C. European Food S. A.，S. C. Starmill S. R. L. and S. C. Multipack S. R. L. v. Romania（2013）（ICSID Case No. ARB/05/20）

选读理由（Selected Reason）

本案米库拉兄弟与罗马尼亚之间就罗马尼亚撤销经济优惠产生争议。本案涉及到东道国吸引投资的优惠措施提前终止后，是否伤害了投资者对投资法律环境所享有的合理预期。本案投资者提出了罗马尼亚违背了保护伞条款和公正公平待遇义务的两项仲裁请求，仲裁庭重点对公平公正待遇问题做了分析。本裁决做出后能否得到承认和执行也存在很大的争议，因为欧盟委员会曾作出一项决定表示，如果罗马尼亚履行了该裁决，将违反欧盟竞争法。

仲裁申请情况（The Request for Arbitration）

There are five claimants in this case：two individual persons （the "Individual Claimants" or "Messrs. Micula"）and three companies （the "Corporate Claimants"）owned directly or indirectly by the Individual Claimants.

The Individual Claimants are：

a. Mr. loan Micula, who is domiciled at Teatrului Street No. 1 – 2, Oradea, Bihor County, Romania （hereinafter referred to as "Claimant 1"）. Mr. Ioan Micula was born in Romania on 8 April 1957. He moved to Sweden in 1987 where he obtained Swedish nationality in 1992 after having renounced his Romanian nationality.

b. Mr. Viorel Micula, who is domiciled at Colinelor Street No. 48, Oradea, Bihor County, Romania (hereinafter referred to as "Claimant 2"). Mr. Viorel Micula is Ioan Micula's twin brother. He left Romania for Sweden in 1989. He obtained Swedish nationality in 1995 after having renounced his Romanian nationality.

The Corporate Claimants are:

a. European Food S. A., with its registered office at 13 Septembrie Street, Ştei, Bihor County, Romania, registered with the trade register under No. J5/892/1999, registration-number 12457015 (hereinafter referred to as "Claimant 3" or "European Food"). Claimant 3 specializes in industrial manufacturing of food products.

b. Starmill S. R. L., with its registered office at 41 Drăgăneşti, Pantasesti Village, Bihor County, Romania, registered with the trade register under No. J5/177/2002, registration number 14467201 (hereinafter referred to as "Claimant 4" or "Starmill"). Claimant 4 specializes in the manufacturing of milling products.

c. Multipack S. R. L., with its registered office at 41 Drăgăneşti, Pantasesti Village, Bihor County, Romania, registered with the trade register under No. J5/178/2002, registration number 14467210 (hereinafter referred to as "Claimant 5" or "Multipack"). Claimant 5 specializes in the manufacturing of plastic packaging.

In its Decision on Jurisdiction and Admissibility of 24 September 2008 (the "Decision on Jurisdiction and Admissibility"), the Tribunal found that the Individual Claimants and the Corporate Claimants (collectively, the "Claimants") are Swedish nationals for the purposes of this arbitration.

本案有 5 个申请人：两个个人（"个人申请人"或"Micula 先生"）和三个公司（"公司申请人"），由个人申请人直接或间接拥有。

个人申请人是：

1. 伊万·米库拉先生，其住所位于罗马尼亚比霍尔县奥拉迪亚市剧院街 1—2 号（以下简称"申请人 1"）。伊万·米库拉先生 1957 年 4 月 8 日出生于罗马尼亚。1987 年他移居瑞典，1992 年放弃罗马尼亚国籍后获得瑞典国籍。

2. 维奥雷·米库拉先生，其住所位于罗马尼亚比霍尔县奥拉迪亚市圆柱街 48 号（以下简称"申请人 2"）。米库拉先生是伊万·米库拉的孪生兄弟。1989 年他离开罗马尼亚前往瑞典。他在 1995 年放弃罗马尼亚国籍后获得瑞典国籍。

公司申请人包括：

1. 欧洲食品有限公司，注册地址罗马尼亚比霍尔县施蒂里亚九月街 13 号，贸易登记号 J5/892/1999，公司注册号：12457015（以下简称"申请人 3"或"欧洲食品"）。

申请人 3 专门从事食品工业生产。

2. 星际面粉有限公司，注册地址罗马尼亚比霍尔县潘塔塞斯蒂村 41 号，贸易登记号：J5/177/2002，公司注册号：14467201（以下简称"申请人 4"或"星际面粉"）。申请人 4 专门从事面粉产品的制造。

3. 多种包装有限公司，注册地址罗马尼亚比霍尔县潘塔塞斯蒂村 41 号，贸易登记号：J5/178/2002，公司注册号：14467210（以下简称"申请人 5"或"多种包装"）。申请人 5 专门从事塑料包装的制造。

在其 2008 年 9 月 24 日关于管辖权和可受理性的决定（"管辖权和可受理性决定"）中，仲裁庭发现，为本次仲裁的目的，个人申请人和公司申请人（统称"申请人"）是瑞典国民。

The present dispute arises from Romania's introduction of certain economic incentives for the development of disfavored regions of Romania, and their subsequent revocation in the context of Romania's accession to the European Union（"EU"）.

Specifically, in 1998, Romania enacted Emergency Government Ordinance 24/1998（"EGO 24/1998" or "EGO 24"）, which made available certain tax incentives, including customs duties exemptions（called alternatively by the Parties the "Incentives" or the "Facilities"）, to investors in certain disfavored regions who met the requirements set out in EGO 24/1998 and its implementing legislation. The Claimants claim that, in reliance on those incentives, and in reliance on the expectation that they would be maintained for a 10 – year period, they made substantial investments in the Ştei-NucetDrăgăneşti disfavored region located in Bihor County, northwestern Romania. The Claimants further claim that Romania's revocation of these incentives（effective 22 February 2005）was in breach of its obligations under the BIT and caused damages to the Claimants, as described further below.

目前的争议源于罗马尼亚为发展罗马尼亚不受欢迎的地区引入了某些经济激励措施，并在罗马尼亚加入欧盟（"欧盟"）的背景下撤销了这些经济激励措施。

具体来说，1998 年，罗马尼亚颁布了《紧急政府条例》24/1998（"EGO 24/1998"或"EGO 24"），向满足 EGO 24/1998 规定的条件并实施该法律的不受欢迎地区的投资者，提供了某些税收优惠，包括关税免税（也被各方称为"优惠"或"措施"）。申请人声称，他们依赖这些激励措施，并依赖于这些措施将维持 10 年的预期，从而对位于罗马尼亚西北部比霍尔县的不受欢迎的坚果地区进行了大量投资。申请人进一步声称，罗马尼亚撤销这些激励措施（2005 年 2 月 22 日生效）违反了其在 BIT 项下的义务，并对申请人造成了损害，如下所述。

Romania does not dispute that in 1998 it passed EGO 24, which offered tax incentives to investors investing in disfavored regions, nor does it dispute that, effective 22 February 2005, it repealed most of the tax incentives offered under EGO 24, with the exception of a profit tax incentive. However, it denies that this revocation breached any of its obligations under the BIT. In addition, it argues that this revocation was necessary to comply with EU state aid obligations, which in turn was necessary for Romania to complete its accession to the EU.

The Claimants began to invest in Romania in 1991, and continued investing throughout the next two decades. During this time, Romania was undergoing its economic transition from communism to a market economy. As stated by the Respondent, during this time "the factual record [...] portrays a government trying to pursue two policies that came into increasing conflict": one directed to the development of its disfavored regions, and another directed to obtaining accession to the EU.

罗马尼亚并不否认 1998 年通过了向投资于不受欢迎地区的投资者提供税收优惠的 EGO 24，也不否认自 2005 年 2 月 22 日起，罗马尼亚废除了 EGO 24 下提供的利润税优惠除外的大部分税收优惠。然而，它否认这种撤销违反了它在 BIT 下的任何义务。此外，该委员会认为，这一撤销是遵守欧盟国家资助义务所必需的，而这反过来又是罗马尼亚完成加入欧盟所必需的。

申请人于 1991 年开始在罗马尼亚投资，并在接下来的 20 年里继续投资。在此期间，罗马尼亚正经历着从共产主义到市场经济的转型。如被申请人所述，在这段时间内，"事实记录……描绘了一个政府试图采取两项政策，这两项政策引起了越来越多的冲突：一项是针对其不受欢迎地区的发展，另一项是针对加入欧盟。

The Individual Claimants allege that their beverage business was initially developed in reliance on the incentive programs established by Law 35 and GO 27, predecessors to EGO 24. Law 35 (C-275) was enacted in 1991 to attract foreign investors to Romania by offering the incentives for new investments, including customs duties and profit tax exemptions. GO 27/1996 (Exh. C-276) was enacted in 1996 to attract investments in Bihor County and other disadvantaged regions, and provided a corporate profit tax incentive ranging from 5 to 10 years, depending on the location of the investment.

个人申请人称，他们的饮料业务最初是依靠 35 号法律和 27 号条例（EGO 24 的前身）制定的激励计划发展起来的。1991 年颁布了第 35 号法律（C-275），通过提供新投资的激励措施（包括关税和利润税免税），吸引外国投资者到罗马尼亚。1996 年颁布了 27 号条例（C-276），以吸引在比哈尔县和其他不利地区的投资，并提供了企业利润。根据投资地点的不同，税收优惠从 5 年到 10 年不等。

The Claimants claim that their beverage business was very successful. By 2001, they state that European Drinks held an estimated 55% of the total carbonated drink market in Romania and a 51% share of the bottled mineral water market.

Specifically, the Claimants allege that, starting in 1998, they expanded their business under a ten-year plan to capitalize on the EGO 24 incentives with the objective of building an integrated food platform, incorporating several companies in the process. In 1999 they incorporated European Food (Claimant 3), which as explained below was the first Corporate Claimant to benefit from the EGO 24 program. The Claimants state that they imported the majority of their raw material products through European Food, which brought them customs duties savings and allowed them to pursue a two-phase expansion plan.

申请人声称他们的饮料生意非常成功。到 2001 年，他们声称欧洲饮料公司占据罗马尼亚碳酸饮料市场总量的 55%，占瓶装矿泉水市场的 51%。

具体来说，申请人声称，从 1998 年开始，他们根据一项十年计划扩大业务，以利用"EGO 24"的激励，目的是建立一个综合食品平台，在这一过程中合并了几家公司。1999 年，他们成立了欧洲食品有限公司（申请人 3），如下文所述，这是第一个从"EGO 24"计划中受益的企业申请人。申请人声明，他们的大部分原材料产品是通过欧洲食品进口的，这为他们节省了关税，并允许他们实行两阶段扩张计划。

On 31 August 2004, by means of Government Ordinance No. 94/2004 ("GO 94/2004", Exh. R-94), Romania repealed Article 6 (1) (b) (d) and (e) of EGO 24/1998, thus repealing/revoking the incentives provided under EGO 24/1998, including the Raw Materials Incentive, with the exception of the Tax Profit Incentive. The repeal was originally to become effective 90 days from the date of entry into force of GO 94/2004 (that is, on 3 December 2004). However, the date of repeal was subsequently extended to 22 February 2005 by means of Law No. 507/2004 of 22 November 2004 (Exh. C-52), which approved and amended GO 94/2004 to that effect.

On 28 July 2005, the Claimants filed their Request for Arbitration. In view of the above, the Claimants argue that Romania has breached the Claimants' rights under the Sweden-Romania BIT and under international law. Specifically, they contend that the premature revocation of the EGO 24 incentives:

a. Breached a clear commitment undertaken by Romania vis-à-vis the Claimants, and therefore breached the BIT's umbrella clause contained in Article 2 (4) of the BIT.

b. Undermined the Claimants' legitimate expectations, upset the stability of the regulatory regime, lacked transparency and consistency, and was taken in bad faith, and therefore breached Romania's obligation under Article 2 (3) of the BIT to afford the Claimants fair and equitable treatment.

c. Impaired by unreasonable measures the management, maintenance, use, enjoyment and disposal of the Claimants' investments, and therefore breached Article 2 (3) of the BIT.

d. Expropriated without compensation the Claimants' right to receive the incentives and substantially deprived their entire investment of value, and therefore breached Article 4 (1) of the BIT.

2004 年 8 月 31 日，根据第 94/2004 号政府条例（"GO 94/2004"），罗马尼亚废除了 EGO 24/1998 第 6 条（1）款（b）项、（d）项和（e）项，从而废除/撤销了 EGO 24/1998 规定的激励，包括原材料激励，但税收利润激励除外。废除本应自 Go 94/2004 生效之日（即 2004 年 12 月 3 日）起 90 天内生效。然而，根据 2004 年 11 月 22 日批准并修订了 GO94/2004 的第 507/2004 号法律，废除日期随后延长至 2005 年 2 月 22 日。

2005 年 7 月 28 日，申请人提出仲裁请求，鉴于上述情况，申请人认为罗马尼亚违约侵害了申请人在瑞典—罗马尼亚 BIT 和国际法规定的权利。具体来说，他们认为过早撤销"EGO24"激励：

a. 违反罗马尼亚对申请人作出的明确承诺，因此违反了 BIT 第 2 条（4）款中包含的 BIT 保护伞条款。

b. 损害了申请人的合法期望，扰乱了监管制度的稳定性，缺乏透明度和一致性，并被恶意对待，因此违反了罗马尼亚在 BIT 第 2 条（3）款下向申请人提供公平和公正待遇的义务。

c. 因不合理措施而损害了申请人投资的管理、维护、使用、享受和处置，因此违反了 BIT 第 2 条（3）款。

d. 申请人获得优惠的权利被无偿征收，并实质上剥夺了其全部价值投资，因此违反了 BIT 第 4 条（1）款。

The Claimants deny that the termination of the incentives was required under EU law. The Claimants allege that, to the contrary, the incentives were one of the factors that allowed Romania to accede to the EU in the first place. Indeed, the Claimants argue that Romania desperately needed economic development, particularly in certain distressed regions, to be able to join the EU. In their view, incentive programs such as EGO 24 greatly contributed to this development.

The Claimants argue that Romania has failed to show how the EGO 24 incentives conflicted with EU law and that Romania has not provided evidence that the EU required the termination of the incentives in order to obtain accession.

申请人否认激励措施是根据欧盟法律要求终止的。申请人声称，与此相反，激励措施是罗马尼亚能够加入欧盟的因素之一。事实上，申请人辩称罗马尼亚迫切需要经济发展，特别是在某些贫困地区，才能加入欧盟。在他们看来，像"EGO 24"这样的激励计划极大地促进了这一发展。

申请人辩称，罗马尼亚未能证明"EGO 24"激励机制与欧盟法律冲突，罗马尼亚也没有提供证据证明欧盟要求终止激励机制以获得加入。

仲裁结果（Award）

For the reasons stated in the body of this Award, the Tribunal makes the following decision:

a. The Claimants' claim that the Respondent has violated Article 2 (4) of the BIT by failing to observe obligations entered into with the Claimants with regard to their investments is dismissed by majority.

b. The Claimants' claim that the Respondent has violated Article 2 (3) of the BIT by failing to ensure fair and equitable treatment of the Claimants' investments is upheld by majority. In view of this decision, the Tribunal does not need to determine whether the Respondent has breached the BIT by impairing the Claimants' investments through unreasonable or discriminatory measures (Article 2 (3) of the BIT, second part) or by expropriating the Claimants' investments without the payment of prompt, adequate, and effective compensation (Article 4 (1) of the BIT).

c. As a result of the Respondent's breach of the BIT, the Claimants are awarded and the Respondent is ordered to pay RON 376,433,229 as damages, broken down as follows:

i. RON 85,100,000 for increased costs of sugar;

ii. RON 17,500,000 for increased costs of raw materials other than sugar or PET;

iii. RON 18,133,229 for the lost opportunity to stockpile sugar; and

iv. RON 255,700,000 for lost profits on sales of finished goods.

d. The Respondent is ordered to pay interest on the amount specified in subparagraph (c) above, at 3 – month ROBOR plus 5%, compounded on a quarterly basis, calculated from the following dates until full payment of the Award:

i. With respect to the claims for increased cost of sugar and other raw materials, interest shall be calculated from 1 March 2007.

ii. With respect to the claim for the lost opportunity to stockpile sugar, interest shall be calculated from 1 November 2009.

iii. With respect to the claim for lost profits on sales of finished goods, interest shall be calculated from 1 May 2008.

e. The Claimants on one side and the Respondent on the other shall bear the costs of the arbitration in equal shares, and each Party shall bear its own legal and other costs incurred in connection with this case.

f. All provisional measures recommended by the Tribunal will cease to have effect as of the date of dispatch of this Award.

g. All other claims or prayers for relief are dismissed.

基于本裁决书正文中所述的理由，仲裁庭作出以下决定：

一、申请人有关被申请人违反了 BIT 第 2 条（4）款未能遵守与申请人就其投资达成的义务的请求，被以多数驳回。

二、申请人有关被申请人因未能确保对申请人投资的公平和公正待遇而违反了 BIT 第 2 条（3）款的规定，获得多数人支持。鉴于这一决定，仲裁庭不需要裁定被申请人是否通过不合理或歧视性措施［BIT 第二部分第 2 条（3）款］损害申请人的投资，或在没有及时、充分和有效的支付补偿的情况下征收了申请人的投资［BIT 第 4 条（1）款］。

三、由于被申请人违反了 BIT，申请人被裁决给且被申请人被命令支付 376433229 列伊的损害赔偿金，具体如下：

（一）85100000 列伊用于糖的成本增加。

（二）17500000 列伊，用于糖或塑料以外的原材料成本的增加。

（三）18133229 列伊，因为失去了储存糖的机会。

（四）销售产成品利润损失 255700000 列伊。

四、要求被申请人支付上述第三项规定金额的利息，利率为 3 个月罗马尼亚同业拆借利率加上 5%，按季度计算复利，从以下日期开始计算，直至全额支付裁决：

（一）糖及其他原材料成本增加的索赔，利息自 2007 年 3 月 1 日起计算。

（二）对于失去储存糖机会的索赔，利息应从 2009 年 11 月 1 日开始计算。

（三）对产成品销售利润损失的索赔，利息自 2008 年 5 月 1 日起计算。

五、申请人一方和被申请人一方应均摊仲裁费用，双方各自承担与本案有关的法律费用和其他费用。

六、仲裁庭建议的所有临时措施自本裁决发出之日起失效。

七、所有其他索赔或请求均被驳回。

裁决原因（Reasons for the Award）

The Claimants argue that, through the EGO 24 framework, Romania entered into a specific obligation with the Claimants with regard to their investment, which consisted of Romania's undertaking with respect to the Claimants to maintain the EGO 24 incentives in the

Ştei-Nucet disfavored region for the full 10 – year period provided by GD 194/1999.

The majority does not find that the Claimants have provided sufficient evidence and legal-arguments on the content of Romanian law for the Tribunal to find the existence of an obligation protected by the umbrella clause. The majority accordingly dismisses the Claimants' umbrella clause claim, and the Tribunal will now address the Claimants' arguments in the context of their fair and equitable treatment claim, which spans the same injuries alleged by the Claimants under the umbrella clause.

申请人辩称，通过"EGO 24"框架，罗马尼亚与申请人就其投资达成了一项具体义务，其中包括罗马尼亚对申请人承诺在"不受欢迎地区"维持"EGO 24"激励直到GD194/1999 规定的全部 10 年期。

多数人认为，申请人没有就罗马尼亚法律的内容提供充分的证据和法律论据，以便仲裁庭发现存在受保护伞条款保护的义务。多数人因此驳回了申请人的保护伞条款索赔，仲裁庭现在将在他们的公平和公正待遇索赔范围内解决申请人的论点，该索赔范围涵盖了申请人根据保护伞条款提出的相同伤害。

Article 2 (3) of the BIT provides:

Each Contracting Party shall at all times ensure fair and equitable treatment of the investments by investors of the other Contracting Party and shall not impair the management, maintenance, use, enjoyment or disposal thereof, as well as the acquisition of goods and services or the sale of their production, through unreasonable or discriminatory measures.

BIT 第 2 条（3）款规定：

每一缔约国均应始终确保对另一缔约国的投资者的投资给予公平和公正的待遇，不得通过不合理或歧视性措施损害其对投资的管理、维护、使用、享受或处置，以及对货物和服务的获取或对其产品的销售。

The Parties agree that, in order to establish a breach of the fair and equitable treatment obligation based on an allegation that Romania undermined the Claimants' legitimate expectations, the Claimants must establish that (a) Romania made a promise or assurance, (b) the Claimants relied on that promise or assurance as a matter of fact, and (c) such reliance (and expectation) was reasonable. This test is consistent with the elements considered by other international tribunals.

In the Tribunal's view, elements (a) and (c) are related. There must be a promise, assurance or representation attributable to a competent organ or representative of the state, which may be explicit or implicit. The crucial point is whether the state, through statements or conduct, has contributed to the creation of a reasonable expectation, in this case, a representation of regulatory stability. It is irrelevant whether the state in fact wished to commit itself; it is sufficient that it acted in a manner that would reasonably be understood to create such an appearance. The element of reasonableness cannot be separated from the promise, assurance or representation, in particular if the promise is not contained in a contract or is otherwise stated explicitly. Whether a state has created a legitimate expectation in an investor is thus a factual assessment which must be undertaken in consideration of all the surrounding circumstances.

双方同意，为了确认罗马尼亚损害了申请人的合法预期从而违反了公平公正待遇的义务，申请人必须证实（a）罗马尼亚作出了承诺或保证；（b）申请人事实上依赖于该承诺或保证；（c）这种信赖（和期望）是合理的。这一衡量标准与其他国际仲裁庭所考虑的因素是一致的。

在仲裁庭看来，要素（a）和（c）是相关的。必须有可归因于主管机关或国家代表的承诺、保证或陈述，可以是明确的或隐含的。关键的一点是，国家是否通过声明或行为，从而创造了一个合理的预期，在本案中是对监管稳定性的陈述。事实上，国家是否愿意承诺是无关紧要的，只要它以将被合理地理解为创造了这样一种外在表现的方式行事就足够了。合理的因素不能与承诺、保证或陈述分开，特别是如果承诺未包含在合同中或另有明确规定。因此，一个国家是否在投资者身上创造了合法的期望，必须考虑到所有周围环境来进行事实上的评估。

As stated above, the Tribunal considers that, in determining whether the Claimants had a legitimate expectation, it must take account of the accepted principle that Romania is free to amend its laws and regulations absent an assurance to the contrary. However, in this case the Tribunal finds that Romania's conduct had included an element of inducement that required Romania to stand by its statements and its conduct. Romania launched a program directed to attract investors to the disfavored regions. To obtain that investment, it offered certain tax benefits for a certain amount of time. In other words, Romania created the appearance of a ten year tax holiday for investors who decided to invest in the disadvantaged area (and this appearance conformed to what Romania did in fact wish to enact). The Tribunal has noted in particular that the former president of the National Agency for Regional Development, Mr. Neculai Liviu Marcu, testified that the incentives were to be understood to be granted for the full duration of the disadvantaged area. In the Tribunal's view, Romania thereby made a representation that gave rise to the Permanent Investor Certificates (PIC) holders' legitimate expectation that during this tax holiday they would receive substantially the same benefits they were offered when they committed their investments.

如上所述，仲裁庭认为，在确定申请人是否有合法期望时，必须考虑到公认的原则，即罗马尼亚可以在没有相反保证的情况下自由修改其法律和法规。然而，在本案中，仲裁庭认为罗马尼亚的行为包括一种诱因，要求罗马尼亚坚持其声明和行为。罗马尼亚发起了一项旨在吸引投资者到不受欢迎地区的计划。为了获得这项投资，它在一定时间内提供了一定的税收优惠。换言之，罗马尼亚为决定投资落后地区的投资者创造了一个为期十年的免税期（这种情况与罗马尼亚实际上希望制定的政策一致）。仲裁庭特别注意到，国家区域发展局前主席内库莱·利维·马库先生作证说，激励措施应理解为允许在弱势地区的整个期间执行。仲裁庭认为，罗马尼亚因此做出了一项陈述，引起了永久投资认证持有人的合法期望，即在这个免税期内，他们将获得与他们进行投资时提供的实质相同的利益。

Taking all of this into consideration, it is clear that (i) not all of the Claimants' investments were predicated on the EGO 24 incentives; and (ii) even when the Claimants'took the EGO 24 incentives into account in making investment decisions, other factors also influenced the Claimants' decisions. However, the Tribunal is satisfied that a significant part of the Claimants' investments (from 2000 to 2004) were made in reliance on the incentives. In particular, the Tribunal is satisfied that the existence of the incentives was one of the reasons for the scale and manner of those investments. It is evident from the record that the Claimants built a large and complex platform for the production of food and drink products, and that its profits depended largely on the reduction of their operating costs resulting from the Raw Materials Incentive. Accordingly, the Tribunal is satisfied that the Claimants in fact relied on the incentives to build and develop their investment in the manner in which it stood at the date of the revocation of those incentives.

考虑到所有这些因素，很明显：（1）并非所有申请人的投资都是基于 EGO 24；（2）即使申请人在作出投资决策时考虑到 EGO 24，其他因素也会影响申请人的决策。但是，仲裁庭认为，申请人的大部分投资（2000 年至 2004 年）是依靠激励措施进行的。特别是，仲裁庭确信，激励措施的存在是这些投资规模和方式的原因之一。从记录中可以明显看出，申请人为食品和饮料产品的生产搭建了一个庞大而复杂的平台，其利润主要取决于原材料激励导致的运营成本的降低。因此，仲裁庭确信，申请人事实上依赖于激励措施，以这些激励措施被撤销时的方式建立和发展其投资。

For the reasons stated above, the Tribunal finds that, with one exception, Romania did not act unreasonably. Romania's decision to revoke the incentives was reasonably tailored to the pursuit of a rational policy (specifically, EU accession), and there was an appropriate correlation between that objective and the measure adopted to achieve it (i. e., the repeal of the EGO 24 incentives). The question is whether Romania could have negotiated a transition period for the incentives or their conversion into compatible aid. However, even if it could have done more, but failed to do so, objectively speaking the Tribunal does not find that it acted unreasonably. Even if Romania could have done more to maintain the incentives, its failure to negotiate transitional periods or compensation was not arbitrary, but appears justified under the specific circumstances of the accession negotiations.

基于上述理由，仲裁庭认为，除一个例外之外，罗马尼亚没有不合理行为。罗马尼亚撤销激励措施的决定是为了追求合理的政策（特别是加入欧盟），这一目标与为实现这一目标而采取的措施（即废除 EGO 24 激励措施）之间存在适当的相关性。问题在于，罗马尼亚是否可以为激励措施谈判获得过渡期或将其转化为可以兼容的资助措施。然而，虽然它本可以做得更多，但却未能做到这一点，客观地说，仲裁庭并不认为它的行为不合理。即使罗马尼亚本可以采取更多措施来维持这些激励措施，它未能谈判过渡期或给予补偿并非武断，且在加入谈判的具体情况下似乎是合理的。

The Tribunal concludes that, by repealing the EGO 24 incentives prior to 1 April 2009, Romania did not act unreasonably or in bad faith (except that the Respondent acted unreasonably by maintaining investors' obligations after terminating the incentives). The Tribunal, however, concludes by majority that Romania violated the Claimants' legitimate expectations that those incentives would be available, in substantially the same form, until 1 April 2009. Romania also failed to act transparently by failing to inform the Claimants in a timely manner that the regime would be terminated prior to its stated date of expiration. As a result, the Tribunal finds that Romania failed to "ensure fair and equitable treatment of the investments" of the Claimants in the meaning of Article 2 (3) of the BIT.

仲裁庭的结论是，通过在 2009 年 4 月 1 日之前废除 EGO 24 激励措施，罗马尼亚没有做出不合理或不诚实的行为（除了被申请人在终止激励措施后不合理地维持投资者的义务）。然而，仲裁庭以多数作出结论，认为罗马尼亚违反了申请人的合法期望，即在 2009 年 4 月 1 日之前，这些激励措施将以基本相同的形式提供。罗马尼亚也未能透明地采取行动，未能及时通知申请人该制度将在其规定的到期日前终止。因此，仲裁庭认为，罗马尼亚未能按照 BIT 第 2 条 （3） 款确保公平和公正地对待申请人投资。

裁决撤销或执行情况 （Annulment or Enforcement of the Award）

Approved Judgment of the English Court of Appeal (Civil Division)

In December 2013, at ICSID, Ioan Micula, Viorel Micula, S. C. European Food S. A, S. C. Starmill S. R. L. and S. C. Multipack S. R. L. v. Romania. The winning bid by investors is about \$2. 5 billion. One particular aspect of the case is the commission's decision in March 2015 to declare a breach of eu competition law if Romania complied with the ruling. This is because the case is brought under the so-called bilateral investment treaty between eu countries, and the commission argues that the document has been replaced by eu law. At the same time, enforcement procedures in the United States have been hampered by procedural problems. In October 2017, the U. S. federal second circuit court of appeals rejected the Micula brothers' enforcement application, arguing that they did not serve Romania properly because they filed a summary ex parte proceedings.

2013 年 12 月，在解决投资争端国际中心，案件是 Viorel Micula 与 Ioan Micula 兄弟与罗马尼亚之间就罗马尼亚撤销经济优惠的行为的争议，投资者胜诉标的额约 25 亿美元。该案的一个特别之处在于，欧盟委员会于 2015 年 3 月曾作出一项决定，表示如果罗马尼亚履行了该裁决，将违反欧盟竞争法。这是因为该案是根据所谓的欧盟国家间双边投资条约提起的，而欧盟委员会则主张该文件已经被欧盟法律取代。同时，在美国进行的执行程序也被程序性问题所阻碍。2017 年 10 月，美国联邦第二巡回上诉法院驳回了 Micula 兄弟的执行申请，认为他们并没有按照正当程序送达罗马尼亚，因为他们提起的是单方简易程序。

Suffice it to say, that the ultimate conclusion on the present appeals, on which all members of the Court are agreed, is that there should be a stay on enforcement until the conclusion of the General Court of the EU proceedings (or further order in the meantime). We also all agree that Romania should provide security in the sum of £ 150m as a term of such stay but on the basis that the sanction for any non-compliance with the order for security (which we would not in any way expect or encourage) will not of itself (save possibly if forinstance there is some exceptional change of circumstances) lead to the termination of the stay which we have ordered.

可以说，本次上诉的最终结论是，法院所有成员都同意在欧盟综合法院程序结束之前（或在此期间进一步的命令）应暂停执行。我们还同意，罗马尼亚应提供 1.5 亿英镑作为该暂停执行裁决期限的担保，其前提是，任何与担保命令不相符的措施（我们不会以任何方式期望或鼓励）不会（除非可能存在情况的特殊变化）导致我们所要求的暂停执行终止。

案件影响（Impact of the Case）

从 2005 年提起仲裁到 2013 年 12 月做出决定，本案争议旷日持久。本案的一个特别之处在于，欧盟委员会于 2015 年 3 月曾作出一项决定，表示如果罗马尼亚履行了该裁决，将违反欧盟竞争法。这是因为该案是根据所谓的欧盟国家间双边投资条约提起的，而欧盟委员会则主张该文件已经被欧盟法律取代。在本案审理过程中，被申请人罗马尼亚也提到这一点抗辩意见，认为取消该税收优惠是应欧盟法律的要求而不得已为之。仲裁庭认为罗马尼亚在取消优惠措施方面虽具有合理性，但在具体努力维护投资者既得的合理期待方面还做得不够，因此裁决罗马尼亚承担违反公平公正待遇的责任。

裁决做出后，申请人米库拉兄弟在美国、英国、瑞典、比利时等国的法院先后提出诉讼要求承认和执行本裁定。在英国的诉讼程序对申请人是有利的，要求罗马尼亚为暂停裁决执行缴纳了保证金。本案裁决涉及的对欧盟国家间的双边投资条约的合法性问题，还有待更权威的结论。

思考问题（Questions）

1. 如何认定投资者对东道国法律或政策的预期是合理的？
2. 关于暂缓执行 ICSID 判决的判定依据是什么？

案例十二 斯塔蒂诉哈萨克斯坦案

Anatolie Stati，Gabriel Stati，Ascom Group S. A. and Terra Raf Trans Traiding Ltd. v. The Republic of Kazakhstan（2013）（SCC Arbitration V（116/2010））

选读理由（Selected Reason）

本案是斯德哥尔摩商事仲裁院仲裁庭根据《能源宪章公约》审理的安纳托利·斯塔蒂等四个申请人与哈萨克斯坦的国际投资争端案件。仲裁庭在实体上支持了申请人有关东道国违反了公平公正待遇义务的诉求，在2013年裁决哈萨克斯坦败诉，裁决书长达400多页，裁决赔偿金额连同应承担的律师费用超过5亿美元。裁决作出后，哈萨克斯坦在瑞典斯维亚上诉法院寻求撤销该仲裁裁决，申请人则寻求在英国和美国执行该裁决，从而围绕裁决结果形成了一系列的法院判决，涉及到了申请人涉嫌欺诈而违反公共政策的禁反言问题，从而对该裁决应否被承认和执行引发了争论。

仲裁申请情况（The Request for Arbitration）

Natural hydrocarbon resources are one of the principal assets of the Republic. Within the next ten years，Kazakhstan will be among the top five oil producers，holding 30 billion barrels of proven oil and 85 trillion cubic feet of gas reserves. Kazpolmunay LLP（KPM）and Tolkyn-neftegaz LLP（TNG）were important to the economic framework of and have played a strategic role in the Mangystau region's economy，providing 80% of the fuel needed for the local power plant and employing a considerable number of people.

Claimant Anatolie Stati is a natural citizen of Moldova and Romania who has invested in Turkmenistan since 1995. Based on his testimony and the testimony of Prof. Olcott at the Hearing on Jurisdiction and Liability, Respondent argues that Anatolie Stati was a "novice" in the oil and gas industry when he entered Kazakhstan. Respondent presents a history of the Stati family's involvement in Moldova's politics, as well as in the politics and businesses of other states. Claimants and Respondent agree that Anatolie Stati is not a political opponent of President Nazarbayev.

天然烃资源是哈萨克斯坦共和国的主要资产之一。在未来十年内，哈萨克斯坦将成为前五大石油生产国之一，拥有 300 亿桶已探明石油和 85 万亿立方英尺的天然气储量。KPM 公司和 TNG 公司对曼格斯套地区的经济框架非常重要，并在该地区的经济中发挥了战略作用，为当地发电厂提供了 80% 的燃料，雇用了大量的人员。

申请人安纳托利·斯塔蒂是摩尔多瓦和罗马尼亚的自然公民，自 1995 年以来一直在土库曼斯坦投资。根据他的证词和奥尔科特教授在管辖权和责任听证会上的证词，被申请人辩称，安纳托利·斯塔蒂进入哈萨克斯坦时是石油和天然气行业的"新手"。被申请人介绍了斯塔蒂家族参与摩尔多瓦政治以及其他国家政治和商业的历史。申请人和被申请人同意安纳托利·斯塔蒂不是纳扎尔巴耶夫总统的政治对手。

Claimant Gabriel Stati is a natural citizen of Moldova and Romania and is the son of Anatolie Stati. Claimant Ascom Group S. A. is a joint stock company incorporated under the laws of Moldova, with headquarters in Moldova. Ascom's operational subsidiaries were located in Kazakhstan. The Parties dispute whether Anatolie Stati owned 100% of Ascom, which owned 100% of KPM or that Ascom has substantial business activities in or is controlled from Moldova. Respondent argued that Anatolie Stati is Ascom's 100% shareholder. Claimant Terra Raf Trans Traiding Ltd. is a limited liability company incorporated under the laws of Gibraltar.

Respondent states that Tristan Oil Ltd. ("Tristan") is an affiliate of KPM and TNG and is 100% owned by Anatolie Stati. Tristan was created as a special purpose vehicle with the purpose of issuing notes.

申请人加布里埃尔斯·塔蒂是摩尔多瓦和罗马尼亚的自然公民，是安纳托利·斯塔蒂的儿子。申请人阿斯康集团公司是一家根据摩尔多瓦法律成立的股份有限公司，总部位于摩尔多瓦。阿斯康的运营子公司位于哈萨克斯坦。仲裁当事双方对安纳托利·斯塔蒂是否拥有阿斯康 100% 的股份（阿斯康拥有 KPM 100% 的股份）或阿斯康在摩尔多瓦境内是否有实质性的商业活动或其控制权是否来自摩尔多瓦存在争议。被申请人辩称，安纳托利·斯塔蒂是阿斯康的 100% 股东。申请人特拉夫特朗贸易有限公司是一家根据直布罗陀法律成立的有限责任公司。

被申请人声明，特里斯坦石油有限公司（以下简称"特里斯坦"）是 KPM 和 TNG

的附属公司，100%由安纳托利·斯塔蒂公司所有。特里斯坦是被创设用来发行债券的特殊目的的公司。

According to Kazakhstan's own figures, between 2000 and 2009, Claimants invested US $473 million in KPM and US $693 million in TNG, a total in excess of US $1.1 billion [and] paid over US $350 million in tax revenues to the Kazakh State. KPM and TNG permanently employed nearly 1,000 Kazakh workers, and TNG employed some 3,000 additional contract workers to construct the LPG Plant.

Claimants' substantial investments transformed the previously fallow Borankol and Tolkyn fields into significant producers of oil, gas, and condensate. By 2010, Claimants had over 70 operational wells in the Borankol field and a total of 40 wells in the Tolkyn field and Contract 302 area. As of 2008, Claimants had produced 12 million barrels of oil and condensate ("MBbls") and 22 billion cubic feet ("bcf") of gas from the Borankol field, and 11 MBbls oil and condensate and 246 bcf of gas from the Tolkyn field. As a result of Claimants' investments, TNG became the fourth largest gas producer in Kazakhstan.

Claimants also invested more than US $240 million in construction of an LPG Plant, which was substantially complete before construction was halted as a result of the State's misconduct. Kazakhstan viewed the LPG Plant as a "strategic asset" for the Mangystau region. Claimants also conducted extensive exploration and production work on TNG's Contract 302 Properties, including drilling the "Munaibay 1" well, shooting 3D seismic, and acquiring a deep drilling rig to explore the considerable "Interoil Reef" prospect.

根据哈萨克斯坦自己的数据，2000年至2009年期间，申请人向KPM投资了4.73亿美元，向TNG投资了6.93亿美元，总计超过11亿美元［和］向哈萨克斯坦支付了3.5亿美元的税收。KPM和TNG永久雇用了近1000名哈萨克斯坦工人，TNG又雇用了约3000名合同工来建造液化石油气工厂。

申请人的大量投资将之前处于闲置的波兰科尔和托尔金油田转变为重要的石油、天然气和凝析油生产者。到2010年，申请人在波兰科尔油田拥有70多口作业井，在托尔金油田和302号合同区共有40口井。截至2008年，申请人已从波兰科尔生产了1200万桶石油、凝析油（"MBbls"）和220亿立方英尺天然气（"BCF"），从托尔金油田生产了1100万桶石油、凝析油和2460亿立方英尺天然气。由于申请人的投资，TNG成为哈萨克斯坦第四大天然气生产商。

申请人还投资超过2.4亿美元建设液化石油气工厂，该工厂在因国家不当行为而暂停建设之前基本完工。哈萨克斯坦将液化石油气工厂视为曼格斯套地区的"战略资产"。申请人还对TNG的302号合同区域进行了广泛的勘探和生产工作，包括钻探穆纳伊湾1号井、拍摄3D地震波，以及购买一台深层钻机以勘探预期前景重大的

"油间礁"。

In summer 2008, Claimants made an "independent business decision" to explore a sale of KPM, TNG, and the LPG Plant, excepting the Contract 302 properties (the so-called Tabyl Block). This was nicknamed "Project Zenith" and Claimants retained Renaissance Capital to facilitate the sale process. They included Kaz Munai Gas (KMG) in the potential purchaser targets, since they would not be in business with the buyer thereafter. Renaissance Capital sent KMG the Information Memorandum and the Due Diligence presentation, both of which contained substantial details about the companies and their assets. On 25 September 2008, KMG submitted an offer of USD 754 million, for KPM and TNG (minus the Contract 302 properties). This was the third lowest offer. Less than three weeks later, however, President Nazarbayev issued his order to investigate Claimants' companies, resulting in a "barrage of investigations, false accusations, exorbitant tax assessments, and criminal prosecutions." Claimants argue that the "timing alone supports a strong inference that President Nazarbayev issued his order to help tip the scales in KazMunaiGaz's favor in the Project Zenith. The events that unfolded over the next 20 months make that inference extremely clear." In particular, Claimants highlight the following events:

2008 年夏季，申请人做出了"独立的商业决定"，以寻求销售 KPM、TNG 和液化石油气工厂，但不包括 302 号合同区域的资产（所谓的泰比区块）。这被称为"天顶项目"，申请人聘请了复兴资本公司以推进销售。他们将哈萨克斯坦国家石油公司（"KMG"）纳入潜在买家目标，因为此后他们将不再与买家开展业务。复兴资本公司向 KMG 发送了信息备忘录和尽职调查报告，两者都包含了公司及其资产的实质性细节。2008 年 9 月 25 日，KMG 向 KPM 和 TNG 提交了 7.54 亿美元的报价（减去 302 号合同区域）。这是第三个最低报价。然而，不到三周后，纳扎尔巴耶夫总统发布了调查申请人公司的命令，导致了"一连串的调查、虚假指控、过高的税务评估和刑事起诉"。申请人辩称，"仅时间要求一项就足以形成这一结论，即纳扎尔巴耶夫总统发布命令，帮助哈萨克斯坦国家石油公司在'天顶项目'中占有优势。接下来 20 个月发生的事件使这一推论非常清楚"。具体而言，申请人强调了以下事件：

• On November 11, 2008, the Financial Police's issuance of a finding that KPM did not have a main pipeline license, paving the way for the criminal trial and US $ 145 million fine on KPM;

• On December 18, 2008, the MEMR's reversal of its pre-emptive rights waiver as to TNG, and issuance of a press release alleging forgery and fraud in connection with the registration of TNG;

• On February 10, 2009, the assessment of US $ 62 million in back taxes, disregarding stabilization guarantees in its Subsoil Use Contracts; and

- On April 29, 2009, the arrest of KPM's general director.

● 2008 年 11 月 11 日,金融警察声称其发现 KPM 没有主管道许可证,这为对 KPM 进行刑事审判和 1.45 亿美元的罚款铺平了道路;

● 2008 年 12 月 18 日,哈萨克斯坦能源和矿产资源部,"MEMR" 撤销了对 TNG 的优先购买权的弃权声明,并发布了一份新闻稿,指控 TNG 注册过程中存在伪造和欺诈行为。

● 2009 年 2 月 10 日,不考虑其底土使用合同中的稳定保证条款,评估出了 6200 万美元的欠缴税款。

● 2009 年 4 月 29 日,逮捕了 KPM 董事长。

On 21 July 2010, the State delivered to KPM and TNG two written notices terminating KPM Subsoil Use Contract 305 covering the Borankol field, and terminating TNG Subsoil Use Contract 210 covering the Tolkyn field. The State did not deliver a specific written notice terminating TNG Subsoil Use Contract 302 covering the Tabyl Block, which the State says expired on 30 March 2009. On the same date, pursuant to the legislation, the MOG and KMG agreed to two trust management agreements over the subsoil areas for the Tolkyn and Borankol. Respondent stressed that these agreements transferred the property into temporary possession of KMG NC as a result of the termination of the contracts until a new subsoil useris found. While terminating the contracts, the State made no claim that KPM and TNG owed outstanding corporate income taxes, transfer pricing taxes or export duties.

2010 年 7 月 21 日,政府向 KPM 和 TNG 发送了两份书面通知,终止 KPM 涉及波兰科尔油田的 305 号底土使用合同,终止 TNG 的涉及托尔金油田的 210 号底土使用合同。政府没有发出具体的书面通知终止 TNG 涉及泰比区块的 302 号底土使用合同,政府方面称该合同于 2009 年 3 月 30 日到期。同一天,根据法律,哈萨克斯坦石油天然气部("MOG")和 KMG 就托尔金和波兰科尔的底土区达成了两项信托管理协议。被申请人强调,由于合同终止,在找到新的底土用户之前,这些协议将财产临时占有权转让给了 KMG 国家公司。在终止合同的同时,国家没有声称 KPM 和 TNG 欠下未付的公司所得税、转让定价税或出口税。

On 22 July 2010, all revenues generated from oil and gas production were put into a separate escrow account held by KMG.

On 23 July 2010, KPM and TNG received letters from the MOG stating that, due to the unilateral termination of the contract from 00 hrs. 00 min. of 22 July 2010 all products produced on the enterprise had been transferred to the ownership of the Republic of Kazakhstan.

On 28 July 2010, Respondent employed the attorney provisions set out in Article 72

(10) of the Subsoil Law and to arrange for an agreement to be entered into for the transfer of property to KMG.

2010 年 7 月 22 日，所有石油和天然气生产产生的收入都存入了 KMG 持有的独立托管账户。

2010 年 7 月 23 日，KPM 和 TNG 收到来自 MOG 的信函，说明由于合同从 00 点单方面终止。2010 年 7 月 22 日 00 点，企业生产的所有产品已转归哈萨克斯坦共和国所有。

2010 年 7 月 28 日，被申请人雇佣律师适用《底土法》第 72 条（10）款规定起草了文本，并安排签订协议，将财产转让给 KMG。

Claimants argue that Respondent runs a "playbook" of harassment to coerce investors and to enrich powerful Kazakhs. The playbook typically commences with an executive-mandated investigative onslaught and ends with a firesale of assets to the State or an outright seizure. Groundless tax claims are an important element of the playbook. Respondent used these harassing and intimidating tactics to coerce Claimants into selling their investments to KMG at a firesale price and, when that failed, seized the investments under the appearance of legitimacy.

As time continued, Respondent simply turned up the pressure. Kazakhstan interfered in the trial of Mr. Cornegruta to ensure a guilty verdict and then sentenced him to four years' incarceration in a notoriously dangerous prison system. Kazakhstan then threatened to do the same to KPM and TNG's other directors. Kazakhstan levied a massive fine against KPM that was large enough to bankrupt the company and provide a ground for seizing the assets. Through the continued inspections, audits, and seizures, Kazakhstan continued to interferewith the day-to-day operations of the business. Then, in November 2009, KMG made another, even lower bid to buy the companies.

申请人诉称，被申请人在按照一个"剧本"骚扰和强迫投资者以使有权力的哈萨克斯坦人获得财富。该剧本通常以执行官授权的调查性袭击开始，以向国家出售资产或直接扣押结束。毫无根据的税务追索是剧本的一个重要组成部分。被申请人使用这些骚扰和恐吓手段，强迫申请人以超低价将其投资给 KMG，在失败后以表面合法的形式没收了这些投资。

Claimants' contentions are taken from their own words, without prejudice to their further arguments：

The campaign against Claimants' investments in KPM and TNG that Kazakhstan commenced in the final quarter of 2008 breached the ECT and international law in multiple respects. It clearly entailed indirect expropriation, because it materially interfered with Claimants' ability to manage, use, and dispose of their investments. The measures Kazakhstan adopted — interference with contractual rights, wrongful exercises of administrative and judicial authority, sequestration of the companies' assets and Claimants' shares, assessment of spurious tax penalties, and harassment and persecution of key personnel — all fall squarely within the bounds of indirect expropriation as understood in international law and treaty practice.

Kazakhstan's campaign was equally a violation of the ECT's fair and equitable treatment and impairment provisions, as well as its "most constant protection and security" clause. Kazakhstan subjected Claimants' investments in KPM and TNG to severe harassment and coercion as well as inconsistent and contradictory conduct, and it created an environment that was thoroughly unstable and unpredictable (if not treacherous).

Kazakhstan also flagrantly violated due process and committed "denial of justice" in relation to KPM and its general director. At the same time, Kazakhstan's state apparatus, led by the Financial Police, utterly failed to provide legal (and in some cases physical) protection and security to Claimants' investments and personnel, much less the "most constant protection and security" required by the ECT.

从申请人自己的文件中摘出如下主张，且不影响其做进一步争辩：

哈萨克斯坦于 2008 年第四季度开始的针对申请人在 KPM 和 TNG 投资的运动在多个方面违反了《能源宪章条约》（ECT）和国际法。这显然是间接征收，因为它严重干扰了申请人管理、使用和处置其投资的能力。哈萨克斯坦采取的措施——干涉合同权利、不当行使行政和司法权力、扣押公司资产和申请人的股份、评估虚假的税收处罚、骚扰和迫害关键人员，全部属于国际法和条约惯例所理解的间接征收范围内。

哈萨克斯坦的运动同样违反了 ECT 的公平公正待遇和减值条款，以及"最持续的保护和保障"条款。哈萨克斯坦使申请人对 KPM 和 TNG 的投资遭受严重的骚扰和胁迫，以及不一致和矛盾的行为，并创造了一个完全不稳定和不可预测的环境（如果不是危险的话）。

哈萨克斯坦还公然违反了正当程序，并在与 KPM 及其董事长有关的问题上"拒绝司法"。与此同时，由金融警察领导的哈萨克斯坦国家机构完全未能为申请人的投资和人员提供法律（在某些情况下是物质上）的保护和保障，更没有提供 ECT 所要求的"最持续的保护和保障"。

Kazakhstan also breached key provisions of Claimants' Subsoil Use Contracts. For example, Kazakhstan imposed groundless and extracontractual tax assessments on KPM and TNG, and perhaps most notably, it terminated those contracts in violation of their termination provisions. Those acts were breaches of the ECT's "umbrella clause".

In July 2010, Kazakhstan directly expropriated Claimants' investments by terminating KPM's and TNG's Subsoil Use Contracts and seizing their assets outright. Like the campaign that preceded it, Kazakhstan's ultimate expropriation was thoroughly groundless and illegal. By that point, however, Claimants' investments had already suffered 20 months of indirect expropriation and other mistreatment that clearly violated the standards of protection afforded by the ECT and international law.

哈萨克斯坦还违反了申请人的底土使用合同的关键条款。例如，哈萨克斯坦对 KPM 和 TNG 进行了无根据的和合同外的税务评估，最值得注意的是，它违反了终止条款终止了这些合同。这些行为违反了 ECT 的"保护伞条款"。

2010 年 7 月，哈萨克斯坦终止了 KPM 和 TNG 的底土使用合同，并直接没收了申请人的投资。就像之前的运动一样，哈萨克斯坦的最终征收是毫无根据和非法的。然而，到那时，申请人的投资已经遭受了 20 个月的间接征收和其他虐待，明显违反了 ECT 和国际法提供的保护标准。

Claimants make the following contentions regarding compensation:

Tolkyn	US \$478,927,000
Borankol	US \$197,013,000
Munaibay Oil	US \$96,808,000
LPG Plant	US \$245,000,000 cost plus discretionary portion of US \$84,077,000
Contract 302 (other than Munaibay Oil)	US \$31,330,000 cost plus discretionary portion of US \$1,498,017,000

Claimants contend that they are entitled to (1) compound interest at an appropriate rate; (2) recovery of principal, interest, and penalties on the Tristan notes; (3) moral damages in the amount of 10% of the total compensatory damages awarded to Claimants; (4) a full award on costs.

申请人提出下列要求赔偿的内容：托尔金油田 478927000 美元；波兰科尔油田 197013000 美元；穆纳伊湾油井 96808000 美元；液化石油气工厂 245000000 美元成本加酌定部分 84077000 美元；302 号合同（不含穆纳伊湾油井）31330000 美元成本加酌定部分 1498017000 美元。

申请人主张，他们有权（1）以适当的利率要求复利；（2）收回特里斯坦票据的本金、利息和罚款；（3）给予申请人的赔偿金总额 10% 的精神损害赔偿金；（4）全额支付费用。

仲裁结果（Award）

For the reasons set out above in this award, the tribunal hereby decides, declares, and awards as follows.

1. The respondent has violated its obligations under the energy charter treaty with respect to the claimant investments.

2. Subtracting the subtotal of debts (USD $ 10,444,899.00) from the subtotal of compensation due (USD $ 508,130,000.00), the tribunal decides that respondent shall pay to claimants a net amount of USD $ 497,685,101.00.

3. This net amount is to be paid from respondent to claimants with interests, defined as the rate of 6 months US Treasury bills from 30 April 2009 to the date of payment, compounded semi-annually.

4.1. Of the costs of arbitration as determined by the Arbitration Institute of The Stockholm Chamber of Commerce (SCC), Respondent shall bear 3/4 and Claimants 1/4. These arbitration costs will be drawn from the advances paid by the Parties to the SCC.

4.2. Further, Respondent shall pay to Claimants 50% of Claimants' costs of legal representation, i.e. an amount of USD 8,975,496.40.

5. All other claims are dismissed.

Place of Arbitration: Stockholm (Sweden)

基于本裁决书中上述理由，仲裁庭特此决定、宣布和裁决如下。

1. 被申请人违反了其在《能源宪章条约》下与申请人投资有关的义务。

2. 从应付赔偿金小计（508130000.00 美元）中减去债务小计（10444899.00 美元），仲裁庭决定被申请人应向申请人支付赔偿净额497685101.00 美元。

3. 净金额将由被申请人连同利息支付给申请人，利息自 2009 年 4 月 30 日至付款日按 6 个月期的美国国债利率计算，每半年复利一次。

4.1. 在斯德哥尔摩商会仲裁院确定的仲裁费用中，被申请人应承担 3/4，申请人应承担 1/4。这些仲裁费用将从各方给斯德哥尔摩商会仲裁院支付的预付款中提取。

4.2. 此外，被申请人应向申请人支付申请人律师费的 50%，即 8975496.40 美元。

5. 驳回所有其他索赔。

仲裁地点：斯德哥尔摩（瑞典）

裁决原因 (Reasons for the Award)

The Tribunal need not opine on whether the pipeline was a field or trunk pipeline in order to find that the procedure surrounding the discovery was in violation of the FET standard. The Parties have presented that Claimants operated a pipeline system that was approved by Kazakh authorities. During routine inspections from 2002 – until November 2008, there was no indication that anyone believed that the pipelines were trunk pipelines and Respondent has provided no indication that the proper authorities were in any way prevented from having made the same discovery sooner. Instead, the evidence demonstrates that, it was not until immediately prior to the "discovery", namely on 12 November 2008, that the Financial Police began to seek information on whether KPM and TNG held licenses to operate trunk pipelines. On Friday, 14 November 2008, the Financial Police received confirmation that neither company held such licenses. Immediately thereafter, on the following Monday, 17 November 2008, the Financial Police "discovered" that KPM and TNG operated a trunk pipeline and ordered the Tax Committee to calculate profit earned from operating that pipeline.

Taking into account the above considerations, the Tribunal concludes that Respondent's measures, seen cumulatively in context to each other and compared with the treatment of Claimants' investments before the Order of the President of the Republic on 14/16 October 2008, constituted a string of measures of coordinated harassment by various institutions of Respondent. These measures must be considered as a breach of the obligation to treat investors fairly and equitably, as required by Art. 10 (1) ECT.

仲裁庭无须就管道是油田管道还是干线管道发表意见，以确认相关程序违反了公平公正待遇标准。双方提出，申请人运营的管道系统经哈萨克斯坦当局批准。在 2002 年至 2008 年 11 月的例行检查中，没有迹象表明有人相信这些管道是主干管道，而被申请人也没有提供任何迹象表明主管当局以任何方式阻止早日做出这样的发现。相反，证据表明，直到 2008 年 11 月 12 日"发现"的很短时间之前，金融警察才开始寻求有关 KPM 和 TNG 是否持有干线管道运营许可证的信息。2008 年 11 月 14 日星期五，金融警察收到确认，两家公司均未持有此类许可证。紧接着，在 2008 年 11 月 17 日的下一个星期一，金融警察"发现"了 KPM 和 TNG 运营的一条主干管道，并命令税务委员会计算运营该管道获得的利润。

综合上述考虑，仲裁庭得出结论，被申请人采取的措施与 2008 年 10 月 14 日或 16 日国家总统命令前给申请人投资的待遇相比，在相互关联的情况下累积出现，构成了一系列由被申请人的各个机构相互协调进行骚扰的措施。这些措施必须被视为违反了 ECT 第 10 条（1）款所要求的公平公正对待投资者的义务。

It is the mandate of the Tribunal to decide on the Relief Sought by the Parties, no less, but also no more. The Tribunal notes that Claimants, in their Relief Sought as cited above in this Award, do not request a separate amount allegedly caused by their prevention from selling the investment, but rather base their amounts requested on alleged violations related to the Borankol and Tolkyn Fields and Munaibay Oil, to the Contract 302 Properties, and to the LPG Plant. Therefore, the Tribunal hereafter will focus on these claims and considers that it does not have to decide whether Respondent's actions prevented Claimants from selling their investments, unless this issue may become relevant for one of the claims raised. This will be taken into account in the Tribunal's examination of the respective claims hereafter.

仲裁庭的任务是决定各当事方所寻求的救济，不可少，也不可多。仲裁庭注意到，申请人在本裁决书上文所述寻求的救济中，并未要求单独计算因出售投资被他们阻止而导致损失金额，其索赔的金额是以与波兰科尔和托尔金油田、穆纳湾油田、302 号合同区域、液化石油气工厂有关的违约行为为基础。因此，仲裁庭此后将关注这些索赔，并认为不必确定被申请人的行为是否阻止了申请人出售其投资，除非该问题可能与所提出的其中一项索赔有关。这将在下文仲裁庭对各项索赔进行审查时予以考虑。

Turning to the question of which is the valuation date to be selected, the Tribunal considers that the date of 14 or 16 October 2008 suggested by Claimants cannot be accepted. Claimants have not shown that, already at that time, any damages were caused by Respondent's breaches of the ETC. Though the President's Order in October almost immediately caused various government actions against Claimants' investment, which were the beginning of a continuing breach of the FET-standard of the ECT, as seen above in the chapter on causation in this Award, the effects of these breaches damaging the investments only started in December 2008.

The Tribunal considers that only by 30 April 2009, when the State sequestration of Claimants' KPM and TNG shares and assets occurred, actual, and permanent damages could be identified for the investments.

关于选择哪一个估价日期的问题，仲裁庭认为不能接受申请人建议的 2008 年 10 月 14 日或 16 日的日期。申请人没有证明，在当时，任何损害都是由于被申请人违反 ETC 造成的。尽管总统在 10 月的命令几乎立即导致了政府对申请人投资的各种行动，这只是对申请人的投资持续违反 ECT 的 FET 标准的开始。如上文中关于本裁决因果关系的章节所述，这些违规行为对投资造成的影响直到 2008 年 12 月才开始。

仲裁庭认为，只有到 2009 年 4 月 30 日，当国家对申请人的 KPM 和 TNG 股份和资产进行扣押时，才能确定投资的实际和永久损害。

The Parties agree that the Discounted Cash Flow (DCF) methodology is an appropriate method of calculation. The Tribunal agrees as well, as this method has been used in many comparable cases and decisions of other Tribunals. This Tribunal sees no reason not to apply it here. The Tribunal now turns to the issues of application of that method disputed between the Parties and their experts.

After evaluation of the timeline of events summarized above in the chapter on causation, the Tribunal accepts Claimants' argument that Respondent's conduct, which was found above to be a breach of the ECT, including the liquidity shortage insofar as it was also caused by Respondent, forced Claimants to reduce development efforts at Borankol and Tolkyn fields and that, in particular, this caused Claimants to decide not to drill or recomplete 13 wells at Borankol and Tolkyn in 2009 – 2010.

1619. In this context, the Tribunal considers that Claimants have provided sufficient proof for three kinds of damages: (1) KPM and TNG lost revenue that they would have earned from their planned production; (2) the gap in the development efforts depressed the production-curve at Tolkyn and Borankol more than it would have been, had Claimants been able to develop the fields without Respondent's breaching conduct; (3) Claimants were unable to sufficiently respond to the watering issues at the Tolkyn field.

双方同意，现金流量折现法是一种适当的计算方法。仲裁庭也同意这一点，因为这种方法已用于许多可类比案件和其他仲裁庭的判决。仲裁庭认为没有理由不在这里适用。现在，仲裁庭将讨论双方及其专家之间存在争议的这种方法的适用问题。

在对因果关系一章中概述的上述事件时间表进行评估后，仲裁庭接受了申请人的论点，即上述被认定为违反 ECT 的被申请人行为，包括因被申请人造成的流动性短缺，迫使申请人减少了波兰科尔和托尔金油田的开发工作，特别是这导致申请人决定在 2009—2010 年不在波兰科尔和托尔金钻取或重新完成 13 口井。

在这种情况下，仲裁庭认为，申请人已经为三种损害提供了充分的证据：(1) KPM 和 TNG 损失了他们从计划生产中获得的收入；(2) 开发工作的差距，降低了与假设申请人能够在没有被申请人违约行为的情况下相比较，开发波兰科尔和托尔金油田的增长态势；(3) 申请人无法对托尔金油田的水回灌问题作出充分的响应。

In particular, before Respondent's interference, it could be expected that export of gas would be possible. The CAC Pipeline-a direct export route-is proximate to the Tolkyn field. At the time, Respondent was forecasting both an expansion of total gas production from 33.7 Bcm^3 in 2008 to 61.5 Bcm^3 by 2015, with a concomitant export volume expansion from 6.2 Bcm^3 in 2008 to 12.9 Bcm^3 in 2015. Claimants' right to export gas is relevant to TNG's and its prospective purchaser's reasonable expectations as of 14 October 2008. The Tripartite Agreement confirms that TNG would be able to export gas. As Respondent itself rightly points out, the Tripartite Agreement represented a bargain-if TNG were to deliver gas to a strategic project, TNG would have the opportunity to sell gas. KMG executed the 17 November 2008 Agreement, giving its clear indication that gas exports could be presumed to be available to a prospective purchaser upon entry into negotiations with KMG, regardless of the KazAzot fertilizer project. The Tribunal is not persuaded by Respondent's argument that an Agreement it effectively executed itself for TNG gas exports and export pricing is no evidence of the right, expectation, and ability to export gas. The non-implemantation of the Agreement was part of and due to the Respondent's conduct found to be in breach of the ECT. The same is true for Respondent's argument that there would have been be a sharp decline in oil production beginning in 2009, brought about by the end of the contract with TNG's biggest customer, Kemikal. As suggested by Respondent itself, Kemikal stopped payments on Claimants' products because of liquidity and insolvency issues, but, as also discussed earlier in this Award, this discontinuance of payments was caused by Respondent's own breaching actions.

具体而言，在被申请人介入之前，可以预期天然气的出口是可能的。CAC 管道——一条直接出口路线——靠近托尔金油田。当时，被申请人预测到 2015 年，天然气总产量将从 2008 年的 337 亿立方米增至 615 亿立方米，同时出口量将从 2008 年的 62 亿立方米增至 2015 年的 129 亿立方米。截至 2008 年 10 月 14 日，申请人出口天然气的权利与 TNG 及其潜在买方的合理预期有关。三方协议确认，TNG 将能够出口天然气。正如被申请人自己正确指出的那样，三方协议代表了一个交易——如果 TNG 将天然气输送给一个战略项目，TNG 将有机会出售天然气。哈萨克斯坦国家石油天然气公司（KMG）执行了 2008 年 11 月 17 日的协议，明确表示，在与哈萨克斯坦国家石油天然气公司进行谈判时，无论卡扎佐的化肥项目如何，都可以假定天然气出口可供潜在买家使用。被申请人的论点不足以说服仲裁庭，即其为 TNG 天然气出口和出口定价而有效执行的协议并不能证明出口天然气的权利、预期和能力。协议的不执行是被申请人违反 ECT 的行为的一部分，也是由于被申请人违反 ECT 的行为造成的。被申请人的观点也是如此，即自 2009 年起，石油产量将大幅下降，这是 TNG 最大客户凯美卡与该公司签订的合同到期后所导致的。正如被申请人本身所指出的，凯美卡因流动性和破产问题停止了对申请人产品的付款，但正如本裁决前面所讨论的，这种付款中断是由被申请人自己的违约行为造成的。

Regarding the prices that could reasonably be expected, the Tribunal considers that Claimants have not fulfilled their burden of proof for the price of USD 180 they allege. Claimants instructed Miller Lents for the 2009 Report, which is closest to the valuation date accepted by this Tribunal, to apply a base price of USD 2.00 starting from the year 2009, which translates into about USD 70 per 1000 m³. This price of USD 70 is also the export price Gas Trade International LLP received. The Tribunal, therefore, considers that a price of USD 70 is appropriate for its calculation of damages.

关于可以合理预期的价格，仲裁庭认为申请人没有履行其所声称的 180 美元价格的举证责任。申请人要求米勒·伦茨提交 2009 年报告，该报告最接近本仲裁庭接受的估价日期，从 2009 年起适用 2.00 美元的基准价，即每 1000 立方米约 70 美元。该价格为 70 美元，也是天然气贸易国际公司收到的出口价格。因此，仲裁庭认为，70 美元的价格适用于其损害赔偿的计算。

The Tribunal considers it to be of particular relevance that an offer was made for the LPG Plant by state-owned KMG at that time for USD 199 million. The Tribunal considers that to be the relatively best source of information for the valuation of the LPG Plant among the various sources of information submitted by the Parties regarding the valuation for the LPG Plant during the relevant period of the valuation date accepted by the Tribunal.

仲裁庭认为，当时国有哈萨克斯坦国家石油天然气公司为液化石油气工厂提供 1.99 亿美元的报价具有特别的相关性。仲裁庭认为，在各方提交的有关液化石油气工厂在仲裁庭接受的估值日期期间内的估值的各种资料来源中，这是液化石油气工厂估值的相对最佳资料来源。

裁决撤销或执行情况（Annulment or Enforcement of the Award）

United States Court of Appeals for The District of Columbia Circuit

September Term, 2018 Filed On: April 19, 2019

From 1999 to 2000, Petitioners-Appellees Anatolie Stati, Gabriel Stati, Ascom Group, S. A., and Terra Raf Trans Trading Ltd. ("the Statis") acquired controlling shares in two Kazakh oil companies: Ascom purchased a 62 percent interest in Kazpolmunay LLP ("KPM"), and the Statis purchased 75 percent interest in Toklynneftagaz LLP ("TNG"). These companies owned subsoil use rights to the Borankol oil and Tolkyn gas fields and the Tabyl exploration block in Kazakhstan. By 2001, the Statis invested an estimated one billion US dollars exploring and developing these projects.

These developments stalled in 2008 when the President of Kazakhstan received a letter from the President of Moldova, the Statis' home country. The letter stated that Anatolie Stati invested in UN-sanctioned areas using proceeds from Kazakhstan's mineral resources and that he was concealing profits in offshore accounts. As a result, the Kazakh government began investigating Anatolie Stati and his companies.

美国哥伦比亚特区巡回上诉法院

2018 年 9 月　提交上诉日期：2019 年 4 月 19 日

从 1999 年到 2000 年，申请人暨被上诉人安纳托利·斯塔蒂、加布里埃尔·斯塔蒂、阿斯康集团公司和特拉夫特朗贸易有限公司（"斯塔蒂"）获得了两家哈萨克斯坦石油公司的控股权：阿斯康收购了 KPM 公司 62% 的股权，斯塔蒂收购了 TNG 公司 75% 权益。这些公司拥有在哈萨克斯坦的波兰科尔油田和托尔金气田以及泰比勘探区块的底土使用权。到 2001 年，斯塔蒂估计投资了 10 亿美元用于勘探和开发这些项目。

这些开发在 2008 年停滞不前，当时哈萨克斯坦总统收到了斯塔蒂母国摩尔多瓦总统的一封信。信中说，安纳托利·斯塔蒂利用哈萨克斯坦矿产资源的收益投资于联合国制裁的地区，并在离岸账户中隐瞒利润。结果，哈萨克斯坦政府开始调查安纳托利斯塔蒂和他的公司。

On September 30, 2014, the Statis filed a Petition to Confirm Arbitral Award in the District Court under the Convention on the Recognition and Enforcement of Foreign Arbitral Awards（"New York Convention"）, which has been incorporated into the Federal Arbitration Act. See 9 U. S. C. § § 201 - 208. On April 5, 2016, after the parties had completed their merits briefings in this case, Kazakhstan filed a motion for leave to file "additional grounds" in support of its opposition to the petition to confirm the arbitral award. The District Court denied Kazakhstan's motion after considering whether justice required permitting it to add new grounds to its opposition to the petition to confirm the award. Kazakhstan then filed a motion for reconsideration of the District Court's denial of its motion to supplement. On March 23, 2018, the District Court issued a memorandum opinion denying the motion for reconsideration and confirming the arbitration award.

We affirm the District Court's grant of the Statis' petition to confirm the arbitral award. There is an "emphatic federal policy in favor of arbitral dispute resolution," thus district courts have "little discretion in refusing or deferring enforcement of foreign arbitral awards: the [New York] Convention is 'clear' that a court 'may refuse to enforce the award only on the grounds explicitly set forth in Article V of the Convention.'" Kazakhstan has failed toshow that any exceptions to enforceability under the New York Convention are appropriate here.

2014 年 9 月 30 日，斯塔蒂根据《承认和执行外国仲裁裁决公约》（《纽约公约》）向地方法院提交了确认仲裁裁决的申请，该公约已纳入《联邦仲裁法》（见《联邦法典》第 9 编第 201—208 节）。2016 年 4 月 5 日，当事各方完成本案的案情简报后，哈萨克斯坦提出了一项申请，要求许可提交"其他理由"，以支持其反对确认仲裁裁决的请求。地方法院在考虑是否需要司法部门允许哈萨克斯坦在反对确认裁决的申请书中增加新的理由后，驳回了哈萨克斯坦的动议。哈萨克斯坦随后就地方法院驳回其补充动议提出了复议申请。2018 年 3 月 23 日，地方法院发布判决意见，驳回复议申请，确认仲裁裁决。

我们确认地方法院批准了斯塔蒂确认仲裁裁决的请求。有一项"有利于仲裁纠纷解决的强调性联邦政策"，因此地区法院"在拒绝或推迟执行外国仲裁裁决方面几乎没有自由裁量权：纽约公约'明确'规定，法院只有在公约第五条明确规定的基础上才能拒绝执行裁决"。哈萨克斯坦未能证明纽约公约规定的任何可执行性例外在这里适用。

案件影响（Impact of the Case）

本案裁决作出后，哈萨克斯坦在瑞典斯维亚上诉法院寻求撤销该仲裁裁决。申请人则寻求在英国和美国执行该裁决。英国高等法院于 2014 年 2 月 28 日作出了准许执行裁决的许可。2015 年 4 月 7 日，哈萨克斯坦以双方没有签署有效的仲裁协议、仲裁庭组成不合法、严重的程序错误使其无法向仲裁庭陈述案情为由（原始的三个理由），向英国高等法院申请撤销准许执行裁决的许可。在美国，申请人寻求美国哥伦比亚特区联邦地区法院执行该裁决。在英国申请发出后不久，哈萨克斯坦成功地在联邦地区法院申请了司法协助。该申请导致法院向第三方发出传票，迫使其出示文件。哈萨克斯坦声称，这些文件显示申请人没有如实阐明与 LPG 厂相关的费用，这些费用并不代表设备和真实工作的实际成本，因此这些费用影响了仲裁庭对裁决中损害赔偿的评估。

据此，2015 年 8 月底，哈萨克斯坦申请修改上述英国申请，增加的请求称，裁决的作出是由于申请人的欺诈，因此执行该裁决将违反英国的公共政策。哈萨克斯坦也向美国和瑞典法院提出申请，要求修正上述程序中的理由，指出理由应该包括基于欺诈指控的公共政策抗辩。美国地区法院拒绝了哈萨克斯坦的修正动议，而瑞典上诉法院则准许了哈萨克斯的修正动议。2016 年 8 月 5 日，美国地区法院停止了执行程序，等待瑞典撤销程序的结果。2016 年 12 月 9 日，瑞典斯维亚上诉法院驳回哈萨克斯坦的撤销仲裁裁决申请，认为哈萨克斯坦提出的三个月的冷却期并不是管辖权的前提条件。至于程序管理的瑕疵问题，法院认为哈萨克斯坦充分知晓《能源宪章公约》以及斯德哥尔摩商会仲裁院的规则，本可以申请延期，以便指定仲裁员，其未能指定仲裁员并不是仲裁机构的错误。法院也驳回了哈萨克斯坦关于违反公共政策的撤销仲裁裁决申请。最终，美国哥伦比亚特区巡回上诉法院也驳回了哈萨克斯坦的有关要求撤销承认该仲裁裁决的上诉请求。

2017 年以来，斯塔蒂在欧洲的比利时、瑞典、荷兰等国有法院先后提出执行裁决的诉讼，法院做出判决冻结了哈萨克斯坦在美国纽约梅隆银行托管的国家基金、哈萨克斯坦相关国家持有的公司股权等资产，并陆续进入处置执行程序。

思考问题（Questions）

1. 斯塔蒂投资的公司在哈萨克斯坦被税务处罚的罚款，仲裁庭没有在计算赔偿额时从损失价值中扣减，仲裁庭不认可罚款的管辖依据是什么？

2. 裁决做出后哈萨克斯坦获得了反证表明申请人欺诈而使仲裁裁决对 LPG 厂的估值不当，而为何无法在外国法院推翻该裁决结果？

案例十三　尤科斯诉俄罗斯案

Yukos Universal Limited（Isle of Man）
v. the Russian Federation（2014）
（PCA Case No. AA 227）

选读理由（Selected Reason）

2014 年 7 月 18 日，由常设仲裁法院（PCA）主持的贸易法委员会仲裁庭裁决俄罗斯支付 500 多亿美元，以补偿其对尤科斯石油公司的间接征收而给尤科斯三家前股东造成的损失。这三家股东分别是赫利企业有限公司（Hulley Enterprises Limited，注册在塞浦路斯）、尤科斯环球有限公司（Yukos Universal Limited，注册在马恩岛）和老兵石油有限公司（Veteran Petroleum Limited，注册在塞浦路斯），他们共同持有尤科斯石油公司（OAO Yukos Oil Company，注册在俄罗斯）70.5% 的股份。仲裁是在 2005 年根据《能源宪章条约》（ECT）启动的，这三个平行仲裁案件的申请人索赔请求不低于 1140 亿美元。三起案件由同一个仲裁庭审理，所形成的裁决是迄今为止在投资条约仲裁中所知的最大的损害赔偿裁决。

仲裁申请情况（The Request for Arbitration）

After the dissolution of the Soviet Union, Yukos was incorporated as a joint stock company in 1993 by Presidential Decree. Fully privatized in 1995 – 1996, it was a vertically integrated group engaging in exploration, production, refining, marketing and distribution of crude oil, natural gas and petroleum products. Its three main production subsidiaries were Yuganskneftegaz（"YNG"）, Samaraneftegaz and, from 1997, Tomskneft. In May 2002, Yukos became the first Russian company to be ranked among the top ten largest oil and gas companies by market capitalization worldwide. In the fourth quarter of 2002, Claimants submit that Yukos became the largest oil company in Russia in terms of daily crude oil production.

苏联解体后，尤科斯作为一家股份公司于 1993 年根据总统令成立。1995 年至 1996 年期间完全私有化以后，尤科斯被整合为一垂直管理的集团，从事原油、天然气和石油产品的勘探、生产、精炼、营销和分销。其三个主要生产性子公司分别是尤甘斯克公司、萨马拉公司和 1997 年设立的托木斯克公司。2002 年 5 月，尤科斯成为全球市值前十大石油和天然气公司中的第一家俄罗斯公司。在 2002 年第四季度，仲裁申请人提出，尤科斯公司成为俄罗斯每日原油产量最大的石油公司。

At its peak in 2003, it had around 100,000 employees, six main refineries and a market capitalization estimated at over USD 33 billion. According to Claimants, after its projected 2003 merger with then Russia's fifth largest oil company Sibneft（"Sibneft"）, Yukos Sibneft would have become the fourth largest private oil producer worldwide, behind BP, Exxon and Shell. At the time of Respondent's alleged adverse actions in the summer of 2003, Yukos was engaged in negotiations with Exxon Mobil and Chevron Texaco for a merger or other form of business combination. Claimants contend that this level of success was the result of efforts to modernize Yukos' operations and implement Western business practices. According to Claimants, Yukos' success and the increasing social and economic influence gained by its management—including financial support given by Mr. Khodorkovsky to opposition parties—were perceived as a political threat by the Russian authorities and ccordingly Yukos would fall from grace and be targeted for destruction. Respondent, however, contends that Yukos was a "criminal enterprise", engaged in a variety of tax evasion schemes and other fraudulent activities.

在 2003 年的巅峰时期，该公司拥有约 10 万名员工，6 家主要炼油厂，市值估计超过 330 亿美元。根据申请人的说法，在 2003 年与当时的俄罗斯第五大石油公司西伯利亚石油公司合并后，尤科斯西伯利亚石油公司将成为全球第四大私人石油生产商，仅次于英国石油公司、埃克森美孚和壳牌。在被申请人于 2003 年夏天采取被指控的不利行动之时，尤科斯正与埃克森美孚和雪佛龙德士古就吸收合并或其他形式的企业联合进行谈判。申请人认为，尤科斯所获得的这一水平的成功是其努力进行业务管理现代化和实施西方商业惯例的结果。根据申请人的说法，尤科斯的成功以及其管理上所获得的社会和经济影响越来越大（包括霍多尔科夫斯基先生向反对党提供财政支持），被俄罗斯当局视为一种政治威胁，因此尤科斯必然会失宠，并成为破坏目标。然而，被申请人辩称尤科斯是一家"犯罪企业"，从事各种逃税计划和其他欺诈活动。

The low-tax region program was established in the 1990s to foster economic development in impoverished areas of the Russian Federation. The Russian low-tax regions were permitted to exempt taxpayers from federal corporate profit tax for the purpose of fostering taxpayers' investments in the low-tax regions, provided the taxpayer complied with certain requirements. The Russian low-tax regions that are relevant to Yukos' "tax optimization" scheme include: Closed Administrative Territorial Units (known as "ZATOs"): Lesnoy and Trekhgorniy; and Other low-tax regions: Mordovia, Kalmykia and Evenkia.

低税区计划于 20 世纪 90 年代建立，旨在促进俄罗斯联邦贫困地区的经济发展。为了促进纳税人在低税地区的投资，俄罗斯低税地区允许免除纳税人的联邦企业利润税，前提是纳税人符合某些要求。与尤科斯"税收优化"计划相关的俄罗斯低税地区包括：封闭的行政区域单元（称为"ZATOs"）：莱斯诺和特里赫戈尼；以及其他低税地区：莫多维亚、卡尔米基亚和埃文基亚。

With respect to the tax benefits available in the ZATOs (Lesnoy and Trekhgorniy), in 1999, the ZATOs were permitted to exempt taxpayers fully from federal corporate profit tax. In 2000, most ZATOs were permitted to exempt taxpayers from the portion of the federal corporate profit tax that was payable to their budget (e. g., up to 19 percent). In 2001, all ZATOs were permitted to exempt taxpayers from the portion of the federal corporate profit tax that was payable to their budget (e. g., also up to 19 percent). In 2002, however, these exemptions were revoked.

With respect to the tax benefits available in other low-tax regions, in 2000 and 2001, Mordovia, Kalmykia and Evenkia were permitted to exempt taxpayers fully from the portion of the federal corporate profit tax that was payable to their budget (e. g., from up to 19 percent to zero percent). From 1 July 2002 until 31 December 2003, low-tax regions were permitted to exempt taxpayers from the portion of the federal corporate profit tax payable to their budget, but only up to four percent. An exception existed for "grandfathered" tax investment agreements entered into prior to 1 July 2001, such that these taxpayers could still receive a zero percent profit tax rate if they fulfilled certain other conditions. As of 1 January 2004, the existing tax investment agreements were terminated, but the Tax Code of the Russian Federation (the "Russian Tax Code") still allowed low-tax regions to reduce the federal corporate profit tax payable to their budget up to four percent.

Zatos（莱斯诺和特里赫戈尼）在 1999 年提供的税收优惠，允许 Zatos 的企业完全免除纳税人的联邦企业利润税。2000 年，大多数 Zatos 企业被允许免除纳税人应缴纳的联邦企业利润税部分（从高达 19% 的税率减至 0 税率）。2001 年，所有的 Zatos 公司都被允许免除纳税人应缴纳的联邦企业利润税部分（同样高达 19%）。然而，在 2002 年，这些豁免被撤销。

关于其他低税地区的税收优惠，在2000年和2001年，莫多维亚、卡尔米基亚和埃文基被允许完全免除纳税人应缴纳的联邦企业利润税部分（从高达19%的税率减至0税率）。从2002年7月1日到2003年12月31日，低税地区被允许免除纳税人应缴纳的联邦企业利润税，但最高仅为4%。2001年7月1日之前签订的"祖父"税收投资协议有一个例外，这样，如果满足某些其他条件，这些纳税人仍然可以获得0%的利润税率。截至2004年1月1日，现有的税务投资协议已终止，但俄罗斯联邦的税法（以下简称"俄罗斯税法"）仍允许低税收地区将应支付给财政部门的联邦企业利润税减少至4%。

Respondent contends that Yukos' restructuring of its trading operations from high-tax jurisdictions, such as Moscow and Nefteyugansk, to trading companies incorporated in the low？tax jurisdictions of Lesnoy, Trekhgorny, Mordovia, Kalmykia and Evenkia was aimed at evading taxes, rather than to achieve any genuine economic result. Respondent alleges that Yukos interposed between Yukos and its customer its "sham" trading shells registered in Russian low-tax regions. Yukos' oil producing subsidiaries sold the extracted oil to the trading companies at a fraction of the market price. The trading companies then sold the oil either abroad at a market price or to Yukos' refineries, and subsequently re-bought it at a reduced price and re-sold it at the market price. Respondent asserts that prices increased step by step from sham shell to sham shell, generating artificially inflated profits through non-arms length transactions. Those profits were then taxed at reduced rates in the low-tax regions, where the sham trading shells were registered. Respondent contends that the tax authorities identified abuses by the Lesnoy trading shells, which resulted in further investigations and, ultimately, in the tax assessments against Yukos and related proceedings.

Claimants contend that Yukos, like other Russian companies at that time, was merely taking advantage of the legislation in place in the low-tax regions. Claimants assert that any findings of "abuse" by the Russian tax authorities was a function of the arbitrary and unpredictable interpretations of the law in Russia.

被申请人辩称，尤科斯将其贸易业务从莫斯科和内夫特尤甘斯克等高税收管辖区重组为在莱斯诺、特里赫戈尼、摩多维亚、卡尔米基亚和埃文基低税收管辖区注册的贸易公司，目的是逃避税收，而不是取得任何真正的经济成果。被申请人称，尤科斯公司介入了尤科斯公司与其客户——在俄罗斯低税收地区注册的壳公司——之间的"虚假"交易。尤科斯的石油生产子公司以市场价格的一小部分将提取的石油出售给贸易公司。然后，贸易公司以市场价格或尤科斯炼油厂的价格将石油出售到国外，随后以低价重新购买，并以市场价格重新出售。被申请人声称，价格从虚假的壳公司一步一步地上涨，通过非常规交易产生人为夸大的利润。然后，这些利润在低税率地区以较低的税率征税，这些地区是虚假壳公司的注册地。被申请人辩称，税务机关确认了莱斯诺交易壳公司的滥用行为，这导致了进一步的调查，并最终导致了针对尤科斯的税务评估和相关诉讼。

申请人辩称，尤科斯和当时的其他俄罗斯公司一样，只是利用了低税收地区的立法。申请人声称，俄罗斯税务机关对"滥用"的任何调查结果都只是在发挥对俄罗斯法律的任意和不可预测的解释的功能。

Starting in July 2003, a series of criminal investigations were initiated by the Russian Federation against Yukos management and activities. According to Claimants, these actions included the "targeting" of Yukos' employees, auditor PwC, in-house counsel, lawyers involved in various Yukos-related cases, as well as searches and seizures, threats to revoke its oil licenses, and mutual legal assistance requests and extradition proceedings against Yukos management. Claimants characterize these actions as harassment, motivated by Mr. Khodorkovsky's participation in Russian opposition politics, that were intended—together with tax reassessments—to lead to the expropriation of Yukos' assets. Respondent contends that its actions were in response to illegal acts committed by Yukos and its officers and shareholders.

从 2003 年 7 月开始，俄罗斯联邦对尤科斯的管理和活动发起了一系列刑事调查。据申请人说，这些行动包括将尤科斯的员工、普华永道的审计师、内部律师、参与各种尤科斯相关案件的律师作为"目标"，同时还进行搜查和扣押、威胁吊销其石油许可证、提出司法协助请求和针对尤科斯管理层的引渡程序。申请人将这些行为描述为骚扰，其动机是霍多尔科夫斯基先生参与俄罗斯反对派政治活动，这些行动，与税收重新评估一起，导致尤科斯的资产被征用。被申请人辩称，其行动只是针对尤科斯及其高管和股东的违法行为。

Between July and October 2003, three key Yukos officers were arrested. In July 2003, Mr. Platon Lebedev, Director of Hulley and YUL, was arrested on charges of embezzlement and fraud; he was sentenced to nine years in prison in May 2005. In October 2003, Mr. Vasily Shakhovsky, President of Yukos-Moscow, was charged with and later convicted of tax evasion. In October 2003, Mr. Khodorkovsky himself was arrested and charged with crimes including forgery, fraud and tax evasion; he was also sentenced to a nine-year prison term in May 2005. As a result of these arrests, a number of high-ranking Yukos executives fled Russia, such as Mr. Leonid Nevzlin, Deputy Chairman of the Yukos Board of Directors until 2003. On 2 February 2007, new charges of embezzlement and money laundering were brought against Messrs. Khodorkovsky and Lebedev, leading to further convictions in December 2010. Messrs. Khodorkovsky and Lebedev were each imprisoned for over a decade.

2003 年 7 月至 10 月，三名重要的尤科斯高管被捕。2003 年 7 月，赫利公司和尤科斯环球公司的董事柏拉图·列别捷夫因贪污和欺诈罪被捕；2005 年 5 月，他被判处 9 年监禁。2003 年 10 月，尤科斯莫斯科的董事长瓦西里·沙霍夫斯基被指控并被以逃税定罪。2003 年 10 月，霍多尔科夫斯基本人被捕，被控犯有伪造、欺诈和逃税罪；2005 年 5 月，他被判处 9 年徒刑。由于这些逮捕，一些尤科斯高级管理人员逃离了俄罗斯，比如尤科斯董事会副主席利昂尼德内兹林先生直到 2003 年都在逃离。2007 年 2 月 2 日，霍多尔科夫斯基和列别捷夫被提出了新的有关贪污和洗钱的指控，在 2010 年 12 月被定罪。霍多尔科夫斯基和列别捷夫分别被监禁十多年。

The Tax Ministry demanded payment from Yukos for approximately USD 3. 5 billion for 2000, which was largely upheld by the Moscow Arbitrazh Court. Similarly large tax reassessments were issued in the period between 2004 and 2006 for subsequent tax years. 2001 taxes were re-assessed in the amount of approximately USD 4. 1 billion, 2002 taxes in the amount of approximately USD 6. 8 billion, 2003 taxes in the amount of approximately USD 6. 1 billion, and 2004 taxes in the amount of approximately USD 3. 7 billion. By the time the Tax Ministry issued the last of these demands, Yukos faced a tax bill of more than USD 24 billion, of which approximately USD 10. 6 billion constituted allegedly evaded revenue-based taxes (including interest and fines), and the remainder (approximately USD 13. 6 billion) comprised of VAT and related, interest and fines.

税务部要求尤科斯支付 2000 年度的大约 35 亿美元税款，这一决定在很大程度上获得了莫斯科仲裁法院的支持。同样，在 2004 年至 2006 年期间，又对随后的纳税年度进行了大规模的重新评估。2001 年的税款经重新评估约 41 亿美元，2002 年的税款约 68 亿美元，2003 年的税款约 61 亿美元，2004 年的税款约 37 亿美元。截至税务部发布上述最后一项要求时，尤科斯面临着 240 多亿美元的税单，其中约 106 亿美元为所逃避的基于营业收入的税款（包括利息和罚款），其余（约 136 亿美元）为增值税和相关的利息及罚款。

In July 2004, the Russian Federation indicated that it intended to appraise and sell YNG to pay off Yukos' back taxes. A valuation carried out by investment bank ZAO Dresdner Bank ("Dresdner") at the request of the Russian Federation valued YNG at between USD 15. 7 billion and USD 18. 3 billion. A valuation carried out by JP Morgan, at the request of Yukos, valued YNG at between USD 16 billion and USD 22 billion. The Russian Ministry of Justice announced that YNG was worth USD 10. 4 billion.

After Yukos' attempts to enjoin the sale of YNG by legal recourse in the United States failed, YNG was sold at auction on 19 December 2004 for USD 9. 37 billion to sole bidder and newly incorporated entity, Baikal Finance Group ("Baikal"), which was quickly bought by Russian State-owned Rosneft ("Rosneft").

2004 年 7 月，俄罗斯联邦表示，它打算评估并出售尤甘斯克公司，以偿还尤科斯的欠税。根据俄罗斯联邦的要求，投资银行德累斯顿银行（"德累斯顿"）作出的估值为 157 亿美元至 183 亿美元。根据尤科斯的要求，摩根大通对尤甘斯克公司的估值在 160 亿美元至 220 亿美元之间。俄罗斯司法部宣布，尤甘斯克公司价值 104 亿美元。

尤科斯试图在美国通过法律手段禁止出售尤甘斯克公司的尝试失败后，尤甘斯克公司于 2004 年 12 月 19 日以 93.7 亿美元的价格拍卖给唯一投标人和新成立的实体贝加尔湖金融集团（"贝加尔湖"），后者很快被俄罗斯国有俄罗斯石油公司（"俄罗斯石油公司"）收购。

On 28 March 2006, bankruptcy proceedings were commenced against Yukos, placing it under external supervision, and on 4 August 2006, Yukos was declared bankrupt.

Yukos' remaining assets were nearly all acquired by State-owned Gazprom and Rosneft, with the bankruptcy auctions raising a total of USD 31.5 billion. In November 2007, Yukos was liquidated and struck off the register of legal entities.

2006 年 3 月 28 日，尤科斯开始破产程序，并接受外部监管，2006 年 8 月 4 日，尤科斯被宣布破产。

尤科斯的剩余资产几乎全部被国有的俄罗斯天然气工业股份公司和俄罗斯石油公司收购，破产拍卖共筹集了 315 亿美元。2007 年 11 月，尤科斯被清算，并从法人实体登记册中除名。

Claimants request that the Tribunal render an Award：

（1）Declaring that the Respondent has breached its obligations under Article 10（1）of the Energy Charter Treaty；

（2）Declaring that the Respondent has breached its obligations under Article 13（1）of the Energy Charter Treaty；

（3）Ordering the Respondent to pay to the Claimants, in full reparation of their damages, an amount to be determined by the Arbitral Tribunal, estimated by the Claimants at no less than US $ 114.174 billion, to be shared between the Claimants in the following proportions：

§ Hulley Enterprises Limited US $ 93.229 billion

§ Yukos Universal Limited US $ 4.666 billion

§ Veteran Petroleum Limited US $ 16.279 billion

（4）Ordering the Respondent to pay post-award interest on the above sums to the Claimants at the rate of Libor + 4% compounded annually from the date of the Award until the date of full payment；

（5）Ordering the Respondent to pay to the Claimants the full costs of these arbitrations, including, without limitation, arbitrators' fees, administrative costs of the PCA, counsel fees, expert fees and all other costs associated with these proceedings.

(6) Dismissing all of the Respondent's defenses.

(7) Ordering any such further relief as it may deem appropriate.

申请人要求法庭作出裁决：

（一）宣布被申请人违反《能源宪章条约》第十条第（1）款义务。

（二）宣布被申请人违反《能源宪章条约》第十三条第（1）款义务。

（三）责令被申请人向申请人支付全部赔偿金，具体数额由仲裁庭确定，但申请人估计不少于1141.74亿美元，由申请人按以下比例分配：赫利公司932.29亿美元；尤科斯环球有限公司46.66亿美元；老兵石油有限公司162.79亿美元。

（四）责令被申请人以伦敦银行同业拆借利率加4%的年复利向申请人支付上述款项的裁决后利息，复利从裁决之日起至全额支付之日止。

（五）责令被申请人向申请人支付仲裁的全部费用，包括但不限于仲裁员费用、常设仲裁法院的行政费用、律师费、专家费以及与这些程序相关的所有其他费用。

（六）驳回被申请人的全部答辩。

（七）责令给予其认为适当的进一步救济。

仲裁结果（Award）

For the reasons set forth above, the Tribunal unanimously:

(a) Dismisses the objections to jurisdiction and/or admissibility, based on Article 21 of the Energy Charter Treaty;

(b) Dismisses the objections to jurisdiction and/or admissibility, pertaining to Respondent's contentions concerning "unclean hands" and "illegal and bad faith conduct";

(c) Dismisses the renewed objections to jurisdiction and/or admissibility based on Article 26 (3) (b) (i) of the Energy Charter Treaty;

(d) Holds that the present dispute is admissible and within the Tribunal's jurisdiction;

(e) Declares that Respondent has breached its obligations under Article 13 (1) of the Energy Charter Treaty;

(f) Orders Respondent to pay to Claimant Yukos Universal Limited damages in the amount of USD 1, 846,000,687;

(g) Orders Respondent to pay the amount of EUR 156,476 to Claimant Yukos Universal Limited as reimbursement for the costs of the arbitration;

（h）Orders Respondent to pay the amount of USD 2,214,277 to Claimant Yukos Universal Limited for a portion of the costs of its legal representation and assistance in the arbitration proceedings; and

（i）Orders Respondent to pay to Claimant Yukos Universal Limited, if within 180 days of the issuance of this Award Respondent fails to pay in full the amounts set forth in paragraphs （f）,（g）and（h）, above post-award interest on any outstanding amount starting from 15 January 2015, compounded annually. Post-award interest shall be determined as the yield on 10 – year U. S. treasury bonds as of 15 January 2015 and then the dates of compounding yearly thereafter.

基于上述原因，仲裁庭一致认为：

（一）驳回根据《能源宪章条约》第21条对管辖权和/或可仲裁性的异议。

（二）驳回与被申请人"不洁之手"和"非法和不诚实行为"的争议有关的管辖权和/或可仲裁性的异议。

（三）驳回根据《能源宪章条约》第26条（3）款（b）项（i）目重新提出的对管辖权和/或可仲裁性的异议。

（四）认为本争议是可仲裁的，并在仲裁庭的司法管辖权范围内。

（五）宣布被申请人违反了《能源宪章条约》第13条（1）款规定的义务。

（六）责令被申请人向申请人尤科斯环球有限公司支付1846000687美元的损害赔偿金。

（七）责令被申请人向申请人尤科斯环球有限公司支付156476欧元以补偿仲裁费用。

（八）责令被申请人向申请人尤科斯环球有限公司支付2214277美元，作为其在仲裁程序中的诉讼代理人及其助理费用的一部分。

（九）责令被申请人向申请人尤科斯环球有限公司支付款项，如果在本裁决书发布后180天内，被申请人未能全额支付上述（六）、（七）和（八）项中规定的金额，则自2015年1月15日起的任何未付金额需自裁决作出后开始按年度计取复利。裁决后的利率应确定为2015年1月15日的10年期美国国债收益率，此后在每年的该日计取复利。

裁决原因（Reasons for the Award）

Claimants' Alleged "Unclean Hands"

Respondent lists 28 instances of alleged "illegal and bad faith conduct" by Claimants or "attributable to" Claimants involving a variety of actors and spanning over ten years, from the privatization of Yukos in the mid-1990s to its liquidation in November 2007. Claimants dispute that any of their conduct (or any conduct attributable to them) was illegal or in bad faith.

申请人涉嫌"不洁双手"的问题

被申请人列举了 28 起申请人的或"可归因于"申请人的各种"非法和不诚实行为"，这些案件跨度超过 10 年，即从 20 世纪 90 年代中期尤科斯的私有化到 2007 年 11 月的清算期间。申请人对他们的任何行为（或归因于他们的任何行为）是非法的或不诚实的观点提出异议。

There is no compelling reason to deny altogether the right to invoke the ECT to any investor who has breached the law of the host State in the course of its investment. If the investor acts illegally, the host state can request it to correct its behavior and impose upon it sanctions available under domestic law, as the Russian Federation indeed purports to have done by reassessing taxes and imposing fines. However, if the investor believes these sanctions to be unjustified (as Claimants do in the present case), it must have the possibility of challenging their validity in accordance with the applicable investment treaty. It would undermine the purpose and object of the ECT to deny the investor the right to make its case before an arbitral tribunal based on the same alleged violations the existence of which the investor seeks to dispute on the merits.

对于任何在投资过程中违反东道国法律的投资者，没有任何令人信服的理由完全剥夺他们援引《能源宪章条约》的权利。如果投资者的行为是非法的，东道国可以要求它纠正自己的行为，并根据国内法对其施加制裁，俄罗斯联邦确实声称已通过重新评估税收和处以罚款来做到这一点。但是，如果投资者认为这些制裁是不合理的（如申请人在本案件中所作的那样），它必须有可能根据适用的投资条约对制裁的有效性提出质疑。如果剥夺投资者就同一被指控的案件向仲裁庭提起诉讼以争辩该些违法的指控是否存在的权利，将破坏《能源宪章条约》的目的和目标。

The Tribunal therefore concludes that "unclean hands" does not exist as a general principle of international law which would bar a claim by an investor, such as Claimants in this case.

因此，仲裁庭的结论是，"不洁双手"并不作为国际法的一般原则而存在，这一原则将禁止投资者，例如本案的申请人提出索赔。

Another important threshold issue in this arbitration arises from Respondent's objection under Article 21 of the ECT. Respondent argues that, pursuant to this complex provision [containing a "carve out" from the ECT for "Taxation Measures" at Article 21 (1) and a "claw back" for Article 13 of the ECT in relation to "taxes" at Article 21 (5)], the Tribunal lacks jurisdiction over claims with respect to "Taxation Measures" other than those based on expropriatory "taxes". Claimants argue that the objection is without merit since, inter alia, Article 21 does not apply to actions—including expropriations—carried out "under the guise of taxation."

本仲裁中另一个重要的门槛问题是被申请人根据《能源宪章条约》第21条提出的异议。被申请人认为，依照这个复杂的条款（包含第21条第（1）款排除在外的税收措施和第21条第（5）款"税"的规定纳入《能源宪章条约》第13条的问题），相较于对以征收为目的的"税"，仲裁庭对基于"税收措施"的索赔缺乏管辖权。1786年，申请人争辩说，被申请人的这一异议毫无根据，除其他理由外，第21条并不适用于"以税收为幌子"进行的行为，包括征收行为。

Having considered the Parties' arguments, the Tribunal concludes that it has jurisdiction to rule on Claimants' claims under Article 13 of the ECT for two independent reasons, each of which in and of itself suffices to justify the jurisdiction of the Tribunal. Firstly, the Tribunal finds that, irrespective of its findings regarding the applicability of Article 21 of the ECT to the present case, it would have "indirect" jurisdiction over claims under Article 13 of the ECT because any measures excluded by the carve-out under Article 21 (1) of the ECT would be brought back within the Tribunal's jurisdiction by the claw-back of Article 21 (5) of the ECT and any referral to the Competent Taxation Authorities within the meaning of this latter provision would clearly have been futile.

Secondly, the Tribunal finds that, in any event, the carve-out of Article 21 (1) can apply only to bona fide taxation actions, i. e. , actions that are motivated by the purpose of raising general revenue for the State. By contrast, actions that are taken only under the guise of taxation, but in reality aim to achieve an entirely unrelated purpose (such as the destruction of a company or the elimination of a political opponent) cannot qualify for exemption from the protection standards of the ECT under the taxation carve-out in Article 21 (1). As a consequence, the Tribunal finds that it does indeed have "direct" jurisdiction over claims under Article 13 (as well as Article 10) in the extraordinary circumstances of this case.

在考虑了双方的论点后，仲裁庭得出结论，它有权根据《能源宪章条约》第13条对申请人的索赔作出裁决，理由有两个，每一个理由本身就足以证明仲裁庭的管辖权是正当的。首先，仲裁庭认为，无论其关于《能源宪章条约》第21条对本案适用性的调查结果如何，它对基于《能源宪章条约》第13条提出的索赔都具有"间接"管辖权，因为根据《能源宪章条约》第21条第（1）款排除在外的任何措施都将根据《能源宪章条约》第21条第（5）款纳入的规定回到仲裁庭的管辖范围内。试图按照后一款的规定将其转回由主管税务机关处理，显然是徒劳的。

其次，仲裁庭认为，在任何情况下，第 21 条第（1）款所述的排除仅适用于善意的税务行为，即出于为国家增加一般收入的目的而采取的行为。相比之下，仅在税收伪装下采取的行动，但实际上旨在实现完全无关的目的（如摧毁公司或消除政治对手），不符合第 21 条第（1）款所述税收排除规定所体现的《能源宪章条约》的保护标准。因此，仲裁庭认为，在本案的特殊情况下，它确实对第 13 条（以及第 10 条）项下的索赔具有"直接"管辖权。

Article 13 (1) of the ECT provides, in relevant part:

Article 13 Expropriation

(1) Investments of Investors of a Contracting Party in the Area of any other Contracting Party shall not be nationalized, expropriated or subjected to a measure or measures having effect equivalent to nationalization or expropriation (hereinafter referred to as "Expropriation") except where such Expropriation is:

(a) for a purpose which is in the public interest;

(b) not discriminatory;

(c) carried out under due process of law; and

(d) accompanied by the payment of prompt, adequate and effective compensation.

Such compensation shall amount to the fair market value of the Investment expropriated at the time immediately before the Expropriation or impending Expropriation became knownin such a way as to affect the value of the Investment (hereinafter referred to as the "Valuation Date").

Such fair market value shall at the request of the Investor be expressed in a Freely Convertible Currency on the basis of the market rate of exchange existing for that currency on the Valuation Date. Compensation shall also include interest at a commercial rate established on a market basis from the date of Expropriation until the date of payment.

《能源宪章条约》第 13 条第（1）款在相关部分中规定：

第 13 条征收

（1）缔约一方投资者在缔约另一方区域内的投资，除下列情形外，不得收归国有、征收或者采取相当于收归国有或者征收的措施（以下简称征收）：

（a）为符合公众利益的目的。

（b）不歧视。

（c）根据适当的法律程序进行。

（d）同时支付及时、充分和有效的款项作为补偿。

补偿金额应当等于投资在被征收或者即将被征收为公众所知前影响着投资价值的那一时刻的公平市场价值（以下简称估价日）。

根据投资者的要求，这种公平的市场价值应以该货币在估价日的现行市场汇率为基础，以可自由兑换的货币表示。补偿还应包括从征收之日起至付款之日止按市场确定的商业利率计算的利息。

The Tribunal has earlier concluded that "the primary objective of the Russian Federation was not to collect taxes but rather to bankrupt Yukos and appropriate its valuable assets." For the reasons that emerge in Part Ⅷ, if the true objective were no more than tax collection, Yukos, its officers and employees, and its properties and facilities, would not have been treated, and mistreated, as in fact they were. Among the many incidents in this train of mistreatment that are within the remit of this Tribunal, two stand out: finding Yukos liable for the payment of more than 13 billion dollars in VAT in respect of oil that had been exported by the trading companies and should have been free of VAT and free of fines in respect of VAT; and the auction of YNG at a price that was far less than its value. But for these actions, for which the Russian Federation for reasons set out above and in preceding chapters was responsible, Yukos would have been able to pay the tax claims of the Russian Federation justified or not; it would not have been bankrupted and liquidated (unless the Russian Fedcration were intent on its liquidation and found still additional grounds for achieving that end, as the second criminal trial of Messrs. Khodorkovsky and Lebedev indeed suggests).

仲裁庭早些时候得出的结论是，"俄罗斯联邦的首要目标不是征税，而是让尤科斯破产，并取得其有价值的资产"。根据第八部分所述的理由，如果真正的目标仅仅是征税，尤科斯、其官员和雇员以及其财产和设施就不会受到事实上已遭受的那些待遇和虐待。在仲裁庭正在审理的一系列的虐待事件中，有两个尤为突出：认定尤科斯应对已由贸易公司出口且应获得免除增值税和罚款待遇的超过 130 亿美元的石油增值税负责；拍卖尤甘斯克公司的价格远远低于它的价值。如果不是因为这些如上文和前几章所述的理由应认定由俄罗斯联邦承担责任的行动，尤科斯就有能力支付俄罗斯联邦提出的合理或不合理的税款要求，它不会破产和清算（除非俄罗斯联邦打算清算它，并为实现这一目标找到更多的理由，正如霍多尔科夫斯基和列别捷夫的第二次刑事审判所表明的那样）。

Respondent has not explicitly expropriated Yukos or the holdings of its shareholders, but the measures that Respondent has taken in respect of Yukos, set forth in detail in Part VIII, in the view of the Tribunal have had an effect "equivalent to nationalization or expropriation". The four conditions specified in Article 13 (1) of the ECT do not qualify that conclusion.

被申请人没有明确征收尤科斯或其股东的财产，但被申请人对尤科斯所采取的措施，如法庭认为的第八部分所详述的，已产生"相当于国有化或征用"的效果。《能源宪章条约》第 13 条第（1）款中规定的四个征收的前提条件均不具备。

As to condition (a), whether the destruction of Russia's leading oil company and largest taxpayer was in the public interest is profoundly questionable. It was in the interest of the largest State-owned oil company, Rosneft, which took over the principal assets of Yukos virtually cost-free, but that is not the same as saying that it was in the public interest of the economy, polity and population of the Russian Federation.

As to condition (b), the treatment of Yukos and the appropriation of its assets by Rosneft (and to a much lesser extent, another State-owned corporation, Gazprom), when compared to the treatment of other Russian oil companies that also took advantage of investments in low-tax jurisdictions, may well have been discriminatory, a question that was inconclusively argued between the Parties and need not be and has not been decided by this Tribunal.

As to condition (c), Yukos was subjected to processes of law, but the Tribunal does not accept that the effective expropriation of Yukos was "carried out under due process of law" for multiple reasons set out above, notably in Section Ⅷ. C. 3. The harsh treatment accorded to Messrs. Khodorkovsky and Lebedev remotely jailed and caged in court, the mistreatment of counsel of Yukos and the difficulties counsel encountered in reading the record and conferring with Messrs. Khodorkovsky and Lebedev, the very pace of the legal proceedings, do not comport with the due process of law. Rather the Russian court proceedings, and most egregiously, the second trial and second sentencing of Messrs. Khodorkovsky and Lebedev on the creative legal theory of their theft of Yukos' oil production, indicate that Russian courts bent to the will of Russian executive authorities to bankrupt Yukos, assign its assets to a Statecontrolled company, and incarcerate a man who gave signs of becoming a political competitor.

As to condition (d), what in any event is incontestable is Respondent's failure to meet its prescription, because the effective expropriation of Yukos was not "accompanied by the payment of prompt, adequate and effective compensation", or, in point of fact, any compensation whatsoever. In order for the Russian Federation to be found in breach of its treaty obligations under Article 13 of the ECT, the foregoing violations of the conditions of Article 13 more than suffice.

关于第一个条件，摧毁俄罗斯最大的石油公司和纳税人是否符合公众利益，是非常值得怀疑的。这只是符合最大的国有石油公司俄罗斯石油公司的利益，该公司几乎毫无成本地接管了尤科斯的主要资产，但这并不等于说这符合俄罗斯联邦经济、政治和民众的公共利益。

关于第二个条件，尤科斯的待遇和其资产被俄罗斯石油公司取得（另一个国有公司俄罗斯天然气工业股份公司取得了少部分），与其他也获取在低税率地区投资好处的其他俄罗斯石油公司相比，很可能是歧视性的，这是一个双方争论未定且仲裁庭也不需要和尚未确定的问题。

关于第三个条件，尤科斯适用了法律程序，但法庭不认为对尤科斯的有效征收是"根据适当的法律程序进行的"，理由有上文所述的多种，特别是在第八部分第 C3 节。霍多尔科夫斯基和列别捷夫被投入偏远的监狱和被法庭囚禁所遭受的残酷的待遇、尤科斯律师受到的虐待、律师在阅卷和会见霍多尔科夫斯基和列别捷夫遇到的困难、诉讼程序的快步骤，与正当法律程序均不相称。最过分的是，俄罗斯法庭在其诉讼程序对霍多尔科夫斯基和列别捷夫的第二次审判和第二次判决中，创造出了有关窃取尤科斯石油产品的法律理论，表明了俄罗斯法院向俄罗斯行政当局屈服以使尤科斯破产，从而将其资产交给国有控股公司和关押一个有迹象成为政治对手的个人。

关于第四个条件，在任何情况下，无可争辩的是被告未能履行其规定，因为对尤科斯的有效征用并没有"同时支付及时、充分和有效的补偿"，事实上也没有任何补偿。为了确认俄罗斯联邦违反了《能源宪章条约》第 13 条所规定的条约义务，上述违反第 13 条条件的行为已经足够了。

On each of these valuation dates, Claimants are entitled to the following heads of damages: (1) the value of Claimants' shares in Yukos valued as of the valuation date; (2) the value of the dividends that the Tribunal determines would have been paid to Claimants by Yukos up to the valuation date but for the expropriation of Yukos; and (3) pre-award simple interest on these amounts.

在每一个估价日，申请人有权获得下列损害赔偿金：（1）申请人在尤科斯的股份在估价日的价值；（2）法庭所确定的，如果没有征收尤科斯，本应由尤科斯在估价日之前支付给申请人的股息的价值；（3）在裁决作出前这些金额的单一利息。

裁决撤销或执行情况（Annulment or Enforcement of the Award）

The first ground for reversal is linked to the meaning of Article 45 paragraph 1 ECT, which forms the basis for the provisional application of the Treaty referred to in this section. According to that provision, each Signatory consents to the provisional application of the ECT "to the extent that such provisional application is not inconsistent with its constitution, laws or regulations". The court designates this restriction hereinafter as the "Limitation Clause", in accordance with the terminology used in the Interim Awards. The Tribunal decided that by signing the ECT the Russian Federation consented to the provisional application of the entire Treaty pending its entry into force, unless the principle of provisional application itself were contrary to the Russian Constitution, laws or other regulations. According to the Tribunal, the Limitation Clause contained in Article 45 paragraph 1 entailed an "all or nothing" approach.

第一个撤销理由与第 45 条 1 款的含义有关，该款构成本节所述条约临时适用的基础。根据该规定，各签字人同意临时适用《能源宪章条约》，"只要该临时适用不违反其宪法、法律或法规"。法院根据中间裁决中使用的术语，在下文中将该限制称为"限制条款"。仲裁庭认定，通过签署《能源宪章条约》，俄罗斯联邦同意在整个条约生效之前临时适用整个条约，除非临时适用原则本身违反俄罗斯宪法、法律或其他条例。根据仲裁庭的说法，第 45 条 1 款所载的时效条款规定了"全部或全否"的做法。

The opinion delivered in this judgment leads to the final conclusion that from Article 45 paragraph 1 ECT it follows that based only on the signature of the ECT, the Russian Federation was not bound by the provisional application of the arbitration regulations of Article 26 ECT. The Russian Federation never made unconditional offer for arbitration, in the sense of Article 26 ECT. As a result, the defendants' "notice of arbitration" did not form a valid arbitration agreement.

依据本判决中的意见得出的最终结论是，按照《能源宪章条约》第 45 条第 1 款的规定，仅凭在《能源宪章条约》的签字，俄罗斯联邦不受《能源宪章条约》第 26 条仲裁条款的约束。俄罗斯联邦从未无条件地接受《能源宪章条约》第 26 条的仲裁条款。因此，被告的"仲裁通知"并不构成有效的仲裁协议。

案件影响（Impact of the Case）

因本案金额巨大，备受关注。在仲裁程序中，仲裁庭以中间裁决解决了部分管辖问题，包括俄罗斯主张本案已触发 ECT 条约第 26 条第 3 款（b）项（i）目规定的"岔路口条款"，认为申请人或其控制人（指霍多尔夫斯基等人）或其所投资企业（指尤科斯石油公司）已经将争议事项提交给了俄罗斯法院和欧洲人权法院，所以不可以将本案再提请仲裁。仲裁庭认为，触发"岔路口条款"必须满足"三重同一性"标准，即争端的当事人、诉由和标的三方面均相同。俄罗斯法院和欧洲人权法院的相关程序并不触发岔路口条款的适用。仲裁庭在最终裁决中还分析并驳回了有关申请人在俄罗斯被指控的"非法和不诚实行为"影响本案受理的观点，也考虑申请人的过错会造成其所获补偿的减少，最终形成了裁决。

但 2014 年 10 月，俄罗斯向海牙地区法院提出申请，认为仲裁申请人与俄罗斯之间不存在有效的仲裁协议，要求撤销仲裁庭的上述裁决。2016 年 4 月 20 日，海牙地区法院支持俄罗斯的主张，以仲裁庭无管辖权为由决定撤销仲裁裁决。尤科斯石油公司的前总裁还在欧洲人权法院获得了要求俄罗斯支付尤科斯前股东18.66亿欧元的判决，但该判决也被俄罗斯宪法法院裁定不予执行。本案裁决虽然被撤销，但尤科斯方面在近几年来仍在不断寻求该裁决在一些国内法院得到承认和执行。

思考问题（Questions）

1. 中国加入《能源宪章公约》的利弊有哪些？

2. 在海牙地区法院撤销仲裁裁决的基础上，尤斯科是否还有法律上的可能性在其他国家法院获得承认和执行该裁决的判决？

案例十四 菲利普莫里斯诉乌拉圭案

Philip Morris Brands Sàrl, Philip Morris Products S. A. and Abal Hermanos S. A. v. Oriental Republic of Uruguay（2016）（ICSID Case No. ARB/10/7）

选读理由（Selected Reason）

作为烟草业巨头的菲利普莫里斯公司近年来频繁通过各种各样的法律手段挑战各国的控烟措施。和其他的跨国烟草企业一样，菲利普莫里斯在澳大利亚、乌拉圭等国的国内法领域推进了一系列诉讼，包括但不限于推进控烟措施上位法的违宪审查，或者推进控烟措施违反上位法或存在其他违法、无效情况的行政诉讼。在国际法领域，它不仅派出旗下不同的法人实体作为申请人在投资仲裁领域推进了诉乌拉圭（即本文所评析的案例）、诉澳大利亚两起案件，还是WTO领域5个挑战澳大利亚政府平装烟草法案的幕后推手之一。本案诉讼涉及间接征收及其赔偿问题、公平合理待遇问题、保护伞条款问题、拒绝司法以及法庭之友等诉讼程序问题。

仲裁申请情况（The Request for Arbitration）

Abal was formally established in its present form in 1945, although in an earlier incarnation it had manufactured and marketed tobacco products in Uruguay since 1877. Its main business after 1945 continued to be manufacturing cigarettes for export and sale in the local market. Abal was acquired by PMI in 1979. Twenty years later, in 1999, it became a wholly owned subsidiary of FTR Holding S. A ("FTR"). On or before 5 October 2010, PMB, as

FTR's successor, became Abal's 100% direct owner.

Abal concluded license agreements to manufacture and sell cigarettes under various Philip Morris brands. PMP was the owner of the Marlboro, Fiesta, L&M and Philip Morris trademarks which it licensed to Abal. Abal also used a number of Uruguayan trademarks registered in its own name to sell tobacco products. In particular, Abal sold the Marlboro, Fiesta, L&M, Philip Morris, Casino, and Premier brands of cigarettes in Uruguay; and it owns the Casino, Premier and associated trademarks.

阿贝尔公司于 1945 年以目前的形式正式成立,虽然在早期的一个前身中,它自 1877 年以来一直在乌拉圭制造和销售烟草产品。1945 年后,该公司的主要业务仍是生产出口卷烟,并在当地市场销售。阿贝尔公司于 1979 年被菲利普莫里斯国际公司收购。二十年后的 1999 年,它成为 FTR 控股有限公司("FTR")的全资子公司。2010 年 10 月 5 日或之前,菲利普莫里斯国际公司作为 FTR 的继承人,成为阿贝尔公司的 100% 直接所有人。

阿贝尔公司签订了生产和销售各种菲利普莫里斯品牌香烟的许可协议。菲利普莫里斯公司是万宝路、节日、L&M 和菲利普莫里斯商标的所有者,该商标已授权给阿贝尔公司。阿贝尔公司还使用了一些以自己名义注册的乌拉圭商标来销售烟草产品。具体而言,阿贝尔在乌拉圭出售万宝路、节日、L&M、菲利普莫里斯、娱乐场和总理品牌的香烟,并拥有娱乐场、总理和相关商标。

At its core, the dispute concerns allegations by the Claimants that, through several tobacco-control measures regulating the tobacco industry, the Respondent violated the BIT in its treatment of the trademarks associated with cigarettes brands in which the Claimants had invested. These measures included the Government's adoption of a single presentation requirement precluding tobacco manufacturers from marketing more than one variant of cigarette per brand family (the "Single Presentation Requirement" or "SPR"), and the increase in the size of graphic health warnings appearing on cigarette packages (the "80/80 Regulation"), jointly referred to as the "Challenged Measures."

这场纠纷的核心在于,申请人指控称,通过几项针对烟草行业的烟草控制措施,被申请人在对待申请人所投资与烟草品牌相关的商标上违反了双边投资协定。这些措施包括政府的单标签展示要求从而排除烟草制造商使用一个商标家族营销多种香烟("单一外观要求"或"SPR"),和加大出现在香烟包装上的健康警示图片的面积("80/80 规则"),这两项措施合称为"被质疑的措施"。

The Single Presentation Requirement was implemented through Ordinance 514 dated 18 August 2008 ("Ordinance 514") of the Uruguayan Ministry of Public Health (the "MPH"). Article 3 of Ordinance 514 requires each cigarette brand to have a "single presentation" and prohibits different packaging or "variants" for cigarettes sold under a given brand. Until the enactment of the SPR, Abal sold multiple product varieties under each of its brands (for example, "Marlboro Red," "Marlboro Gold," "Marlboro Blue" and "Marlboro Green (Fresh Mint)"). As a result of Ordinance 514, Abal ceased selling all but one of the product variants of each brand that it owns or holds licenses to (e. g. only Marlboro Red). The Claimants allege that the measure and lack of variant sales have substantially impacted the value of the company.

单一外观要求是通过 2008 年 8 月 18 日乌拉圭公共卫生部发布的第 514 号条例实施的（简称 514 条例）。514 条例第 3 条规定每个香烟品牌必须有一个"单一标签"，并禁止以某一品牌出售的香烟有不同的包装或"变体"。在单一外观要求颁布之前，阿贝尔公司在每个品牌下都销售多种产品［例如"万宝路红""万宝路金""万宝路蓝"和"万宝路绿（鲜薄荷）"］。实施 514 条例的后果是，阿贝尔公司只能销售其拥有或持有许可的每个品牌的所有产品变体中的一种（例如只保留万宝路红）。申请人声称，这一措施和缺少变体的销售对公司的价值产生了重大影响。

The 80/80 Regulation was implemented through the enactment of Presidential Decree No. 287/009 dated 15 June 2009 ("Decree 287"). Decree 287 imposes an increase in the size of prescribed health warnings of the surface of the front and back of the cigarette packages from 50% to 80%, leaving only 20% of the cigarette pack for trademarks, logos and other information. According to the Claimants, this wrongfully limits Abal's right to use its legally protected trademarks and prevents Abal from displaying them in their proper form. This, in the Claimants' view, caused a deprivation of PMP's and Abal's intellectual property rights, further reducing the value of their investment.

80/80 规则是通过 2009 年 6 月 15 日颁布的第 287/009 号总统令来执行的（简称"第 287 号法令"）。第 287 号法令规定，在香烟盒正面和背面的健康警告的尺寸从 50% 增加到 80%，只剩下 20% 的香烟盒用于商标、标志和其他信息。根据申请人的说法，这错误地限制了阿贝尔公司使用其受法律保护的商标的权利，并阻止阿贝尔公司以正确的形式展示它们。在申请人看来，这导致菲利普莫里斯公司和阿贝尔公司的知识产权被剥夺，进一步降低了他们投资的价值。

According to the Claimants, the Challenged Measures constitute breaches of the Respondent's obligations under BIT Articles 3 (1) (impairment of use and enjoyment of investments), 3 (2) (fair and equitable treatment and denial of justice), 5 (expropriation) and 11 (observance of commitments), entitling the Claimants to compensation under the Treaty and international law. They further claim damages arising from these alleged breaches. On this basis, the Claimants request that this Tribunal:

Either：

Order that Respondent withdraw the challenged regulations or refrain from applying them against Claimants' investments, and award damages incurred through the date of such withdrawal; or, in the alternative

Award Claimants damages of at least US ＄22. 267 million, plus compound interest running from the date of breach to the date of Respondent's payment of the award; and

Award Claimants all of their fees and expenses, including attorney's fees, incurred in connection with this arbitration; and

Award such other relief as the Tribunal deems just and appropriate.

根据申请人的说法，被质疑的措施违反了双边投资协定中被申请人在第 3 条（1）款（投资使用和享有的减损）、第 3 条（2）款（公平公正待遇和拒绝司法）、第 5 条（征收）和第 11 条（遵守承诺）中规定的义务，使申请人有权根据条约以及国际法获得赔偿。他们进一步要求赔偿因这些所谓的违约行为而产生的损失。在此基础上，申请人要求本仲裁庭或者责令被申请人撤销被质疑的法规或不将其适用于申请人的投资，并裁决在撤销之日之前所产生的损害；或者裁决给申请人至少 2226.7 万美元的损害赔偿金，加上从违约之日起至被申请人支付裁决之日止的复利，裁决给申请人与本仲裁有关的所有费用和开支，包括律师费，以及裁决仲裁庭认为公正和适当的其他救济。

Uruguay in turn holds that the Challenged Measures were adopted in compliance with Uruguay's international obligations, including the BIT, for the single purpose of protecting public health. According to Uruguay, both regulations were applied in a nondiscriminatory manner to all tobacco companies, and they amounted to a reasonable, good faith exercise of Uruguay's sovereign prerogatives. The SPR was adopted to mitigate the ongoing adverse effects of tobacco promotion, including the Claimants' false marketing that certain brand variants are safer than others, even after misleading descriptors such as "light," "mild," "ultra-light" were banned. The 80/80 Regulation was adopted to increase consumer awareness of the health risks of tobacco consumption and to encourage people, including younger people, to quit or not to take up smoking, while still leaving room on packages for brand names and logos. Thus for the Respondent, this case is "about protection of public health, not interference with foreign investment."

乌拉圭则认为，这些受到质疑的措施是按照乌拉圭的国际义务，包括双边投资协定，为保护公共卫生而采取的。根据乌拉圭的规定，这两项规定都以非歧视性的方式适用于所有烟草公司，它们是在合理、真诚地行使乌拉圭的主权。采用单一展示规则是为了减轻烟草促销持续产生的不利影响，包括申请人虚假营销某些品牌变体比其他品牌更安全，即使在"轻""淡""超轻"等具有误导性的描述被禁止之后。80/80 规则的通过是为了提高消费者对烟草消费的健康风险的认识，并鼓励包括年轻人在内的人们戒烟或不吸烟，同时在包装上仍留有品牌名称和标识的空间。因此，对于被申请人来说，这个案件是"关于保护公众健康，而不是干涉外国投资"。

On this basis the Oriental Republic of Uruguay, submits that: Claimants' claims should be dismissed in their entirety; and Uruguay should be awarded compensation for all the expenses and costs associated with defending against these claims.

在此基础上，乌拉圭东岸共和国提出：申请人的索赔要求应予全部驳回；乌拉圭应获得抗辩这些索赔有关的所有费用和支出的赔偿。

仲裁结果（Award）

For the reasons set forth above, the Tribunal decides as follows:

(1) The Claimants' claims are dismissed.

(2) The Claimants shall pay to the Respondent an amount of US $ 7 million on account of its own costs, and shall be responsible for all the fees and expenses of the Tribunal and ICSID's administrative fees and expenses, reimbursing to the Respondent all the amounts paid by it to the Centre on that account.

Arbitrator Born attaches a statement of dissent.

基于上述理由，仲裁庭决定如下：

(1) 被申请人的请求被驳回。

(2) 申请人应支付给被申请人 700 万美元以作为成本，并负责仲裁庭所有的费用和支出、争端解决中心的管理费用和开支，偿付被申请人所有的金额通过其在中心的账户支付。

仲裁员波恩附上了一份异议声明。

裁决原因（Reasons for the Award）

Article 5 (1) of the BIT refers to "any other measure having the same nature or the same effect" as an expropriation or a nationalization. Thus, indirect expropriation under the Treaty is defined in a different and apparently stricter way than in other treaties that make reference to measures, the effect of which, would be "tantamount" or "equivalent" to nationalization or expropriation. Be that as it may, in order to be considered an indirect expropriation, the government's measures interference with the investor's rights must have a major adverse impact on the Claimants' investments. As mentioned by other investment treaty decisions, the State's measures should amount to a "substantial deprivation" of its value, use or enjoyment, "determinative factors" to that effect being "the intensity and duration of the economic deprivation suffered by the investor as a result of such measures."

双边投资协定第 5 条（1）款是指与征收或国有化"具有相同性质或效果的任何其他措施"。因此，本条约中间接征收的定义与其他提及该类措施的条约不同，明显更为严格，要求这些措施的效果"无异于"或"等同于"国有化或征收。尽管如此，为了被视为间接征收，政府对投资者权利的干预措施必须对申请人的投资产生重大不利影响。正如对其他投资条约的裁决所述，国家的措施应相当于"实质性剥夺"其价值、使用权或享用权，这种影响的"决定性因素"是"投资者因此类措施而遭受的经济剥夺的强度和持续时间"。

As a matter of fact, Abal made use of all of its thirteen trademark variants before SP Reffectively banned seven of them, and the 80/80 Regulation limited "the space available for Claimants to display the visual elements of their remaining brands to only 20% of the front and back of the package." As to the Respondent's allegation regarding the Claimants' lack of valid title to the banned trademarks, the Tribunal refers to its ruling in that regard. The Tribunal concludes that the Claimants had property rights regarding their trademarks capable of being expropriated. It must now examine whether the Challenged Measures had an expropriatory character with regard to the Claimants' investment.

Regarding the 80/80 Regulation, the Claimants argue that it reduced the brand equity of those products that survived the implementation of the SPR, "depriving Abal of its ability to charge a premium price."

事实上，阿贝尔公司使用的 13 种商标变体在单一外观要求实施后被禁止使用了 7 种，而 80/80 规则限制了"申请人展示其剩余的品牌视觉元素的空间仅为包装正面和背面的 20%"。关于被申请人有关权利人对被取缔商标缺乏有效的所有权的主张，仲裁庭参照了这方面的裁决。仲裁庭的结论是，申请人对其商标拥有财产权，可以被没收。它现在必须审查被质疑的措施是否对申请人的投资具有征收的性质。

对于 80/80 规则，申请人争辩称其减少了那些在实施单一外观要求后幸存的产品的品牌资产，"剥夺了阿贝尔公司收取溢价的能力"。

In the Tribunal's view there is not even a prima facie case of indirect expropriation by the80/80 Regulation. The Marlboro brand and other distinctive elements continued to appear on cigarette packs in Uruguay, recognizable as such. A limitation to 20% of the space available to such purpose could not have a substantial effect on the Claimants' business since it consisted only in a limitation imposed by the law on the modalities of use of the relevant trademarks. The claim that the 80/80 Regulation breached Article 5 of the BIT consequently fails.

在仲裁庭看来，甚至没有 80/80 规则构成间接征收的初步证据。万宝路品牌和其他独特的元素继续出现在乌拉圭的香烟包装上，可以识别。限制 20% 的可用于该目的的空间不会对申请人的业务产生实质性影响，因为它仅包括法律对相关商标使用方式的限制。80/80 规则违反双边投资协定第 5 条的主张因此失败。

In the Tribunal's view, in respect of a claim based on indirect expropriation, as long as sufficient value remains after the Challenged Measures are implemented, there is no expropriation. As confirmed by investment treaty decisions, a partial loss of the profits that the investment would have yielded absent the measure does not confer an expropriatory character on the measure. In LG&E v. Argentina, for example, the tribunal held: Interference with the investment's ability to carry on its business is not satisfied where the investment continues to operate, even if profits are diminished. The impact must be substantial in order that compensation may be claimed for expropriation.

仲裁庭认为，对于基于间接征收的索赔，只要在被质疑的措施实施后仍有足够的价值，就没有征收。有些投资条约的裁决确认，如果没有该措施，投资将产生的部分利润损失不会赋予该措施征收性质。例如，在 LG&E 诉阿根廷案中，仲裁庭认为：如果投资继续经营，即使利润减少，对投资继续经营的能力的干扰也不满足条件。影响必须是实质性的，以便可以为征收要求赔偿。

In light of the foregoing, the Tribunal concludes that the Challenged Measures were a valid exercise by Uruguay of its police powers for the protection of public health. As such, they cannot constitute an expropriation of the Claimants' investment. For this reason also, the Claimants' claim regarding the expropriation of their investment must be rejected.

根据上述规定，仲裁庭得出结论，被质疑的措施是乌拉圭为保护公共卫生而有效行使其警察权的行为。因此，它们不能构成对申请人投资的征收。因此，申请人有关其投资被征收的请求也必须被驳回。

The Tribunal will proceed to determine whether the treatment afforded to the Claimants' investment by the Challenged Measures was in accordance with the FET standard, interpreted as indicated above. To this purpose, it will review each measure taking into account all relevant circumstances, including the margin of appreciation enjoyed by national regulatory agencies when dealing with public policy determinations.

仲裁庭将继续裁定，被质疑措施对申请人投资的待遇是否符合如上文所解释的公平公正待遇标准。为此，它将考虑所有相关情况，包括国家监管机构在处理公共政策决定时所享有的裁量权，以来审查每项措施。

The Tribunal agrees with the Respondent that the "margin of appreciation" is not limitedto the context of the ECHR but "applies equally to claims arising under BITs," at least in contexts such as public health. The responsibility for public health measures rests with the government and investment tribunals should pay great deference to governmental judgments of national needs in matters such as the protection of public health. In such cases respect is due to the "discretionary exercise of sovereign power, not made irrationally and not exercised in bad faith... involving many complex factors." As held by another investment tribunal, "the sole inquiry for the Tribunal... is whether or not there was a manifest lack of reasons for the legislation."

仲裁庭同意被申请人的意见，"裁量权"不仅限于《欧洲人权公约》的背景，而且"同样适用于双边投资协定引起的索赔"，至少在公共卫生等背景下。公共卫生措施的责任由政府承担，投资仲裁庭应在保护公共卫生等事项上对政府基于国家需要做出的判断予以极大的尊重。这种情况下，这是种尊重是由于"主权的自由行使，不是非理性的，也不是恶意的……涉及许多复杂因素"。另一个投资仲裁庭认为，"仲裁庭唯一需要调查的……是是否明显的缺乏立法的理由"。

Article 11 of the BIT, under the rubric "Observance of Commitments," provides: Either Contracting Party shall constantly guarantee the observance of the commitments it has entered into with respect to the investments of the investors of the other Contracting Party. The Tribunal concludes that Article 11 operates as an umbrella clause, at least for contract claims.

双边投资协定第11条在"遵守承诺"标题下规定：任何一缔约国应持续保证遵守其就另一缔约国投资者的投资所作出的承诺。仲裁庭得出结论，第11条作为一项"保护伞"条款，至少对合同索赔有效。

In addition, the scope of any such commitment remains uncertain. As compared to a contract, where the host State enters into specific, quantifiable obligations in relation to an investment, a trademark is not a promise by the host State to perform an obligation. It is simply a part of its general intellectual property law framework. A trademark gives rise to rights, but their extent, being subject to the applicable law, is liable to changes which may not be excluded by an umbrella clause: if investors want stabilization they have to contract for it.

The Tribunal concludes that trademarks are not "commitments" falling within the intended scope of Article 11 of the BIT. Accordingly, the Claimants' claim of breach by the Respondent of Article 11 by the adoption of the Challenged Measures is rejected.

此外，任何此类承诺的范围仍不确定。与合同相比，东道国对一项投资在合同项下承担具体的、可量化的义务，而商标不是东道国履行义务的承诺。它只是其一般知识产权法框架的一部分。商标产生了权利，但其范围受适用法律的制约，可能会发生变化，这一变化不会被排除"保护伞"条款之外，前提是：投资者通过签订合同将其确定下来。

仲裁庭得出结论，商标不属于双边投资协定第11条预期范围内的"承诺"。因此，申请人提出的被申请人通过实施被质疑的措施违反了第11条的主张驳回。

In the Tribunal's view, it is unusual that the Uruguayan judicial system separates out the mechanisms of review in this way, without any system for resolving conflicts of reasoning. The Tribunal believes, however, that it would not be appropriate to find a denial of justice because of this discrepancy. The Claimants were able to have their day (or days) in court, and there was an available judicial body with jurisdiction to hear their challenge to the 80/80 Regulation and which gave a properly reasoned decision. The fact that there is no further recourse from the TCA decision, which did not follow the reasoning of the SCJ, seems to be a quirk of the judicial system.

Under the Uruguayan judicial system, the SCJ can uphold the constitutionality of a law based on an interpretation of the scope of that law, in application of constitutional principles. That interpretation, however, does not bind the TCA when it determines, on the basis of the principles provided by administrative law, the legality of decrees rendered under that same law. That position does not seem to be manifestly unjust or improper, either in general or in the context of this case. Here both courts separately upheld the legality of the measure the Claimants sought to challenge, each under its own jurisdiction and applying its own legal criteria. In the Tribunal's view this does not rise to the level of a denial of justice.

在仲裁庭看来，乌拉圭司法系统不存在任何解决推理冲突的系统，以这种方式将审查机制分离出来是不寻常的。然而，仲裁庭认为，仅以这种不一致性而裁定构成拒绝司法是不恰当的。申请人能够在法庭上度过他们的一天（或几天），并且能得到一个有管辖权的司法机构来审理他们对80/80规则的质疑且给出了有正当推理的决定。事实上，对于没有遵循最高法院的推理而由行政争议法院所做出的决定，没有进一步的救济途径，这似乎是司法系统的怪异情况。

在乌拉圭司法制度下，最高法院可以在适用宪法原则的情况下，对法律在可解释的范围内维护法律的合宪性。但是该种解释对行政争议法院不构成约束，行政争议法院有权根据行政法规定的原则，基于同一法律而认定法令的合法性。无论是在一般情况下还是在本案的背景下，这种状况似乎并不明显、不公正或不适当。在这里，两个法院分别支持申请人所质疑的措施的合法性，每一个决定都在其自己的管辖范围内，并适用其自己的法律标准。在仲裁庭看来，这并没有上升到拒绝司法的程度。

On 30 January 2015, the World Health Organization (the "WHO") and the WHO Framework Convention on Tobacco Control Secretariat (the "FCTC Secretariat") submitted a request to file a written submission as a non-disputing party, pursuant to ICSID Arbitration Rule 37 (2).

On 12 February 2015, the WHO and the FCTC Secretariat's amicus curiae brief dated 28 January 2015 (the "WHO Amicus Brief") was transmitted to the Parties and the Tribunal. In their amicus brief, the WHO and the FCTC Secretariat concluded that: The action taken by Uruguay was taken in light of a substantial body of evidence that large graphic health warnings are an effective means of informing consumers of the risks associated with tobacco consumption and of discouraging tobacco consumption. There is also a substantial body of evidence [sic] that prohibiting brand variants is an effective means of preventing misleading branding of tobacco products. These bodies of evidence, which are consistent with statepractice, support the conclusion that the Uruguayan measures in question are effective means of protecting public health.

2015 年 1 月 30 日，世界卫生组织（以下简称"世卫组织"）和《世界卫生组织烟草控制框架公约》秘书处（以下简称"烟草控制框架公约秘书处"）根据 ICSID 仲裁规则第 37 条（2）款，提交了一份作为非争端当事方提交书面意见的请求。

2015 年 2 月 12 日，世卫组织和烟草控制框架公约秘书处签署日期为 2015 年 1 月 28 日的法庭之友简报（"世卫组织之友简报"）已转交给各方和仲裁庭。世卫组织和烟草控制框架公约秘书处在其中得出结论：乌拉圭采取的措施体现了一种"大面积的健康风险警示图片是提示消费者烟草消费的风险和劝阻烟草消费的有效手段"的理念，也存在大量的可靠证据证明禁止品牌的子牌是防止对烟草品牌的误解的有效手段，这些证据与众多缔约国的国家实践相一致，证明乌拉圭所采取的被挑战措施是保护公共健康的有效手段。

案件影响 (Impact of the Case)

各国烟草控制措施引发了关于外国投资保护与东道国公共健康管制权冲突与协调的重大争议。较早版本的双边投资协定所规定的，不受限制的公平公正待遇和间接征收条款，不利于东道国行使正当公共健康管制权。本案仲裁庭适用《维也纳条约法公约》（VCLT）第 31 条（3）款（c）项，援引习惯国际法解释和适用公平公正待遇和间接征收条款，认定东道国善意、合理、非歧视、合比例地行使公共健康管制权，不违反投资条约中不受限制的公平公正待遇和间接征收条款。2016 年 7 月 8 日，ICSID 仲裁庭做出的本案裁决，驳回了烟草企业一方（申诉方）的全部仲裁请求，判令其承担全部的仲裁费用和乌拉圭一方的费用。本案体现了仲裁庭通过条约解释平衡保护投资者私人权益和东道国公共健康的努力。

思考问题（Questions）

1. 部分利润的损失不构成征收的裁判观点，你是否同意这一说法？为什么？
2. 仲裁庭接受和拒绝法庭之友书面意见的标准是什么？

案例十五　乌巴塞诉阿根廷案

Urbaser S. A. and Consorcio de Aguas Bilbao Bizkaia，Bilbao Biskaia Ur Partzuergoav. The Argentine Republic （ICSID Case No. ARB/07/26）

选读理由（Selected Reason）

本案是关于 ICSID 东道国人权反诉的争议案件。投资仲裁实践中鲜有基于国际人权法来审判有关东道国人权争议的。此次裁决是第一个对东道国人权反诉进行详尽讨论的案例。因此，此项裁决更是给充分理解投资仲裁中的人权问题提供了一个机会。总之，本案在研究东道国人权反诉问题上具有前沿性与重要的指导意义。

仲裁申请情况（The Request for Arbitration）

On July 20，2007，the International Centre for Settlement of Investment Disputes（"IC-SID" or the "Centre"）received a Request for Arbitration（"the Request"）dated July 6，2007，presented in Spanish（"Solicitud de Arbitraje"）and submitted by Urbaser S. A. and Consorcio de Aguas Bilbao Bizkaia，Bilbao Biskaia Ur Partzuergoa（"Claimants" respectively "Urbaser" and "CABB"）against the Argentine Republic（"Argentina" or "Respondent"）. The Claimants submitted the Request pursuant to Article X of the Agreement on the Reciprocal Promotion and Protection of Investments between the Argentine Republic and the Kingdom of Spain signed on October 3，1991（"Argentina-Spain BIT" or "the BIT"）.

2007 年 7 月 20 日，国际解决投资争端中心（"ICSID"或"中心"）收到了一份西班牙语的仲裁申请书，上面签署的日期为 2007 年 7 月 6 日，由乌巴塞公司和比斯开省毕尔巴鄂水务集团公司提交（申请人，分别简称为"乌巴塞"和"CABB"），相对方即被申请人为阿根廷共和国（简称"阿根廷"或者"被申请人"）。申请人根据阿根廷和西班牙签署于 1991 年 10 月 3 日的《相互促进和保护投资协定》（简称"阿根廷—西班牙 BIT"或者"BIT"）中的第 10 条提交了此项申请。

Summarized to its shortest expression, the dispute submitted to this Tribunal relates to a Concession for water and sewage services to be provided in the Province of Greater Buenos Aires. It was granted in early 2000 to Aguas Del Gran Buenos Aires S. A. （AGBA）, a Company established by foreign investors and shareholders, including Claimants in the present proceeding. Claimants assert that they faced numerous obstructions on the part of the Province's authorities, which rendered the efficient and profitable operation of the Concession extremely difficult. The Concession was running into deadlock when Argentine suffered its economic crisis beginning in mid-2001, culminating in the emergency measures taken in January 2002, including a conversion of 1∶1 between USD and Argentine Peso at a time whenthe Peso had depreciated by more than two thirds of its value. AGBA's numerous requests for a new valuation of its tariffs and for a complete review of the Concession all failed in front of the Province's lack of any serious commitment to bring the required renegotiation process to a successful end. Political reasons related to the fate of other concessions finally caused the Province to declare AGBA's Concession terminated in July 2006. This was just the final step of a long process of persistent neglect of AGBA's shareholders' interests on the part of the Province, comprising several violations by the Argentine Republic of Articles Ⅲ, Ⅳ and Ⅴ of the Spain-Argentine BIT.

最简短的概括，提交本仲裁庭的争议涉及在大布宜诺斯艾利斯省提供供水和污水服务的特许权。2000 年初，特许权被授予布宜诺斯艾利斯水务公司（AGBA）——一家由外国投资者和股东（包括本仲裁程序中的申请人）设立的公司。申请人声称，他们面临着该省当局的许多阻挠，这使得特许经营的效率和盈利极为困难。从 2001 年中期开始，阿根廷人遭受经济危机时，特许经营陷入了僵局，2002 年 1 月采取了紧急措施，其中包括比索贬值超过三分之二时将美元与阿根廷比索以 1∶1 做了兑换。由于该省没有认真承诺成功结束所需的重新谈判进程，AGBA 提出的对其关税进行新估价和对特许权进行全面审查的众多请求均宣告失败。与其他特许权相关的政治原因最终导致该省宣布 AGBA 的特许权于 2006 年 7 月终止。这只是在该省部分长期忽视 AGBA 股东利益行为中的最后一步，另外阿根廷共和国还多次违反西班牙和阿根廷双边投资协定的第三条、第四条和第五条。

Claimants' Prayer for Relief is stated in their Memorial on the Merits and has been amended in their Reply on the Merits and Answer to Counterclaim as follows:

A) As regards the complaint filed by CABB and URBASER:

1. A declaration that the Argentine Republic breached the provisions of the Bilateral Investment Treaty executed between the Argentine Republic and the Kingdom of Spain on October 3, 1991 and, in particular, the following obligations of the referred Treaty: Article Ⅲ. 1 on the obligation to protect foreign investments and the prohibition to adopt unjustified or discriminatory measures; Article Ⅳ. 1 on the obligation to afford fair and equitable treatment to the referred investments; and Article Ⅴ, which forbids any illegal and discriminatory expropriation of foreign investments and imposes the obligation to compensate the investor in the event of expropriation or any other measure of similar characteristics and effects.

2. An order for the Argentine Republic to compensate CABB and URBASER

for all damages caused by the referred breaches and, consequently, to pay the following amounts:

2. 1 USD 152,798, 862 (one hundred fifty two million, seven hundred ninety eight thousand eight hundred and sixty two U. S. dollars) to urbaser S. A.

2. 2 USD 163,619,810 (one hundred sixty three million, six hundred nineteen thousand eight hundred and ten U. S. dollars to consorcio de aguas bilbao bizkaia, bilbao bizkaia urpartzuergoa.

2. 3. The interest accrued on the amounts mentioned in items 2. 1 and 2. 2 aboveat a compound interest rate of 15% (Fifteen Percent), to be counted from November 15, 2013 until the effective payment.

申请人的请求在其案情提要中陈述, 并在其案情答复和反请求答复中作了如下修改:

a) 关于 CABB 和 Urbaser 提出的诉求:

1. 阿根廷共和国违反阿根廷共和国与西班牙王国于 1991 年 10 月 3 日签订的双边投资条约的规定, 特别是所指条约的以下义务: 第 3 条 1 款关于保护外国投资和禁止采取不正当或歧视性措施的义务; 第 4 条 1 款关于公平公正对待投资的义务; 第 5 条禁止对外国投资进行任何非法和歧视性的征收, 并要求如果发生征用或其他类似特征和效果的措施, 有义务补偿投资者。

2. 裁令阿根廷共和国对于因上述违约行为造成的所有损害赔偿 CABB 和乌巴塞, 并支付以下金额:

2.1 向乌巴塞支付 152798862 美元。

2.2 向 CABB 支付 163619810 美元。

2.3. 上述第 2 条 1 款和第 2 条 2 款所述金额的应计利息按 15% 的复利率计算, 从

2013 年 11 月 15 日开始计算，直至实际支付完为止。

3. An order instructing the Argentine Republic to make any additional compensation as may be required to remedy the damages caused to the Claimants, as deemed just and adequate by the Tribunal.

4. The mandate for the Argentine Republic to bear the costs of this arbitration, including the fees payable to the ICSID, the fees and costs incurred by the Arbitral Tribunal and all legal costs, experts' fees, and any other expenses incurred by the Claimants in this proceeding under the concept of full compensation.

This request for relief and payment of interest contemplates any amounts resulting from the evidence produced in this arbitration, as deemed appropriate by the Arbitral Tribunal.

The Claimants hereby expressly reserve the right to supplement, add to or amend the claims asserted in this Memorial, according to the circumstances considered in the course of the arbitration proceeding, pursuant to Article 46 of the ICSID Convention.

Alternatively, Claimants fully reiterate their requests stated in their Memorial on the Merits of January 27, 2001, retaining the damages and interest amounts as established in said Memorial.

B) As regards the counterclaim presented by the Argentine Republic, we hereby request that it be fully dismissed by the Arbitral Tribunal, with an award against Respondent for all costs and expenses arising therefrom, in line with the principle of full compensation.

3. 裁决指示阿根廷共和国按照仲裁庭认为用公正和适当的方式，对申请人造成的损害进行补救，并作出可能需要的任何额外赔偿。

4. 要求阿根廷共和国承担本次仲裁费用，包括应支付给 ICSID 的费用、仲裁庭产生的费用和开支以及所有法律费用、专家费用和申请人在本程序中根据全部赔偿的概念所产生的任何其他费用。

本项利息的减少或支付考虑本次仲裁中的证据所可以证明的金额，以仲裁庭认为适当的为准。

根据《ICSID 公约》第 46 条，申请人在此明确保留根据仲裁程序中考虑的情况补充、增加或修改本法律意见中主张的索赔的权利。

或者，申请人充分重申其在 2001 年 1 月 27 日案情法律意见中提出的请求，保留该法律意见中确定的损害赔偿金和利息金额。

b) 关于阿根廷共和国提出的反诉，我们在此要求仲裁庭完全驳回该反诉，并根据全额赔偿的原则，裁决被申请人因此产生的所有费用和开支。

Respondent denies all claims submitted to this Tribunal by Claimants. Respondent rejects all of Claimants' allegations in relation to purported violations of the Concession Contract on part of the Argentine's authorities, all of which are in any event not under the jurisdiction of this Tribunal. The difficulties the Concession was faced with were in large part grounded on AGBA's and its shareholders' deficient management, most expressly demonstrated by their incapacity to proceed efficiently in collecting bills from the network's users. In addition, and even more importantly, the Concession was fundamentally undermined by the investors' failure to perform their obligations when it was confirmed that nothing efficient had been done to provide even minimal investment for the first years of operation, with resources either from third-parties or from the shareholders themselves. After one and a half year of operation, AGBA was already compelled to declare its incapacity to fulfil its undertakings in view of the expansion of the network. This situation having never been remedied, even with the assistance of the Province during a renegotiation process conducted over more than a year, there remained no other solution than to declare the Concession Contract terminated. The Argentine Republic raises a Counterclaim based on Claimants' alleged failure to provide the necessary investment into the Concession, thus violating its commitments and its obligations under international law based on the human right to water.

被申请人否认申请人向本法庭提交的所有索赔。被申请人拒绝所有申请人声称阿根廷当局违反特许合同的指控，这些指控在任何情况下均不属于本仲裁庭的管辖范围。特许经营所面临的困难很大程度上是由于 AGBA 及其股东管理不善，最明显的表现是他们无法有效地向网络用户收取账单费用。此外，更重要的是，投资者未能履行其义务，没有有效地从第三方或投资者自身获得资源提供甚至最少的投资用于最初几年的运营，从根本上破坏了特许经营权。经过一年半的运营，乌巴塞已经被迫宣布其无能力履行其在网络扩展方面的承诺。这种情况从未得到纠正，即使在一年多的重新谈判过程中，在该省的协助下，仍然没有其他解决办法，只能宣布特许合同终止。阿根廷共和国提出反诉，理由是申请人未能向特许经营提供必要的投资，从而违反了其在国际法下基于水的人权的承诺和义务。

Respondent's Prayer for Relief is stated in both of its Counter-Memorial and Re-joinder Submissions on the Merits and in its Post-Hearing Brief, which contains the latest amended drafting requesting that the Tribunal:

(a) dismiss each and every claim submitted by Claimants.

(b) allow the Counterclaim submitted by Argentina and award damages, plus pre-award and post-award interest, as from the moment the harm was caused to Argentina until the time of actual payment.

(c) grant Argentina any other remedies the Tribunal may deem fair.

(d) order Claimants to pay for all costs and expenses arising from these arbitration proceedings.

被申请人的救济请求在其关于案情的抗辩法律意见和重新合并的意见书以及其听证会后摘要意见中均有陈述，其中载有最新修订的申请文本，要求仲裁庭：

1. 驳回申请人所呈交的每项申请。

2. 允许阿根廷提出反诉并支持阿根廷的损害赔偿请求，自阿根廷造成损害的那一刻起直至实际付款时支付裁决前和裁决后的利息。

3. 给予阿根廷仲裁庭认为公平的任何其他补救措施。

4. 命令申请人支付仲裁程序产生的所有费用和开支。

仲裁结果（Award）

The tribunal awards as follows:

1. To confirm its Decision on Jurisdiction of December 19, 2012 and to assert that the Centre has jurisdiction and the Tribunal has competence over the Argentine Republic's Counterclaim.

2. To declare that the Argentine Republic breached Article IV (1) of the Bilateral Investment Treaty executed between the Argentine Republic and the Kingdom of Spain on October 3, 1991 in not affording fair and equitable treatment to Claimants in relation to the renegotiation of the Concession Contract in the period between 2003 and 2005.

3. To dismiss URBASER's and CABB's other claims for a declaration on a breach of this Bilateral Investment Treaty.

4. To dismiss in their entirety URBASER's and CABB's claims to order the Argentine Republic to pay compensatory damages.

5. To dismiss the Counterclaim submitted by the Argentine Republic and related to the human right to access to drinking water and sanitation.

6. To order the Argentine Republic to pay to URBASER and CABB a contribution to their legal fees and costs incurred in respect of the jurisdiction phase in the amount of USD 400,000, and Claimants' share of the advance for costs paid to ICSID during the jurisdictional phase in the amount of USD 647,000 together with annual interest of 3% as from 60 days after the date of the issuance of this Award.

7. To decide that the costs incurred by ICSID as from the end of the jurisdictional phase, including the Arbitrators' fees and expenses, shall be born in equal parts by both URBASER and CABB and by the Argentine Republic.

8. To dismiss any other claim submitted by any Party.

仲裁庭裁决如下：

1. 确认 2012 年 12 月 19 日仲裁庭所做出的管辖权裁决，并且确认国际解决投资争端中心与仲裁庭对阿根廷共和国政府提出的反诉拥有管辖权。

2. 宣告由于阿根廷共和国政府在 2003 年到 2005 年间重新谈判特许权合同中，没有给申请人提供公平公正的待遇，因此违反了阿根廷共和国政府与西班牙王国政府于 1991 年 10 月 3 日签署的《双边投资协议》的第 5 条（1）款。

3. 驳回乌巴塞和 CABB 关于宣告被申请人违反了《双边投资协议》的其他请求。

4. 驳回乌巴塞和 CABB 要求阿根廷政府赔偿其所遭受损失的请求。

5. 驳回阿根廷政府提出的有关于获得饮用水以及清洁卫生的人权的反诉。

6. 裁决被申请人阿根廷政府承担乌巴塞和 CABB 在管辖权仲裁阶段的仲裁过程中产生的合法的费用与支出，数额为 400000 美元，以及在管辖权仲裁阶段申请人支付给 ICSID 的相应部分，数额为 647000 美元，以及自本裁决作出后 60 日起按照每年 3% 所计算的相应利息。

7. 决定 ICSID 在管辖权裁决阶段后产生的费用，包括仲裁员的费用与支出，需要由申请人与被申请人共同承担。

8. 驳回双方当事人其他的仲裁请求。

裁决原因（Reasons for the Award）

The nature of the "dispute" to be decided "on the substance" within 18 months

The Tribunal finds that Claimants have furnished important evidence based upon the results of a statistical study undertaken within the office of Argentina's Attorney General. Indeed, Mr. Rosatti commented on this study while serving as Argentina's Attorney General. The study covered about 1,600 proceedings directed against the Federal Government from 1985 to 2000 similar in nature and complexity to investment disputes. The study yielded two significant propositions. Firstly, the average time in which a ruling on the merits took place was six years and one month. Secondly, none of the cases considered was adjudicated on the merits at the trial court level within 18 months. It is important to note here that this evidence is uncontroverted. In fact, Respondent has not objected to its content. In addition, Respondent has not disputed the factual basis or any assumption upon which the study is premised. Respondent also has refrained from objecting to the study's methodology, content, conclusions, or quality. In this connection, Respondent did not offer a more recent study or analysis that would somehow mitigate the 1985 to 2000 findings with facts of more contemporary vintage. In light of this uncontested evidence, the Tribunal can draw no conclusion other than to admit that the average duration of proceedings involving the State farexceeds 18 months and that it is extremely rare, if not altogether impossible, to have a proceeding of the nature of an investment dispute conclude, even at the trial court level, within 18 months.

争议应在 18 个月内在实体上做出决定的性质

仲裁庭认为，申请人根据阿根廷司法部长办公室内进行的统计研究的结果提供了重要证据。事实上，罗萨蒂在担任阿根廷司法部长期间对这项研究发表了评论。这项研究涵盖了从 1985 年到 2000 年针对联邦政府的大约 1600 项诉讼，其性质和复杂性与投资争端相似。这项研究提出了两个重要的论点。第一，对案件作出实体决定的平均时间是六年零一个月。第二，在 18 个月内，所有被考虑的案件都没有在初审法院层面作出实体判决。重要的是要注意，这一证据是无可争议的。事实上，被申请人并没有反对其内容。此外，被申请人没有对研究所依据的事实依据或任何假设提出异议。被申请人也避免反对研究的方法、内容、结论或质量。在这方面，被申请人没有提供一个更新的研究或分析，以某种方式证明近年来的情况比 1985 年至 2000 年的调查结果有所减轻。鉴于这一没有争议的证据，除承认涉及该国的诉讼平均持续时间远远超过 18 个月外，仲裁庭无法得出任何结论，而且即使并非完全不可能，具有投资争端性质的诉讼在 18 个月内结束初审法院层面的程序也极为罕见。

Based on the findings explained above, it appears that clearly none of the various possible alternative means for litigating before the domestic courts of the Argentine Republic, as presented by Respondent and supported by Prof. Mata, are suitable to meet the requirements of Article X (2) and (3) of the BIT. An investor-state dispute before the courts of Argentina would far exceed the 18 months fixed by Article X (3) of the BIT for purposes of reaching a "decision on the substance." A proceeding that can in no reasonable way be expected to reach that target is useless and unfair to the investor. Claimants were not required to engage in such a "proceeding" pursuant to the provisions of Article X (2) and (3) of the BIT. This conclusion is further supported by the Republic of Argentina's position under domestic law pursuant to which Claimants in any event would lackjus standi before the Republic's domestic courts because they are claiming rights allegedly belonging exclusively to AGBA and not to its shareholders. This matter has also to be examined in light of the Republic of Argentina's second objection to the Tribunal's jurisdiction.

In light of the foregoing conclusion, there is no need to examine whether the Most Favoured Nation Clause (MFN clause) contained in Article IV (2) of the BIT is here applicable. As Claimants were not required to comply with the 18 month rule under the facts presented to this Tribunal, the question of the applicability of the MFN clause is moot.

根据以上解释的调查结果，显然，在阿根廷共和国国内法院进行诉讼的由被申请人提出并由 Mata 教授支持的各种可能的替代方式中，没有一种是适合于满足 BIT 第 10 条第（2）款和第（3）款要求的。在阿根廷法院审理的投资者—国家纠纷将远远超过 BIT 第 10 条（3）款以达成"实体性决定"为目标的 18 个月。一项无法以合理方式预期从而达到该目标的诉讼对投资者来说是无用和不公平的。根据 BIT 第 10 条第（2）款和第（3）款的规定，申请人无须参与此类"诉讼程序"。阿根廷共和国在国内法下的立场进一步支持了这一结论，根据该立场，在任何情况下，申请人在共和国国内法院面前都将缺乏出庭资格，因为他们声称权利仅属于 AGBA，而不是属于其股东。鉴于阿根廷共和国对仲裁庭管辖权第二次提出反对，对这一问题应进行审查。

鉴于上述结论，无须检查 BIT 第 4 条第（2）款中包含的最惠国条款（最惠国条款）是否适用于此。由于根据提交给本仲裁庭的事实，申请人无须遵守 18 个月的规则，因此最惠国待遇条款的适用性问题是没有意义的。

The failure of the renegotiation

Shortly after the New Regulatory Framework took effect, on June 12, 2003, the Federal Government, the Province and nine Municipalities, some of which belong to Region B, signed a Master Agreement（"Acuerdo Marco"）providing for joint work to be undertaken for solutions to the sanitary emergency affecting the population of Greater Buenos Aires and to carry out negotiations in order to obtain funds from the World Bank. The Agreement was later approved by Decree No. 2397/03 of December 5, 2003, which relied on the NRF（CU-139）. The Province took responsibility for the construction of another part of the network to serve 870,000 inhabitants that were to be incorporated to the wastewater service, covering an investment of ARS 160 million from loans granted by the World Bank, budget funds and revenues accumulated in the infrastructure trust fund held by the Province. Consequently, AGBA was invited by a letter of January 29, 2004（CU-140）to a meeting to assess the progress of the projects performed with the sums loaned by the World Bank in seven districts that were part of the Concession Area under AGBA's charge. On June 28, 2004, AGBA approved the text of an agreement to be subscribed with the Province. AGBA was designated therein as the "Concessionaria", however with a role limited to advise on technical feasibility and supervision. The works were undertaken in parallel to AGBA's presence on the network and they have thus certainly affected the negotiations between AGBA and the Province. For Witness Seillant, this was the first success of the renegotiation. The size of the projects submitted to the World Bank was important and represented for the five concerned districts in AGBA's Zone 2 an increase of the expansion of the water service of 36,556 connections（25%）and for the sewerage service of

98，436 connections（115%）．

重新谈判的失败

新的监管框架生效后不久，2003 年 6 月 12 日，联邦政府、省和 9 个市（其中一些属于 B 类地区）签署了一项框架协议（"框架协议"），规定为解决影响大布宜诺斯艾利斯人口卫生的紧急情况而开展联合工作并进行谈判，以便从世界银行获得资金。该协议后来获得 2003 年 12 月 5 日第 2397/03 号法令的批准，该法令依赖于 NRF（CU-139）。该省负责建设供水网络的另一部分，为拟纳入污水处理服务的 87 万居民提供服务，投资的 1.6 亿比索来自世界银行发放的贷款、预算基金和省持有的基础设施建设基金的积累收入。因此，2004 年 1 月 29 日的一封信（CU-140）邀请 AGBA 参加一次会议，以评估由世界银行贷款的七个地区项目的进展情况，这些地区是 AGBA 负责的特许经营区域的一部分。2004 年 6 月 28 日，AGBA 批准了与省签署的协议文本。其中，AGBA 被指定为"特许经营机构"，但其作用仅限于就技术可行性和监督提供建议。这项工作与 AGBA 在网络上的存在并行进行，因此肯定影响了阿格巴和该省之间的谈判。对于目击者塞兰来说，这是重新谈判的第一次成功。向世界银行提交的项目规模非常重要，代表了 AGBA2 区的五个相关地区供水系统扩建 36556 个连接点（25%），排水系统扩建 98436 个连接点（115%）。

In the context of renegotiations that were initially caused by Argentina's emergency and the measures taken thereafter, the Concessionaire could expect to be treated with more deference when it had waited more than a year for the renegotiation to start and contributed to it with substantial proposals that have been seriously taken into consideration by the Province. If the Province's policy shifted towards aligning the outcome of the Concession for Zone 2 with the fate of the concession of Zone 1 and others on the national scale, one could expect that in one way or the other, AGBA as counterpart in the negotiation would have been told so clearly and officially. This did not happen and despite a number of other requests for renewal of the talks, the Province remained closed off from further exchanges of views on this topic until in March 2006 when AGBA got to learn that the outcome of Aguas Argentinas' concession was the signal for the termination of AGBA's Concession. It was then also told by Mr. Sanguinetti at the meeting of March 22, 2006 that it was expected to accept, without further negotiation, to request termination based on an agreement with the Province, as explained by Witness Hernando at the hearing. AGBA declined to act accordingly. There was no ground for keeping AGBA on hold from February until the end of 2005 without informing the Concessionaire about the policy that then came to prevail and that was of a nature to most probably determine AGBA's future. Nor was it fair and equitable to invite AGBA to submit proposals for a renegotiation and to entertain intensive discussions, which were put to an end abruptly in reliance on federal policies unrelated to the Concession under negotiation and producing an impact that the Province must have been aware of in advance but did not inform AGBA's representatives appropriately.

在最初由阿根廷紧急情况引起的重新谈判和随后采取的措施的背景下，特许权享有人在等待重新谈判开始一年多的时间内贡献了实质性的被该省认真考虑的建议，本来期望得到更多的尊重。如果该省的政策转向将2区特许权的结果与1区和其他国家范围内的特许权的命运保持一致，人们可以预期，无论以何种方式，谈判中作为对手的AGBA将都会被明确和正式地告知。但这并没有发生，尽管有许多其他要求重新举行会谈的要求，但该省一直不再就这一问题交换意见。直到2006年3月，AGBA得知阿古斯阿根廷的特许权的结果是终止AGBA的信号时。随后，按照证人赫尔南多在听证会上的解释，桑吉内蒂先生在2006年3月22日的会议上也被告知，将不再进一步协商而是被要求终止与该省的协议。AGBA拒绝照此办理。从2005年2月到2005年底，在没有告知特许权享有人当时的被广泛要求接受的政策的情况下，没有理由让AGBA一直处于停顿状态，这很可能决定了AGBA的未来。邀请AGBA提出重新谈判和进行深入讨论的建议也不是公平和公正的，这些建议由于依赖与正在谈判的特许权无关的联邦政策而突然终止，并产生了该省必须意识到的影响，但没有适当地通知AGBA的代表。

The situation became different as from the end of 2005 and early 2006, when the Province must have been informed of the two Notices of dispute Claimants had submitted to the Government of the Argentine Republic. According to these formal documents, Claimants were envisaging the filing of claims for arbitration. Such an initiative must have been understood as a sign that Claimants were not interested in pursuing with the Concession any longer.

The Tribunal therefore concludes that in light of these circumstances, Respondent-acting through the Province-failed in the period covering the Concession's renegotiation between 2003 and 2005 to provide AGBA and Claimants with a transparent treatment that could reasonably be expected from the host State in its relation to foreign investors. This amount to a violation of the standard of fair and equitable treatment under the BIT and the Tribunal will so declare.

The protection afforded by the standard of fair and equitable treatment cannot provide redress where the failure of the Concession is predominantly attributable to the failure on part of Claimants to make the required investment, resulting in a situation where no expansion work or other development could be envisaged any longer on the basis of the undertakings initially agreed upon. Consequently, the Tribunal dismisses Claimants' requests for payment of damages in this respect.

从2005年底到2006年初，情况有所不同，当时该省应当已收到向阿根廷共和国政府提交的两份争端索赔通知。根据这些正式文件，申请人准备提出仲裁要求。这种主动作为必须被理解为一种迹象，表明申请人不再有兴趣继续寻求特许权。

因此，仲裁庭得出结论，鉴于这些情况，被申请人（通过省行事）未能在2003年至2005年期间就特许权的重新谈判提供一种透明的待遇，这本来是可以合理地从东道国与外国投资者的关系之中来预期。这相当于违反了BIT的公平和公正待遇标准，仲裁庭将作出这一宣告。

如果特许经营权的失败主要是由于部分申请人未能进行所需投资，导致无法按照最初同意的设想进行扩建工程或其他开发，则公平和公正待遇标准提供的保护无法提供补救。因此，仲裁庭驳回了申请人在这方面的损害赔偿请求。

Respondent's Counterclaim

The Tribunal observes that Claimants explain their basic position by the asymmetric nature of BITs, which in their view prevents a host State from invoking any right based on such a treaty, including through the submission of a counterclaim. The Tribunal finds that this submission conflicts with the simple wording of the dispute resolution provisions of Article X of the BIT invoked in the instant case. Indeed, Article X (1) provides:

"1. Disputes arising between a Party and an investor of the other Party in connection with investments within the meaning of this Agreement shall, as far as possible, be settled amicably between the parties to the dispute."

It further follows from the dual possibility to initiate an arbitration that the BIT does include in the dispute resolution mechanisms retained in Article X the hypothesis of a counterclaim, provided that the requirements defined by the provisions governing such mechanism are met. Indeed, when both parties are entitled to lodge a claim, it cannot happen that in acting first one party could prevent the other from raising its claim. This can be avoided only by admitting the possibility of a counterclaim.

被申请人的反诉

仲裁庭注意到，申请人解释他们的基本立场是基于BIT的不对称性，他们认为BIT的不对称性阻止东道国援引任何基于此类条约的权利，包括通过提出反诉。仲裁庭认为，该提交与当前案件中援引的BIT第10条争议解决条款的简单措辞相冲突。实际上，第10条（1）款规定：

"1. 一方与另一方投资者之间发生的与本协议含义内的投资有关的争议，应尽可能在争议双方之间友好解决。"

此外，从提起仲裁的双重可能性来看，只要符合管辖该机制的规定所规定的要求，则BIT将反诉假设纳入第10条所保留的争端解决机制。事实上，当双方都有权提出索赔时，不可能一方作为第一方阻止另一方提出索赔。这只能通过承认反诉的可能性来避免。

However, this does not answer the question whether Claimants' as investors werc bound by an obligation based on international law to provide the population living on the territory of the Concession with drinking water and sanitation services. Respondent does not, in fact, go so far. Indeed, it argues that such human right was incumbent on Claimants because providing for water and sewage was AGBA's and therefore its shareholders' obligation under the Concession. Even if this obligation could be imposed upon Claimants, Respondent does not state that such obligation is based on international law. It merely asserts that the performance obligation under the Concession had the effect of supplying the services that are part of the population's human right to access to water. Respondent also states that Claimants had violated human rights obligations clearly applicable to international companies. This argument does not reference any particular international law obligation, but relies only on AGBA's obligations based on the Concession Contract. And while Respondent correctly introduces the principle of pacta sunt servanda as a principle of international law, it identifies the relevant pactum as Claimants' obligation to invest in expansion work, thus relying again on the Concession Contract and admitting that international law does not provide a cause of action for the Counterclaim.

但是，这并不能回答申请人作为投资者是否是基于国际法规定而受到向居住在特许区领土上的居民提供饮用水和卫生服务的义务的约束。事实上，被申请人并没有证明这一点。事实上，它认为，这种人权是权利人的责任，因为提供水和污水处理服务是 AGBA 的，因此也是其股东在特许权下的义务。即使该义务可以强加给申请人，被申请人也没有说明该义务是基于国际法的。它仅声称，特许权下的履行义务产生了提供服务的效果，这些服务是人民获得水的人权的一部分。被申请人还指出，申请人违反了明确适用于国际公司的人权义务。该论点并未提及任何具体的国际法义务，而是仅依赖于 AGBA 基于特许合同的义务。虽然被申请人正确地将"条约必须遵守"的原则作为国际法的一项原则加以介绍，但它将相关的"条约"确定为权利人投资扩建工程的义务，从而再次依赖特许权合同，也就承认了国际法未提供提出反诉的诉由。

The Tribunal also notes that Respondent does not state any legal ground for any individual's right to claim damages as a consequence of an alleged violation of the human right to water. Respondent does not demonstrate either that the alleged violation of such human right entails a duty of reparation equally based on international law, with the effect that the individuals concerned by such an alleged harm obtain an appropriate compensation. Respondent failed to state such a claim. This would be a reason sufficient to dismiss Respondent's Counterclaim. The Tribunal adds that such failure can also be explained by the lack of any legal ground based on international law that would entitle a group of individuals to raise a claim for performance for delivery of water and sewage services directed against a company or any other private party. Accordingly, there does not exist a claim for compensation in case of lack of such performance not based on an obligation under international law.

For the reasons given above, Respondent's Counterclaim must fail.

仲裁庭还注意到，被申请人没有陈述任何个人因水的人权被侵犯而有权要求损害赔偿的法律依据。被申请人也没有证明，被指控侵犯水的人权会导致赔偿责任是有国际法基础的，从而可使被指控的损害所涉个人获得适当的赔偿。被申请人没有陈述这样的索赔理由。这将是驳回被申请人反诉的充分理由。法庭补充说，这种失败也可以解释为缺乏任何基于国际法的法律依据，这种依据将使一组个人有权针对一家公司或任何其他私人方提出履行供水和污水服务的索赔。因此，不存在不履行国际法规定义务情况下的索赔事由。

基于上述原因，被申请人的反请求必须失败。

案件影响（Impact of the Case）

本案申请人西班牙的投资方乌巴塞因在阿根廷投资受损而提起仲裁。其提起仲裁的原因包括在阿根廷遭遇金融危机，货币大幅贬值，投资大幅缩水；融资困难遭遇很多偷水盗水不愿付费的用户，导致业务难以开展；希望与当地政府重谈特许合同但未获成功。最终，仲裁庭虽认定了在重新谈判过程中政府未与投资者保持充分沟通从而违背了公平公正待遇，但因特许经营合同被终止的根本原因仍然是投资者投资不足未能全面履约扩大供水覆盖范围。因此仲裁庭未要求阿根廷赔偿，这一裁决结果适当平衡了在很多仲裁案件中涉嫌被过度扩张的 FET 义务。

阿根廷在此案里提出了一个罕见的反诉，主张投资者违反国际人权法，未能向所涉地区提供足够的水，损害了该地居民的水权。仲裁庭经充分论证确认了对反诉的管辖权，该案开人权反诉之先河，这是第一次因为 ICSID 条约允许任何一方提出索赔，从而允许提出反诉。另外，本案还涉及仲裁员独立性等问题。

思考问题（Questions）

1. 反诉是否属于该仲裁中心的管辖范围？
2. 哪些人权应当对国际投资者具有约束力？

案例十六　韩国安城公司诉中国案

Ansung Housing Co., Ltd. v. People's Republic of China
(ICSID Case No. ARB/14/25)

选读理由（Selected Reason）

本案是关于 ICSID 仲裁时效的争议案件。韩国安城公司在与江苏省射阳港口产业园区管委会达成的一份土地投资开发合同的履行过程中发生争议。故此，2014 年 10 月 7 日安城公司根据中韩双边投资保护协定（中韩 BIT）向 ICSID 申请仲裁。在当前中韩关系敏感时期，该案尤其引人关注。本案涉及投资仲裁时效的争议事项，仲裁庭在本案裁决中体现的观点对理解仲裁时效及在最惠国待遇条款中仲裁时效的适用问题具有重要指导意义。

仲裁申请情况（The Request for Arbitration）

This case concerns a dispute submitted to the International Centre for Settlement of Investment Disputes ("ICSID" or the "Centre") by Ansung Housing Co., Ltd. ("Ansung" or "Claimant"), a privately-owned company incorporated under the laws of the Republic of Korea, against the People's Republic of China ("China" or "Respondent").

本案涉及安城住房产业有限公司（"安城"或"申请人"），一家根据大韩民国法律成立的私人公司，向国际投资争端解决中心（"ICSID"或"中心"）提交的针对中华人民共和国（"中国"或"被申请人"）的纠纷。

In April 2005 and April 2006, Mr. Jin Woo Pae, Ansung's CEO, attended several presentations held in Korea by representatives from Yancheng-Shi, China, where he learned about possible investment opportunities to develop and operate a golf course in the Yancheng-Shi district.

On or around September 13, 2006, Ansung identified a 1,500 mu parcel of land for a project in Sheyang-Xian (a sub-district of Yancheng-Shi) that had been partially developed by a joint venture company called "Sheyang Seashore International Golf Course Co. Ltd." ("Sheyang Seashore"). In November 2006, Ansung's management decided to build a golf resort in Sheyang-Xian by acquiring the Sheyang Seashore joint venture. Ansung planned to build a 27 - hole golf course and related facilities on 3,000 mu, which included Sheyang Seashore's 1,500 mu land and an additional 1,500 mu in adjacent lands. Ansung filed an application with the Communist Party of the Sheyang Harbor Industrial Zone Administration Committee ("Committee") to obtain an investment approval from the local Sheyang-Xian government, which application attached a report outlining Ansung's overall scheme for a golf course project with more than 18 holes and not more than 36 holes.

2005 年 4 月和 2006 年 4 月, 安城首席执行官金宇佩参加了中国盐城市代表在韩国举行的几次演讲, 了解了在盐城市开发和运营高尔夫球场的可能投资机会。

2006 年 9 月 13 日前后, 安城在射阳县 (一个盐城市的下辖地区) 为一个项目确定了一块 1500 亩的地块, 该地块部分由一家名为 "射阳海滨国际高尔夫球场有限公司" ("射阳海滨") 的合资公司开发。2006 年 11 月, 安城的管理层决定通过收购射阳海滨合资企业, 在射阳县建立一个高尔夫度假村。安城计划在 3000 亩地上建设 27 洞高尔夫球场及相关设施, 包括射阳海滨 1500 亩地和相邻 1500 亩地。安城向射阳县临港工业区管理委员会 (以下简称 "管委会") 的中共党委提出申请, 以获得当地射阳县政府的投资批准, 该申请随附了一份报告, 概述了安城的 18 洞以上 36 洞以下高尔夫球场项目的总体方案。

On December 12, 2006, Ansung entered into an Investment Agreement with the Committee "under which the Committee acknowledged that the related authorities of Jiangsu-Sheng and Sheyang-Xian had approved the development of the 1,500 mu" (referred to as the "first phase" of the project), with "1,200 mu, for the development of an 18 - hole golf course and 300 mu for related facilities." The related facilities were to be luxury condominiums and a clubhouse to house employees and serve administrative functions. The Investment Agreement also provided that the Committee "would reserve an additional 1,500 mu adjacent to the first phase land," as the joint venture "intended to develop another 9 - hole golf course on that 1,500 mu once the first phase of the project had been completed" (the "second phase" of the project).

As requested by the Committee, on January 16, 2007, Ansung's officers briefed local government officials on Ansung's "master plan" to build a 27 – hole golf course on 3,000 mu. On January 29, 2007, Ansung's officers met with Committee Secretary You Dao-jun to ask whether the local government could provide the entire 3,000 mu at the outset, but Secretary You informed the officers that "the government would provide the additional 1,500 mu for the second phase immediately after the completion of the first phase."

2006 年 12 月 12 日，安城与管委会签订投资协议，"根据该协议，管委会承认江苏省和射阳县有关部门已批准开发 1500 亩"（简称项目的"一期"），"1200 亩，用于开发 18 洞高尔夫球场，300 亩用于相关设施，"相关设施为豪华公寓和俱乐部，供员工住宿并提供行政服务。投资协议还规定，管委会"将在第一阶段土地附近额外保留 1500 亩土地"，作为合资企业"计划在项目第一阶段完成后，在 1500 亩土地上开发另一个 9 洞高尔夫球场"（项目的"二期"）。

根据管委会的要求，2007 年 1 月 16 日，安城的官员向当地政府官员简要介绍了安城在 3000 亩土地上修建 27 洞高尔夫球场的"总体规划"。2007 年 1 月 29 日，安城的官员会见了管委会工委书记尤道俊，询问当地政府能否在一开始就提供全部 3000 亩土地，但尤书记告诉他们，"政府将在一期项目完成后立即提供另外的 1500 亩土地用于二期建设。"

On March 5, 2007, Ansung commenced construction work for the first phase of the project. Throughout the work, blueprints and concept drawings for the 27 – hole golf course andrelated facilities were posted in front of the construction site.

In March 2007, shortly after initiating construction of the first phase, Ansung observed that a nearby park called "Sheyang Island Park," which was to be operated by a Chinese company, was apparently being developed as a golf course. On April 5, 2007, Ansung's CEO, Mr. Jin Woo Pae, expressed his concern to Committee Secretary You Dao-jun about "the illegal development of a golf course in Sheyang Island Park." Secretary You reassured him that no other golf course could be legally developed or operated in Sheyang-Xian and Sheyang Island Park was being developed as an amusement park. In April and May 2007, several other local government officials confirmed Secretary You's message about the nature of development in Sheyang Island Park.

2007 年 3 月 5 日，安城开始了一期的建设工作。整个工程期间，27 洞高尔夫球场和相关设施的设计图和概念图都张贴在施工现场前。

2007 年 3 月，在一期工程开工后不久，安城观察到附近一个名为"射阳岛公园"的公园显然正在开发成一个高尔夫球场，该公园将由一家中国公司运营。2007 年 4 月 5 日，安城首席执行官金友佩先生向管委会书记尤道俊表示了对"射阳岛公园非法开发的高尔夫球场"的关注。尤书记向他保证，射阳县没有其他的高尔夫球场可以合法开发或运营，射阳岛公园正在开发为游乐园。2007年4月和5月，一些地方政府官员证实了尤书记关于射阳岛公园开发性质的消息。

On or around June 27, 2007, when Ansung requested the 300 mu necessary for the related facilities for the first phase, Secretary You explained that China had changed its real estate policy so the Committee could no longer provide the land at the price stipulated in the Investment Agreement and Ansung would have to apply for land use rights through a public sale at higher prices. He informed Ansung that the joint venture would not be eligible to develop a clubhouse and condominiums on this 300 mu without establishing a Chinese subsidiary.

On July 10, 2007, after further discussions with Secretary You, Ansung established a Chinese company, "Sheyang Mirage Field Co., Ltd." ("Mirage"), for the sole purpose of building a clubhouse and condominiums on the 300 mu as part of the first phase.

On May 20, 2008, the Committee requested Ansung, through Mirage, to agree to pay a substantially higher price for the 300 mu. Given its already substantial investment and the importance of a clubhouse, "despite the Committee's outright repudiation of the Investment Agreement, Ansung had no alternative but to build the clubhouse" by paying the higher price.

On May 27, 2008, the Sheyang-Xian government awarded Ansung the land use rights for100 mu at a price higher than originally agreed, and refused to provide the further 200 mu. This left Ansung unable to develop the condominiums.

2007年6月27日前后，安城申请建设一期项目附属设施用地300亩。尤书记解释说由于中国的房地产政策调整，管委会无法按照投资协议约定的价格提供土地，安城需要通过公开竞买程序以更高的价格获得土地使用权。他告诉安城合资企业将不具有在这300亩地上开发俱乐部和公寓的资格，除非设立一家中国子公司开发建设。

2007年7月10日，经过与尤书记的进一步讨论，安城设立了一家中国公司射阳美来知球场管理有限公司（"美来知"），以在第一期项目的300亩地上建设俱乐部和公寓为唯一目标。

2008年3月20日，管委会通过美来知要求安城同意支付较高价格以获得300亩土地使用权。考虑到已经进行的投资和俱乐部的重要性，"尽管管委会完全否认了投资协议，但安城除了支付更高的价格建造俱乐部会所外，别无选择。"

2008年5月27日，射阳政府出让100亩土地使用权给安城，价格比最初协议的要高，并拒绝提供另外的200亩。安城因此无法建设公寓。

On June 30, 2009, with the first phase almost complete, the Committee arranged for a third-party development company to loan funds to Mirage to expedite construction of the clubhouse.

In August 2009, Ansung learned that Sheyang Island Park had become an operating 18 - hole golf course, and complained to various government officials. Although the officials represented that they would intervene, "it is clear that the Sheyang-Xian government took no measures to enjoin the illegal operation of the golf course in the Park as it has been illegally operating the golf course up to the present date. "

Ansung completed the 18 - hole first phase of the project in November 2010. At that time, Ansung repeatedly requested the Committee to provide the additional land necessary for the second phase, in order to avoid bearing costly construction-related expenses, but "officials avoided giving clear answers and only advised Ansung to wait" or rejected Ansung's meeting requests.

2009 年 6 月 30 日，一期项目基本完成，管委会安排第三方开发公司向美来知贷款，加快俱乐部建设。

2009 年 8 月，安城得知射阳岛公园已成为一个经营 18 洞高尔夫球场，并向各政府官员投诉。尽管官员表示将进行干预，"很明显，射阳县政府没有采取任何措施禁止在公园内经营高尔夫球场的违法行为，因为到目前为止，该球场一直在非法经营"。

安城于 2010 年 11 月完成了 18 洞一期工程。当时，安城一再要求管委会提供二期所需的额外土地，以避免承担昂贵的建设相关费用，但"官员们避免给出明确的答案，只建议安城等待"或拒绝了安城的会议要求。

On March 24, 2011, Ansung's Chairman Jin Woo Pae visited Secretary Xu Chao, the Communist Party Secretary of Sheyang-Xian, to request the additional land. Chairman Pae received assurances from Secretary Xu that he would "take the steps necessary to address the problem. " On March 25, 2011, "the very next day, Secretary You contacted Chairman Pae to inform him that Secretary Xu... had no authority to address the issue... and he was the only person with the actual power to handle all land-related issues in this project" and, yet, Secretary You took no action and thereafter "he has refused to meet with Ansung for any matter".

2011 年 3 月 24 日，安城董事长裴金吾拜访了射阳县党委书记徐超，要求提供额外土地。裴董事长收到徐书记的保证，他将"采取必要的步骤来解决这个问题。"2011 年 3 月 25 日，"就在第二天，尤书记联系了裴主席，通知他徐书记……无权解决这个问题……他是唯一有实际权力处理本项目中所有与土地有关的问题的人"。然而，尤书记没有采取任何行动，此后"他拒绝就任何问题与安城会面"。

In June 2011, Mirage was unable to repay the loan arranged by the Committee, because, with only an 18 - hole golf course, "Ansung was unable to produce sufficient returns from its investments in the JV and Mirage as to justify their continued existence... [or] contribute additional financing from Korea into its Subsidiaries, including Mirage, given the Sheyang-Xian government's manifest failure to honor its aforementioned commitments and assurances. "

Also in June 2011, Ansung employees reported that Committee officials visited the golf course to demand repayment of the debt by "unlawful means" such as "blockad [ing] the main gate of the golf course and even assault [ing] Ansung's employees," with requests for police protection going unheeded, "leaving Ansung's officers and employees in perpetual danger. "

Without the planned full 27 - hole golf course with luxury condominiums, and facing the competing illegal golf course at Sheyang Island Park and harassment by local officials, Ansung found itself unable to sell memberships to the golf course and hence "incapable of sustaining a profitable and stable golf business in Sheyang-Xian. " Consequently, in October 2011, "Ansung had no alternative but to dispose of its entire assets of the golf business, including its shareholding in [Mirage], to a Chinese purchaser at a price significantly lower than the amount that Ansung had invested toward the project, causing serious financial losses and damage to Ansung. "

As also pleaded in the introduction to the Request for Arbitration: "As a consequence of the foregoing, Ansung was forced to dispose of its entire investment in Sheyang-Xian in October 2011 in order to avoid further losses. "

2011 年 6 月，美来知无法偿还管委会安排的贷款，因为只有一个 18 洞的高尔夫球场，"安城无法从其在合资企业和美来知的投资中获得足够的回报，以实现其持续经营……从韩国获得额外的融资投入到包括美来知在内的子公司，原因在于射阳县政府明显未能履行其上述承诺和保证"。

同样在 2011 年 6 月，安城员工报告说，管委会官员访问了高尔夫球场，以"非法手段"要求偿还债务，如"封锁高尔夫球场的大门，甚至殴打安城的员工"，在要求警方保护未受到重视的情况下，"让安城的官员和雇员永远处于危险之中"。

没有计划中的 27 洞高尔夫球场，没有豪华公寓，还面临射阳岛公园的非法高尔夫球场竞争和当地官员的骚扰，安城发现自己无法发展高尔夫球场的会员，因此"无法在射阳县维持盈利和稳定的高尔夫业务"。因此，2011 年 10 月，"安城除了以远低于安城投资于项目的价格向中国买方处置高尔天经营的全部资产包括美来知的股权外，安城没有别的选择，这给安城造成严重的经济损失和损害"。

正如仲裁请求引言中所述："由于上述原因，安城被迫于 2011 年 10 月处置其在射阳县的全部投资，以避免进一步的损失。"

The factual background in Claimant's Request for Arbitration ends at October 2011. In Ansung's letter of November 3, 2014 to the ICSID Secretary-General and in its First Observations, Ansung describes the sales transactions that it alleges took place in November and December 2011.

申请人申请仲裁的事实背景截止于 2011 年 10 月。安城在 2014 年 11 月 3 日致 IC-SID 秘书长的信中以及在其第一份意见书中,描述了其声称于 2011 年 11 月和 12 月进行的销售交易。

Ansung provides the following description of events in its November 3, 2014 letter:

a) "On 2 November 2011, Claimant entered into a share transfer agreement with a Chinese purchaser to sell its shareholdings in the Subsidiaries. However, the agreement did not set a fixed price for the share transfer. "

b) "On 17 December 2011, the parties reached agreement on the final price for the transfer arrangement as well as the date on which the transfer would occur; and this was reduced to writing and reflected in an instrument called a 'supplementary agreement. '"

c) "On 19 December 2011, pursuant to the supplementary agreement, Claimant transferred the shares of the Subsidiaries to the Chinese purchaser. "

In Claimant's First Observations, the alleged November and December 2011 events were described as follows:

a) "[O]n 2 November 2011, Ansung tentatively agreed to transfer the shares. However it was yet to sell the Project, because the share price for the sale was not yet settled. "

b) "After further negotiations, in mid-December 2011, the parties arrived at the final price for the share transfer and decided the date on which the transfer would occur. "

c) "On 17 December 2011, considering that the additional land was not still provided by the local government, Ansung finally agreed to transfer the shares at the agreed price. "

安城在其 2014 年 11 月 3 日的信函中提供了以下事件说明:

a) "2011 年 11 月 2 日,申请人与中国买家签订了股份转让协议,出售其在子公司中的股份。但是,该协议并未为股份转让设定固定价格。"

b) "2011 年 12 月 17 日,双方就转让安排的最终价格以及转让将发生的日期达成了协议;这已简化了条款,并反映在一份称为'补充协议'的文书中。"

c) "2011 年 12 月 19 日,根据补充协议,申请人将子公司的股份转让给中国买方。"

在申请人的第一次观察中,所指控的 2011 年 11 月和 12 月事件描述如下:

a) "2011 年 11 月 2 日,安城暂时同意转让股份。但是,由于出售的股票价格尚未结算,因此尚未出售该项目。"

b) "经过进一步协商,双方于 2011 年 12 月中旬达成了股份转让的最终价格,并决定了转让的日期。"

c) "2011 年 12 月 17 日,考虑到当地政府尚未提供额外的土地,安城最终同意以商定的价格转让股份。"

仲裁结果（Award）

For the reasons set forth above, the Tribunal decides as follows:

（1）Dismisses with prejudice all claims made by Claimant, Ansung Housing Co.,Ltd., inits Request for Arbitration, pursuant to ICSID Arbitration Rule 41 (5).

（2）Awards Respondent, the People's Republic of China, its share of the direct costs ofthe proceeding in the amount of US \$ 69,760.55, plus 75 percent of its legal fees andexpenses in the amount of USS 4,853.25 plus EUR 267,443.10 plus CNY 1,387,500, plus interest at the rate of three-month LIBOR plus two percent, compounded quarterly, such interest to run from the 90th day after the date of dispatch of this Award on any unpaid portion of the amounts due under this Award until the date of payment.

基于上述理由，仲裁庭裁决如下：

（1）根据 ICSID 仲裁规则第 41 条（5）款，驳回申请人安城住房产业有限公司在其仲裁请求中提出的所有索赔。

（2）裁决给被申请人中华人民共和国在诉讼直接费用中所占份额 69760.55 美元，加上其法律费用和开支的 75%，即 4853.25 美元加上 267443.10 欧元加人民币 1387500 元，另加 3 个月伦敦同业拆借利率上浮 2% 的利率，按季度复利，该利息在本裁决发出日 90 天起计算，基数为本裁决到期应付的款额中任何未付部分，直至付清之日止。

裁决原因（Reasons for the Award）

ICSID Arbitration Rule 41 (5) and (6) provides:

（5）Unless the parties have agreed to another expedited procedure for making preliminary objections, a party may, no later than 30 days after the constitution of the Tribunal, and in any event before the first session of the Tribunal, file an objection that a claim is manifestly without legal merit. The party shall specify as precisely as possible the basis for the objection. The Tribunal, after giving the parties the opportunity to present their observations on the objection, shall, at its first session or promptly thereafter, notify the parties of its decision on the objection. The decision of the Tribunal shall be without prejudice to the right of a party to file an objection pursuant to paragraph (1) or to object, in the course of the proceeding, that a claim lacks legal merit.

（6）If the Tribunal decides that the dispute is not within the jurisdiction of the Centre or not within its own competence, or that all claims are manifestly without legal merit, it shall render an award to that effect.

ICSID 仲裁规则第 41 条（5）款和（6）款为：

（5）除非双方同意以另一个快速程序提出初步异议，一方可在不迟于仲裁庭组成后 30 天，以及在任何情况下，在仲裁庭第一次会议之前，提出仲裁请求显然无法律依据的异议。当事人应当尽可能准确地说明反对理由。仲裁庭在给予当事人提出异议的机会后，应在第一次会议上或其后及时将其对异议的决定通知当事人。仲裁庭的决定不影响一方根据第（1）款提出异议的权利，或在仲裁过程中继续反对一项索赔缺乏法律依据。

（6）如果仲裁庭认为争议不在 ICSID 管辖范围内，或不在其本身管辖范围内，或所有主张均显然无法律依据，则仲裁庭应作出相应裁决。

Article 9 of the China-Korea BIT, headed "Settlement of Disputes Between Investors and One Contracting Party," provides in relevant part：

7. Notwithstanding the provisions of paragraph 3 of this Article, an investor may not make a claim pursuant to paragraph 3 of this Article if more than three years have elapsed from the date on which the investor first acquired, or should have first acquired, knowledge that the investor had incurred loss or damage.

《中韩双边投资协定》第 9 条，标题为"投资者与缔约一方之间的争端解决"，在相关部分规定：

7. 尽管有本条第 3 款的规定，如果从投资者首次知晓或应当首次知晓投资者已经发生损失或损害之日起超过三年，则不得根据本条第 3 款提出索赔。

Article3 of the China-Korea BIT, headed "Treatment of Investment" "Most-Favoured Nation Treatment" or "MFN Clause"）, provides：

3. Each Contracting Party shall in its territory accord to investors of the other Contracting Party and to their investments and activities associated with such investments by the investors of the other Contracting Party treatment no less favourable than that accorded in like circumstances to the investors and investments and associated activities by the investors of any third State（hereinafter referred to as "most-favoured-nation treatment"）with respect to investments and business activities［defined in paragraph 1 as "the expansion, operation, management, maintenance, use, enjoyment, and sale or other disposal of investments"］, including the admission of investment.

5. Treatment accorded to investors of one Contracting Party within the territory of the other

Contracting Party with respect to access to the courts of justice and administrative tribunals and authorities both in pursuit and in defence of their rights shall not be less favourable than that accorded to investors of the latter Contracting Party or to investors of any third State.

中韩双边投资协定第 3 条，标题为"投资待遇"或"最惠国待遇"，规定：

3. 每一缔约国应在其领土内给予另一缔约国的投资者、投资及与投资相关活动的待遇不低于对在类似条件下给予任何第三国投资者、投资及投资相关活动在投资和其他商业活动方面（在第 1 款中定义为"投资的扩张、运营、管理、维持、使用、享受、销售和其他处置行为"，包括投资准入）的待遇（以下简称最惠国待遇）。

5. 一缔约国在另一缔约国领土内的投资者在寻求和捍卫其权利的过程中进入司法、行政法庭和当局程序的待遇不得低于给予后一缔约国的投资者或任何第三国的投资者的待遇。

The test for a preliminary objection under ICSID Arbitration Rule 41 (5) is whether "a claim is manifestly without legal merit." The Tribunal agrees with the Parties that the test of "manifestly" is well articulated by the Trans-Global tribunal, and so will require Respondent to establish its objection "clearly and obviously, with relative ease and despatch."

In deciding the objection, the Tribunal accepts the facts as pleaded by Ansung. The Tribunal need not decide China's argument that it must ignore facts that are "incredible, frivolous, vexatious or inaccurate or made in bad faith," as it does not find that the facts pleaded by Ansung fall into these categories.

根据国际投资争端解决中心仲裁规则第 41 条（5）款，初步反对意见的检验标准是是否"一项索赔显然没有法律依据。"仲裁庭同意当事各方的意见，即"显然"的检验标准已由国际性法庭清楚阐述，因此将要求被申请人以"相对容易和明确的方式"确定其反对意见。

仲裁庭在决定反对意见时，接纳了安城所提出的事实，而无须裁定中国有关这些事实必须被忽略因其"令人难以置信、轻率、烦扰、不准确或恶意做出"的观点，因为仲裁庭认为安城所提出的事实不属于这一问题的范围。

Turning first to the start date for the three-year limitation period in Article 9 (7), the record is clear that Claimant repeatedly pleaded facts setting the date at which it "first acquired... the knowledge... that [it] had incurred loss or damage" to be before October 2011. As set out in the Factual Background section above, which is based on the facts as pleaded by Claimant:

a) Most important, in the Request for Arbitration (paragraph 12), Ansung pleaded that it "was forced to dispose of its entire investment in Sheyang Xian in October 2011 in order to avoid further losses. Specifically, Ansung was forced to sell its shareholdings in the Subsidiaries to a Chinese purchaser at a price significantly lower than the amount that Ansung had invested toward the project". This indicates Ansung had knowledge that it had incurred loss or damage before October 2011.

首先讨论第 9 条（7）款规定的三年时效期间的开始日期，记录清楚地表明，申请人反复陈述事实，确定其"首次获得……所知……其已在 2011 年 10 月之前遭受损失或损害"的日期。如上文"事实背景"一节所述，该节基于申请人所陈述的事实：

a）最重要的是，在仲裁申请书（第 12 段）中，安城辩称"为了避免进一步的损失，2011 年 10 月被迫处置其在射阳县的全部投资。具体来说，安城被迫以明显低于安城对该项目投资金额的价格将其在子公司中的股权出售给中国买家"。这表明安城知道它在 2011 年 10 月之前遭受了损失或损害。

b）In the Request for Arbitration（paragraph 55），Ansung pleaded that its subsidiary Mirage "was unable to meet the repayment date of June 2011 for the［loan］arranged by the Committee", and "Ansung was unable to produce sufficient returns from its investments in the［joint venture］and Mirage as to justify their continued existence." It was also in June 2011 that Ansung cemployces suffered harassment from Committee officials and the local government refused to provide police protection. This indicates Ansung had knowledge of loss or damage incurred by June 2011.

c）In the Request for Arbitration（paragraph 60），Ansung pleaded that "in October 2011, Ansung had no alternative but to dispose of its entire assets of the golf business, including its shareholding in the Subsidiaries, to a Chinese purchaser at a price significantly lower than the amount that Ansung had invested toward the project, causing serious financial losses and damage to Ansung"（emphasis added）. This indicates Ansung had knowledge of incurred loss or damage by October 2011.

d）Ansung pleaded several other facts indicating knowledge of incurred damage, at least to the prospects of its golf course project, well before October 2011. As early as 2007, it observed the development of a competing golf course at Sheyang Island Park, which went into operation in 2009. In 2007 and 2008, Ansung was compelled to pay a higher price for the additional 300 mu of land for phase one than originally agreed, following what Ansung described as "the Committee's outright repudiation" of the Investment Agreement.

b）在仲裁请求书（第 55 段）中，安城辩称其子公司美来知"无法满足管委会安排的贷款 2011 年 6 月的还款日期"，"安城无法从其在合资公司的投资中获得足够的回报。安城的雇员也在 2011 年 6 月遭到委员会官员的骚扰，当地政府拒绝提供警察保护"。这表明安城知道 2011 年 6 月之前发生的损失或损害。

c）在仲裁请求书（第 60 段）中，安城辩称，"2011 年 10 月，安城别无选择，只能以远低于其对该项目投资的价格将其全部投资包括对子公司的持股转让给中国买方，给安城造成了严重的经济损失和损害"。这表明安城在 2011 年 10 月之前已经知道发生了损失或损害。

d) 安城还提出了其他几个事实，至少表明在 2011 年 10 月之前就知道了高尔夫球场项目的前景受到了损害。早在 2007 年，安城就观察到射阳岛公园一座有竞争的高尔夫球场的发展状况，该项于 2009 年投入运营。2007 年和 2008 年，安城被迫为一期项目增加的 300 亩土地支付比最初商定的更高的价格，因为安城称这是"管委会对投资协议的彻底否定"。

Turning to the dies ad quem for the applicable three-year limitation period, the Tribunal finds that, on the basis of the plain language in Article 9 (7) of the China-Korea BIT, the end date is the date on which an investor deposits its request for arbitration with ICSID.

Claimant deposited the Request for Arbitration with ICSID electronically on October 7, 2014 and physically on October 8, 2014. Either date is more than three years after late summer or early autumn 2011, or the beginning of October 2011.

Consequently, Ansung submitted its dispute to ICSID and made its claim for purposes of Article 9 (3) and (7) of the Treaty after more than three years had elapsed from the date on which Ansung first acquired knowledge of loss or damage. The claim is time-barred and, as such, is manifestly without legal merit.

关于适用的三年时效期限，仲裁庭认为根据中韩双边投资协定第 9 条第 7 款的明确措辞，结束日期是投资者向争端解决中心提交仲裁请求的日期。

申请人于 2014 年 10 月 7 日以电子方式向 ICSID 提交了仲裁请求书，并于 2014 年 10 月 8 日以实物方式提交了仲裁请求书。这两个日期都是 2011 年夏末秋初或 2011 年 10 月初之后的三年多。

因此，自安城第一次获悉损失或损害之日起超过三年后，安城将其争端提交了 ICSID，并根据该协定第 9 条 3 款和 7 款提出了索赔。这一仲裁请求受时间限制，因此显然没有法律依据。

Ansung's alternative defense to China's Rule 41 (5) Objection is that, because China has entered into other bilateral investment treaties with third States that do not prescribe a temporal limitation for an investor initiating an arbitration claim against the host State, Ansung is entitled to invoke the MFN Clause in Article 3 (3) of the China-Korea BIT to disregard the three-year limitation period in Article 9 (7) of the Treaty.

安城对中国第 41 条（5）款规则的另一抗辩是，由于中国与第三国签订了其他双边投资条约，这些条约没有规定投资者对东道国提出仲裁请求的时间限制，因此安城有权根据中韩双边投资协定第 3 条（3）款中的最惠国待遇条款对该协定第 9 条（7）

款中的三年时效期限不予理会。

The Tribunal's conclusion in relation to the MFN Clause in Article 3（3）of the China Korea BIT also becomes clear by reference to Article 3（5）of the Treaty. This Article offers specific MFN protection in relation to an investor's "access to courts of justice and administrative tribunals and authorities." In marked contrast to those domestic avenues, such express reference to international dispute resolution is conspicuously absent in the MFN Clause in Article 3（3）.

For these reasons the Tribunal does not consider that Article 3（3）of the China-Korea BIT assists Claimant in preventing its claim from being manifestly time-barred under Article 9（7）of the Treaty.

根据中韩双边投资协定第3条（5）款，仲裁庭对该协定第3条（3）款中最惠国条款的结论也变得清晰。本条就投资者"进入司法、行政法庭和当局"提供了具体的最惠国待遇保护。与这些国内途径相比，第3条（3）款中最惠国待遇条款中明显没有提及国际争端解决。

基于这些原因，仲裁庭不认为中韩双边投资协定第3条（3）款有助于申请人防止其索赔被该协定第9条（7）款明显禁止。

案件影响（Impact of the Case）

该案中中国政府是投资东道国，安城公司作为投资者依据中韩两国签署的《关于促进和保护投资协定》（中韩 BIT）提起投资仲裁。在正式进入实体审理程序前，中方就 ICSID 和/或仲裁庭的管辖权提出异议，为此仲裁庭将管辖异议问题作为前期先决事项进行审理，争议的焦点是投资者提起的仲裁请求是否因超过时效而显然无法律依据而予以驳回。

该案所涉及的争议由中国房地产开发政策的变动而引发。因 ICSID 未公布申请人的仲裁请求和答辩、庭审笔录及各自交换的文件等，韩国安城提出的诉求未能查阅，但正如仲裁庭在裁定中所述，在本案管辖异议的审理中无需对实体诉求做考虑。安城的申请根据中韩双边投资协定第9条第（7）款的规定时间已被限制，而不受协定第3条第（3）款最惠国条款的保障，因此仲裁庭认为，根据 ICSID 仲裁规则第41条（5）款，该申请显然是没有法律依据的。本案中国政府的胜诉，显示出中国政府在律师协助下具备了一定的应对投资争端案件的能力。

思考问题（Questions）

1. 安城公司对其投资遭受损失的诉求如在中国国内处理，可适用哪种法律程序？
2. 如何避免国际投资争端案件触及诉讼时效限制？

参考文献

姚梅镇：《国际投资法成案研究》，武汉大学出版社 1989 年版。

赵秀文：《国际商事仲裁案例评析》，中国法制出版社 1999 年版。

陈安：《国际投资争端案例精选》，复旦大学出版社 2001 年版。

陈安：《国际投资争端仲裁："解决投资争端国际中心"机制研究》，复旦大学出版社 2001 年版。

余劲松：《国际投资法》（第 5 版），法律出版社 2018 年版。

万猛：《国际投资争端解决中心案例导读》，法律出版社 2015 年版。

张正怡：《能源类国际投资争端案例集——能源宪章条约争端解决机制 20 年》，法律出版社 2016 年版。

朱明新：《国际投资争端赔偿的法律问题研究》，中国政法大学出版社 2016 年版。

田海：《最惠国条款适用于国际投资争端解决程序问题研究》，中国社会科学出版社 2017 年版。

袁海勇：《中国海外投资政治风险的国际法应对——以中外 BIT 及国际投资争端案例为研究视角》，上海人民出版社 2018 年版。

网络资源

https：//icsid. worldbank. org.

https：//pca-cpa. org.

http：//www. naftaclaims. com/.

https：//www. italaw. com.